The Paris Review

Founded in 1953.

Publisher Drue Heinz

Editors

George Plimpton, Peter Matthiessen, Donald Hall, Robert Silvers, Blair Fuller,
Maxine Groffsky, Jeanne McCulloch, James Linville

Managing Editor	Daniel Kunitz
Editor at Large	Elizabeth Gaffney
Senior Editors	Gia Kourlas, Elissa Schappell
Assistant Editors	Andy Bellin, Brigid Hughes
Poetry Editor	Richard Howard
Art Editor	Joan Krawczyk
London Editor Shusha Guppy	**Paris Editor** Harry Mathews
Business Manager Lillian von Nickern	**Treasurer** Marjorie Kalman
Design Consultant	Chip Kidd

Editorial Assistants

Nell Freudenberger, Anne Fulenwider, Steve King, Nicole Krauss,
Joseph Mackin (*Internet*)

Readers

Caroline Cheng, David Rosenthal

Special Consultants

Robert Phillips, Ben Sonnenberg, Remar Sutton

Advisory Editors

Nelson Aldrich, Lawrence M. Bensky, Patrick Bowles, Christopher Cerf, Jonathan
Dee, Timothy Dickinson, Joan Dillon, Beth Drenning, David Evanier, Rowan Gaither,
David Gimbel, Francine du Plessix Gray, Lindy Guinness, Fayette Hickox, Susan-
nah Hunnewell, Ben Johnson, Mary B. Lumet, Larissa MacFarquhar, Molly
McKaughan, Jonathan Miller, Ron Padgett, Maggie Paley, John Phillips, Kevin
Richardson, David Robbins, Philip Roth, Frederick Seidel, Mona Simpson, Terry
Southern, Max Steele, Rose Styron, William Styron, Tim Sultan, Hallie Gay Walden,
Eugene Walter, Antonio Weiss

Contributing Editors

Agha Shahid Ali, Kip Azzoni, Sara Barrett, Helen Bartlett, Robert Becker, Adam
Begley, Magda Bogin, Chris Calhoun, Morgan Entrekin, Jill Fox, Walker Gaffney,
Jamey Gambrell, John Glusman, Edward Hirsch, Gerald Howard, Tom Jenks, Bar-
bara Jones, Fran Kiernan, Joanna Laufer, Mary Maguire, Lucas Matthiessen, Dan
Max, Joanie McDonnell, Molly McQuade, Christopher Merrill, David Michaelis, Dini
von Mueffling, Barry Munger, Elise Paschen, Allen Peacock, William Plumber,
Charles Russell, Michael Sagalyn, Elisabeth Sifton, Ileene Smith, Patsy Southgate,
Rose Styron, William Wadsworth, Julia Myer Ward

Poetry Editors

Donald Hall (1953–1961), X.J. Kennedy (1962–1964),
Thomas Clark (1964–1973), Michael Benedikt (1974–1978),
Jonathan Galassi (1978–1988), Patricia Storace (1988–1992)

Art Editors

William Pène du Bois (1953–1960), Paris Editors (1961–1974),
Alexandra Anderson (1974–1978), Richard Marshall (1978–1993)

Founding Publisher Sadruddin Aga Khan

Former Publishers

Bernard F. Conners, Ron Dante, Deborah S. Pease

Founding Editors

Peter Matthiessen, Harold L. Humes, George Plimpton,
William Pène du Bois, Thomas H. Guinzburg, John Train

The Paris Review is published quarterly by The Paris Review, Inc. Vol. 37, No. 135, Summer 1995.
Business Office: 45–39 171 Place, Flushing, New York 11358 (ISSN #0031-2037). Paris Office:
Harry Matthews, 67 rue de Grenelle, Paris 75007 France. London Office: Shusha Guppy, 8 Shawfield
St., London, SW3. US distributors: Random House, Inc. 1(800)733-3000. Typeset and printed in
USA by Capital City Press, Montpelier, VT. Price for single issue in USA: $10.00. $14.00 in Canada.
Post-paid subscription for four issues $34.00, lifetime subscription $1000. Postal surcharge of $7.00
per four issues outside USA (excluding life subscriptions). Subscription card is bound within magazine. Please give six weeks notice of change of address using subscription card. *While The Paris
Review welcomes the submission of unsolicited manuscripts, it cannot accept responsibility for
their loss or delay, or engage in related correspondence. Manuscripts will not be returned or
responded to unless accompanied by self-addressed, stamped envelope. Fiction manuscripts
should be submitted to George Plimpton, poetry to Richard Howard, The Paris Review, 541 East
72nd Street, New York, N.Y. 10021.* Charter member of the Council of Literary Magazines and
Presses. This publication is made possible, in part, with public funds from the New York State Council
on the Arts and the National Endowment for the Arts. Second Class postage paid at Flushing,
New York, and at additional mailing offices. **Postmaster:** Please send address changes to 45-39
171st Place, Flushing, N.Y. 11358.

The
Paris
Review

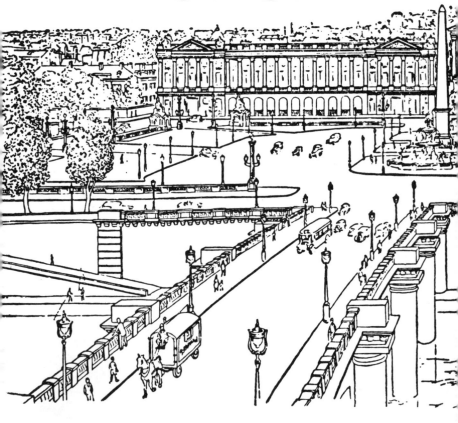

Editorial Office:
541 East 72 Street
New York, New York 10021

Business & Circulation:
45-39 171 Place
Flushing, New York 11358

Distributed by Random House
201 East 50 Street
New York, N.Y. 10022
(800) 733-3000

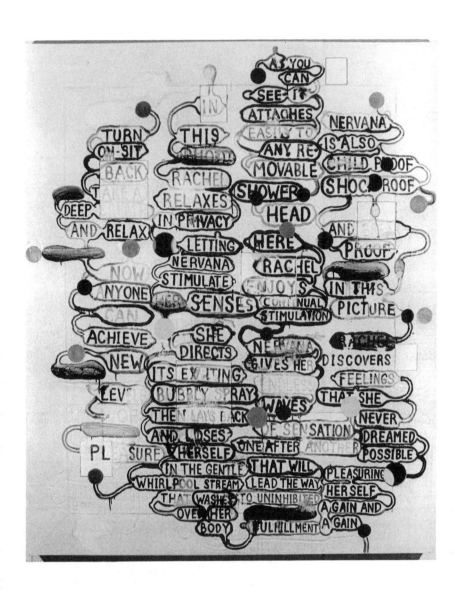

Table of contents illustration by Graham Gilmore, *Nervana*.
Frontispiece by William Pène du Bois.
Cover by Raffaele, *Kali*, oil on panel, 1993.

Number 135

The Fine Art of Sighing

Bernard Cooper

You feel a gradual welling up of pleasure, or boredom, or melancholy. Whatever the emotion, it's more abundant than you ever dreamed. You can no more contain it than your hands can cup a lake. And so you surrender and suck the air. Your esophagus opens, diaphragm expands. Poised at the crest of an exhalation, your body is about to be unburdened, second by second, cell by cell. A kettle hisses. A balloon deflates. Your shoulders fall like two ripe pears, muscles slack at last.

My mother stared out the kitchen window, ashes from her cigarette dribbling into the sink. A sentry guarding her solitude, she'd turned her back on the rest of the house. I'd tiptoe across the linoleum and make my lunch without making a sound. Sometimes I saw her back expand, then heard her let loose one plummeting note, a sigh so long and weary it might have been her last. Beyond our backyard, above telephone poles and apartment buildings, rose the brown horizon of the city; across it glided an occasional bird, or the blimp that advertised Goodyear tires. She might have been drifting into the distance, or lamenting her separation from it. She might have been wishing she were somewhere else, or wishing she could be happy where she was, a middle-aged housewife dreaming at her sink.

My father's sighs were more melodic. What began as a somber sigh could abruptly change pitch, turn gusty and loose, and suggest by its very transformation that what begins in sorrow might end in relief. He could prolong the rounded vowel of OY, or let it ricochet like an echo, as if he were shouting in a tunnel or a cave. Where my mother sighed from ineffable sadness, my father sighed at simple things: the coldness of a drink, the softness of a pillow, or an itch that my mother, following the frantic map of his words, finally found on his back and scratched.

A friend of mine once mentioned that I was given to long and ponderous sighs. Once I became aware of this habit, I heard my father's sighs in my own and knew for a moment his small satisfactions. At other times, I felt my mother's restlessness and wished I could leave my body with my breath, or be happy in the body my breath left behind.

It's a reflex and a legacy, this soulful species of breathing. Listen closely: my ancestors lungs are pumping like bellows, men towing boats along the banks of the Volga, women lugging baskets of rye bread and pike. At the end of each day, they lift their weary arms in a toast; as thanks for the heat and sting of vodka, their *a-h-h*s condense in the cold Russian air.

At any given moment, there must be thousands of people sighing. A man in Milwaukee heaves and shivers and blesses the head of the second wife who's not too shy to lick his toes. A judge in Munich groans with pleasure after tasting again the silky bratwurst she ate as a child. Every day, meaningful sighs are expelled from schoolchildren, driving instructors, forensic experts, certified public accountants, and dental hygienists, just to name a few. The sighs of widows and widowers alone must account for a significant portion of the carbon dioxide released into the atmosphere. Every time a girdle is removed, a foot is submerged in a tub of warm water, or a restroom is reached on a desolate road . . . you'd think the sheer velocity of it would create mistrals, siroccos, hurricanes;

arrows should be swarming over satellite maps, weathermen
talking a mile a minute, ties flapping from their necks like
flags.

Before I learned that Venetian prisoners were led across it
to their execution, I imagined that the Bridge of Sighs was a
feat of invisible engineering, a structure vaulting above the
earth, the girders and trusses, the stay ropes and cables, the
counterweights and safety rails connecting one human breath
to the next.

Incidents

Daniil Kharms

The life of the Russian avant-garde author Daniil Kharms (1905–1942) was every bit as absurd, as abrupt and as symbolically charged as one of his stories. The son of a populist-radical writer with religious leanings, he began a promising career as a poet in the freewheeling artistic scene of late-twenties Leningrad; he knew the great avant-garde artists Malevich, Tatlin, and Filonov, the formalist critic Viktor Shklovsky and the famous children's authors Evgenii Shvartz and Samuil Marshak. Kharms was one of the founders of OBERIU, the Union of Real Art, an artistic society heavily influenced by constructivism, futurism and the za'um (Trans-sense) poets. OBERIU's vaguely absurdist experimental performances ran afoul of the increasingly conservative Soviet artistic apparat, and by 1930 they were being denounced as counterrevolutionary. At their final performance, the OBERIU poets unveiled an amusing Soviet-style banner reading We Are Not Pirogis! Asked to explain this slogan, they responded, "So . . . we are pirogis?" In 1931, Kharms was arrested and sentenced to a year's internal exile in the Siberian city of Kursk.

When Kharms returned to Leningrad, the thriving artistic

*scene of the twenties had been atomized, replaced by an atmo-
sphere of isolation and despair. It had become impossible to
publish experimental literature, and Kharms eked out a living
writing children's stories for his friend Marshak's magazines.
He continued to write serious work, to read it for small circles
of friends, and then to commit it to his desk drawer. He began
to suffer from fits of depression and apparently from actual
hunger. He shambled about in threadbare clothes of a deliberately outdated aristocratic style, and occasionally in the paranoid mood of the time was taken for a spy. His ex-wife, Esther
Rusakova, was arrested and died in a labor camp; his friend
Nikolai Oleinikov was purged and shot. Kharms himself was
finally arrested soon after the German invasion. According to
rumor, he was accused of the fantastic charge of spying for
the Japanese. He feigned psychiatric illness to avoid the firing
squad, and died in a prison hospital, probably of hunger.*

*Kharms's ex-OBERIU colleague, Y.S. Druskin, went to his
empty apartment in the winter of 1942 and stuffed a suitcase
full of Kharms's manuscripts. Gradually, some of these manuscripts were published, first in the cultural thaw of the Khrush-
chev years, and then in small editions by foreign academic
presses. In the late 1980s, Kharms's writings were finally published in large volumes in Russia, where they enjoy a continu-
ing vogue.*

The Plunge

Two men fell off a roof. They both fell off the roof of a
five-story building which was under construction. A school,
apparently. They slid along the roof in a sitting position right
to the edge, and then began to fall.

Ida Markovna noticed their fall before anyone else. She was
standing next to the window in a building across the street,
blowing her nose into a cup. And suddenly, she saw someone
begin to fall from the roof of the opposite building. Looking
closer, Ida Markovna saw that there were two of them, and

that they had begun to fall at the same moment. Thoroughly disconcerted, Ida Markovna tore off her shirt and commenced wiping the shirt on the spotted glass of the windowpane in order better to see who was falling off the roof. But realizing that the falling men might perhaps be able, from their side, to see her naked, and think God only knows what of her, she sprang away from the window and hid herself behind a wicker stand on which a flowerpot had once stood.

At the same time, the falling men were seen by another personage living in the same building as Ida Markovna, only two floors lower down. This personage was also called Ida Markovna. She at this precise moment was sitting with her legs on the windowsill sewing a button onto her shoe. Glancing at the window, she saw the men falling off the roof. Ida Markovna squealed and, sliding off the windowsill, began hurriedly opening the window in order to be able to see better when the men hit the ground. But the window wouldn't open. Ida Markovna remembered that she had nailed the window shut and dashed off to the stove where she kept her tools: four hammers, a chisel and a pair of pliers.

Grabbing the pliers, Ida Markovna ran back to the window and pulled out the nail. Now the window was easily flung open. Ida Markovna leaned out the window and saw the falling men whistling through the air as they fell earthwards.

On the street a small crowd had already gathered. Whistles were already being handed out, and a rather short policeman was unhurriedly strolling towards the scene of the expected incident. A big-nosed doorman was bustling about, pushing people around and announcing that those who had gathered were in danger of being hit on the head by the men falling off the roof.

At this point both Ida Markovnas, one in a dress, the other naked, leaning out the window, screamed and stamped their feet in excitement.

And, at last, arms spread and eyes bulging, the men falling off the roof crashed to earth.

Thus sometimes we, too, falling from the heights of our achievements, crash against the dismal cage of our future.

Pushkin and Gogol

Gogol falls onstage from the wings and lies there immobile.

Pushkin (enters, trips on Gogol and falls): Damn! Don't tell me—on Gogol!

Gogol (rising): What a dirty trick! They won't even let you sleep. (Walks, trips on Pushkin and falls.) Don't tell me I tripped on Pushkin!

Pushkin (rising): Not a minute's peace! (Walks, trips on Gogol and falls.) Damn! Don't tell me—on Gogol again!

Gogol (rising): Always something in the way! (Walks, trips on Pushkin and falls.) What a dirty trick! On Pushkin again!

Pushkin (rising): Hooligans! Utter hooligans! (Walks, trips on Gogol and falls.) Damn! On Gogol again!

Gogol (rising): It's simply an insult! (Walks, trips on Pushkin and falls.) On Pushkin again!

Pushkin (rising): Damn! Honestly—damn! (Walks, trips on Gogol and falls.) On Gogol!

Gogol (rising): What a dirty trick! (Walks, trips on Pushkin and falls.) On Pushkin!

Pushkin (rising): Damn! (Walks, trips on Gogol and falls offstage.) On Gogol!

Gogol (rising): What a dirty trick! (Walks offstage.)

From offstage is heard the voice of Gogol: "On Pushkin!"

Curtain

(20 February 1934)

An Historical Episode

for V.N. Petrov

Ivan Ivanovich Susanin (that same historical personage who risked his life for the Tsar and as a result was immortalized in an opera by Glinka) went into a Russian tavern one day and ordered a steak. While the tavernkeeper was cooking the steak, Ivan Ivanovich sat chewing on his beard and musing quietly, as was his habit.

Thirty clicks of time went by, and the tavernkeeper brought Ivan Ivanovich his steak on a round wooden board. Ivan Ivanovich was hungry and as was the custom in those times seized the steak in his hands and began to eat. But in his rush to assuage his hunger Ivan Ivanovich threw himself on the steak so greedily that he forgot to remove his beard from his mouth, thus swallowing his steak along with a chunk of his beard.

At this point a certain unpleasantness took place, as not more than fifty clicks of time had gone by before Ivan Ivanovich's stomach began to experience sharp pains. Ivan Ivanovich tore himself from the table and rushed into the courtyard. The tavernkeeper shouted after him: "Hoy, yer whiskers is all a-patchy!" But Ivan Ivanovich, paying no attention to anything, ran out into the courtyard.

Then the boyar prince Kovshegub, sitting in the corner of the tavern drinking wort, struck the table with his fist and shouted: "Who is yon gentleman?" And the tavernkeeper, bowing low, answered the boyar: "Yon gentleman is our patriot Ivan Ivanovich Susanin." — "Thus, is't!" said the prince, finishing his wort.

"Might I offer you some fish?" asked the tavernkeeper. "Go to hell!" cried the prince and threw the ladle at the tavernkeeper. The ladle whistled by the tavernkeeper's head, flew out the window into the courtyard and caught Ivan Ivanovich, who was squatting eagle-style, in the teeth. Ivan Ivanovich grabbed his cheek with his hand and fell over on his side.

At this point, Carp came running out of the shed on the right and jumping over the washtub in which a sow was lying and washing herself ran off shouting towards the gate. The keeper looked out of the tavern. "What are you yelling about?" he asked Carp. But Carp, without answering, dashed off.

The tavernkeeper came out into the courtyard and saw Susanin lying motionless on the ground. The tavernkeeper walked up to him and looked him in the face. Susanin gazed fixedly at the tavernkeeper. "So you're alive?" asked the tavernkeeper. "Ay, alive, only I'm afeard they'll hit me with something else," said Susanin. "No," said the tavernkeeper, "Never fear. That was just Prince Kovshegub almost killed you, but now he's gone off."

"Praise be to God!" said Ivan Susanin, rising from the ground. "I'm a brave man, but I don't like to scrape my belly in the mud for nothing. See, I dropped to the ground and waited: what'll happen next? I'd have crawled on my belly clear to Yeldyrina village. . . . There, look how swollen my cheek is. My god! Half my beard is gone!" "That was the way it was before," said the tavernkeeper. "What do you mean, before?" cried the patriot Susanin. "Are you trying to tell me I was walking around with my beard in patches?" "Ay, in patches," said the tavernkeeper. "Ach, you old woman," said Ivan Susanin. The tavernkeeper squinted his eyes and, wiping his hands, with one great stroke smacked Susanin in the ear. "There! Who's an old woman!" said the tavernkeeper, and retreated into the tavern.

For several clicks of time Susanin lay on the ground and listened but not hearing anything suspicious he cautiously raised his head and looked about. There was nobody in the courtyard other than the sow who, having climbed out of the washtub, was rolling around in a dirty puddle. Ivan Susanin, looking around, moved towards the gate. The gate, fortunately, was open, and the patriot Ivan Susanin, coiling along the ground like a worm, crawled off in the direction of Yeldyrina village.

This was an episode in the life of the famous historical personage who risked his life for the Tsar and, as a result, was immortalized in an opera by Glinka.

The Meeting

So one day this guy was going to work, and on the way he met another guy who having bought a loaf of Polish bread went back home where he came from.

And that's basically it.

Unsuccessful Performance

Petrakov-Gorbunov comes onstage and begins to say something, but he hiccups. He begins to vomit. He exits. Pritykin comes on.

Pritykin: The respected Petrakov-Gorbunov wishes to expr . . . (He begins to vomit, and runs off)

Makarov comes on.

Makarov: Yegor . . . (Makarov vomits. He runs off)

Serpukhov comes on.

Serpukhov: In order not to be . . . (He vomits, runs off)

Kurova comes on.

Kurova: I would be . . . (She vomits, runs off.)

A small girl comes on.

Small girl: Papa asked me to tell you all that the theater is closed. Everybody feels nauseous!

Curtain

(1934)

Sonnet

An amazing thing happened to me: I suddenly forgot which came first, seven or eight.

I headed off to my neighbors and asked them what they thought on the subject.

Imagine their and my surprise when they suddenly discovered that they couldn't remember the order of the numbers either. They could remember one, two, three, four, five, and six, but had forgotten the rest.

We all went down to Gastronom, the commercial store on the corner of Znamensky and Basseiny Streets, and explained our problem to the cashier. The cashier smiled sadly, removed a tiny hammer from her mouth and moving her nose slightly said: "In my opinion, seven comes after eight in those cases in which eight comes after seven."

We thanked the cashier and ran joyfully out of the store. But then reflecting on the cashier's words we again fell into despondence, inasmuch as her words appeared to be entirely devoid of meaning.

What could we do? We went to the Summer Gardens and began counting the trees. But when our count reached six, we stopped and began to argue: some thought seven should come next, others—eight.

The argument lasted a long time, but then fortunately a child fell off a bench and broke both his jaws. This diverted us from our argument.

Then we went our separate ways.

(12 November 1935)

Butz and Knatz

Butz: Hey, Knatz!
       Let's catch some gnats!

Knatz: No, I'm still not ready for that.
       What do you say we catch some cats?

Kushakov the Carpenter

Once upon a time there was a carpenter. His name was Kushakov.

One day he went out to the store to buy carpenter's glue.

The thaw had started, and the street was very slippery.

The carpenter walked several steps, slipped, fell, and cracked his forehead.

—Ecch!—said the carpenter, got up, went to the pharmacy, bought a sticking plaster and stuck it to his forehead.

But when he went out on the street and walked several steps, he slipped again, fell, and smashed his nose.

—Phoo!—said the carpenter, went to the pharmacy, bought a sticking plaster and stuck it to his nose.

Then he again stepped out onto the street, again slipped, fell, and smashed his cheek.

He was forced to go back to the pharmacy and put a sticking plaster on his cheek.

—Look,—said the pharmacist to the carpenter,—you fall and smash yourself so often, I would advise you to buy several sticking plasters at once.

—No,—said the carpenter,—I won't fall any more!

But when he stepped out onto the street, he again slipped, fell, and smashed his chin.

—Lousy ice!—cried the carpenter and again ran to the pharmacy.

—There, you see?—said the pharmacist.—You fell again.

—No!—cried the carpenter.—I don't want to hear it! Just give me the plaster.

The pharmacist gave him the plaster, and the carpenter covered his chin and ran home.

But at home they didn't recognize him and wouldn't let him in the apartment.

—I'm Kushakov, the carpenter!—the carpenter cried.

—Sure you are!—they answered from the apartment, and locked the door bolt and chain.

Kushakov the carpenter stood on the stairs for a while, spat, and went out into the street.

(1935)

Old Women Falling

Overpowered by curiosity, an old woman leaned out of the window, fell, and smashed herself to pieces.

Another old woman stuck her head out the window to look down at the first one, but, overpowered by curiosity, also leaned too far, fell, and was smashed to pieces.

Then a third old woman fell out the window, then a fourth, then a fifth.

By the time the sixth old woman fell, I had gotten tired of watching them, and I went over to Maltsevsky market, where, they say, a certain blind man had been given a knit shawl.

(1937)

Symphony No. 2

Anton Mikhailovich spat, said "ecch," spat again, said "ecch" again, spat again, said "ecch" again and left. And to hell with him. Let me tell you about Ilya Pavlovich instead.

Ilya Pavlovich was born in 1893, in Constantinople. When he was still a young child, he was brought to St. Petersburg, and there he graduated from the German school on Kirochny St. Then he worked in some store, then he did something else, and at the beginning of the revolution he emigrated abroad. So the hell with him. Let me tell you about Anna Ignatevna instead.

But it's not so easy to talk about Anna Ignatevna. First of all, I don't know anything about her, and second of all, I just fell off my chair and forgot what I was going to say. Let me tell you about myself instead.

I am tall, not stupid, dress elegantly and with taste, don't drink, and don't play the horses, but I have a weakness for women. And the women don't avoid me. They even like it when I go out with them. Serafima Izmailovna has invited me over several times, and Zinaida Yakovlevna has also said she's always glad to see me. But something funny happened to me with Marina Petrovna that I'd like to tell you about. Something completely ordinary, but still, funny, namely, thanks to me Marina Petrovna has gone completely bald, bald as the palm of your hand. This is how it happened: one day I went over to Marina Petrovna's, and wham! — she went bald. And that's it.

(June 9–10, 1941)

The Beginning of a Lovely Summer Day
(Symphony)

As soon as the cock had crowed, Timothy crawled out of the window onto the roof and frightened everyone who was passing on the street. Khariton the peasant stopped, picked up a rock and threw it at Timothy. Timothy disappeared somewhere. "He dodged it!" — shouted the crowd, and a certain Zubov got a running start and slammed his head into a wall as hard as he could. "Ecch!" — cried a woman with an abscessed tooth. But Komarov gave that woman the old one–two, and she ran off crying into an entranceway. Fetelyushin was walking by, and snickered. Komarov went up to him and said, "Hey you, fatso!" — and hit Fetelyushin in the stomach. Fetelyushin leaned against the wall and started to hiccup. Romashkin spit out of the upstairs window, trying to hit Fetelyushin. Not far off, a woman with a big nose was beating her child with a washtub. And a plump young mother was rubbing a pretty girl's face against a brick wall. A small dog, having broken its thin little leg, was rolling around on the pavement. A small boy was eating some kind of filth out of a spittoon. At the grocery store there was a long line for sugar. Women were cursing loudly and hitting each other with their shopping bags. Khariton the peasant, drunk on methyl alcohol, was standing in front of the women with his pants unbuttoned, pronouncing impolite words.

Thus began a lovely summer day.

—introduced and translated from the Russian
by Matt Steinglass

A Coincidence at the Vet's

Francine Prose

Twice this summer rabid raccoons have crawled down people's chimneys and in both cases bit old women, in both cases on the face. This is the reason that A. has brought her cat, B., to the veterinarian.

The waiting room is crowded, but A. can't tell how many pet owners have brought in their pets for rabies boosters. For one thing, no one mentions the article that appeared yesterday in the local paper and that focused — wrongly, it seems to A. — on the second raccoon attack, when the real news, it seems to her, is that the same thing happened twice, though this fact was only mentioned once in the last paragraph of the article.

Also, many pets in the waiting room seem to have something seriously wrong with them, or rather many pet owners seem to believe that they do. The office is very crowded, and during the long wait A. sees a woman announce to the whole waiting room that her dog is deaf, but when the receptionist calls them, that is, calls the dog's name, the dog turns its head and barks. A. also sees a man tell the receptionist that his cat is blind even as the cat paws with cruel accuracy at a ladybug on the counter.

So even here at the veterinarian's, things are not what they seem, even here where it should be so simple: pet lovers and loving pets. Partly what's caused the long delay was the young couple, much too young to own the old cat that—you could see on their faces—was dying. The receptionist took them first, ahead of everyone waiting, all of whom understood at once that this too was an act of mercy. It strikes A. that this must be regul . procedure at this office, which tips her feelings briefly on the side of veterinarian, Dr. C., whom on the one hand she admires for how good he is with B., even though she knows he will not give B. a rabies shot without insisting on feeling his lymph nodes and checking for many nonexistent conditions while A. looks on in a panic at how much this is going to cost.

The couple returns—without their cat. The receptionist says, "No charge." The couple is weeping, both of them— but you cannot tell. Just as, watching A. stroke B.'s orange fur, you could not possibly tell that this pet owner and her pet have been having a little trouble. In the past weeks, B. has smashed A.'s favorite vase, shit on her best black dress, killed a squirrel—a squirrel!—and left its headless body at the foot of A.'s bed. A. removed the corpse with a shovel. The rabies shot is a must!

For years B. has been a good cat, affectionate, even loyal. A. knows it is stupid to imagine an animal capable of something like human malice. One thing animals teach you is to accept things for what they are, and anyone can see that B. is simply being catlike. It is crazy to think that this is happening because A. laughed at a photograph in a supermarket-tabloid article about a woman whose sweet white kitty began to resemble Hitler: the diagonal shock of dark hair, the little black brush mustache. And finally it is paranoid to imagine that the trouble A. is having with her cat is in any way related to the trouble she is having with people—specifically, with her boyfriend, D. Your warm understanding with your pet is supposed to remain constant, comforting and sustaining you throughout your misunderstandings with people. Your pet, A. thinks, shouldn't turn on you when it sees that you are wounded, though of course A. has to wonder if that is animal nature, too.

Eventually A. is the last one left in the waiting room, though others — and not just the owners of the cat who was put away — came in after her. Once they're alone, the receptionist compliments A. on what a smart thing she is doing, how few people watch out, really watch out, for their pets' well-being. Clearly she has no idea of A.'s new ambivalence about B., or maybe if she did she would say it doesn't matter, what absolves A. is that she is here, getting B. a rabies booster, when most people don't even know that they and their pet need not actually be bitten but can get infected merely from blood or saliva. A.'s stomach lurches sickeningly as she tries to remember if the squirrel B. beheaded could have bled or drooled on the rug, and she is preparing to hide her dread by bringing up the two old women bitten on the face, weeks and dozens of miles apart, both by rabid raccoons . . .

Just at that moment the phone rings. Answering, the receptionist says, "Oh, hello, Mr. E."

A. knows the rules of politeness: she should pretend not to listen, but feels that at this moment the rules have been suspended, because Mr. E. is the last name of A.'s boyfriend, D.

D. is not, strictly speaking, her boyfriend. Or maybe he is her boyfriend. He used to be her boyfriend but hasn't called for two weeks, and she fears they may have broken up, but without her knowing. In fact she doesn't want to know, which is why she hasn't called him, and the longer this goes on . . . well, it could go on forever.

From hearing the receptionist's end of the conversation, A. concludes that something is critically wrong with D.'s (Mr. E.'s) parrot, F. In the year that A. has been in love with D., this parrot has suffered and recovered from several life-threatening ailments that caused all its feathers to drop out and a milky film to cover its eyes. A. has heard, from the other side, several such conversations — essentially the other half of the conversa-

tion that the receptionist is now having with D. And yet,
surprisingly, it never came up that A. and D. have the same
veterinarian. A. always preferred to say as little as possible
about the fact that she has a cat and D. has a bird. It was
supposedly one of the reasons for their not living together.

A. is only mildly surprised by the coincidence of D.'s calling
the veterinarian while she and B. are there. After a week of
D.'s not calling, A. happened to phone her brother-in-law, G.,
a friend of D.'s — and D. was there when she phoned; this is
how she knows he's not dead, just not calling. At the start
of their love everything was coincidental — their meeting, their
both dropping by N.'s party though each had a cold, their having
the same thoughts at the same time even with their small city
between them, and of course A. always thinking of D., the
second before he called. Lately she has been thinking of him
at many seconds when he doesn't call. So his phoning the vet
while she is there may be a step in the right direction, back
toward a time when destiny seemed to have nothing to do
but fling them together.

At last the receptionist calls B.'s name, and A. carries her
cat into the vet's examining room. Dr. C. is a plump little
wombat of a man with a curly red beard and hair, and strong
stubby hands into which A. gratefully surrenders B. The doctor
sets B. on the table and shines a light in his ears as A. struggles
against the desire to shout out loud that all B. needs — that
all A. can afford — is a rabies booster.

But now the doctor is complimenting A. on her concern
for her pet, most people don't know you can get infected
merely from blood or saliva, just as people don't want to admit
how much Lyme disease is around. Dr. C. never goes hiking
without rubber bands around his cuffs. But A. is hardly listening, she no longer even worries as the doctor checks B.'s
teeth and give his testicles a squeeze. She is thinking that
having overheard the news of the parrot's illness is a perfect
excuse to call D. She would call a friend — a distant friend —
in a similar situation.

Dr. C. pinches B.'s fur and sticks it with the syringe. The
cat recoils from the needle. A. is overcome by a wave of love

for B. that intensifies as she realizes that her cat could not
have been purposefully cruel, at worst he was acting out the
pain he'd felt streaming out of A. Her cat would never have
hurt her just because she'd been hurt by D.

That evening A. dials D.'s number and then turns out the
lights; she sits in her dark kitchen, stroking B.'s fur—sleepy
from the vaccination, he's dozing on her lap—and listening
to D.'s phone ring. Finally D. answers.

There is no way for A. to convince herself that D. sounds
happy to hear from her.

"How is F.?" she asks.

"What do you mean?" D. says, warily.

"I'm worried about him," A. says.

"What do you *mean*?" D. repeats.

Already they have gotten off on the wrong footing—this
is not the tone a man uses when his lover calls to ask after
his ill pet. "I'm worried he's sick again," says A.

"What makes you think that?" says D.

Why can't A. just tell him that she's overheard his call to
the vet? Why can't she point out that this coincidence signals
a return to that happy time when what seemed like pure chance
was in fact a conspiracy of fate to knit them tighter and tighter?
It would probably annoy him—he might think she was making
it up about being at the vet. Something is terribly wrong! A
nice gesture, an ordinary act of human kindness and concern
has been made to seem inappropriate, pushy—sexually aggressive!

"How did you know he's sick?" asks D.

"I dreamed it," A. hears herself saying. "It was the strangest
thing. Last night I dreamed a parrot was perched on my hand
and all its feathers started—"

"Oh, Jesus," says D. "He's convulsing again. I'll call you
back, okay?"

A. is still holding the phone long after D. has hung up.
The most humiliating part is that she feels herself mouthing
the question: When? A siren blares inside her head, set off
by the knowledge that D. so clearly loves a dumb bird more
than he loves her. In the very beginning, she'd mistaken this

for a good sign, a sign of his ability to love, to care about a parrot.

A female voice—a computer voice—tells her: please hang up. Startled, A. leans forward to replace the receiver and, in doing so, forgets about B. Abruptly woken, B. cries out and bites A. on the hand. Now A. cries out, too, and half rising, spills B. onto the floor. B. makes no effort to cling to her lap. As A. sinks back into her chair, she hears B. pad out of the room.

The pain is so searing, so terrifying A. thinks at once of rabies. Did she get B. vaccinated too late? Or, by some freak accident, too early? Could B. be harboring the rabies bacillus, a result of the vaccination, and in a one-in-a-million coincidence, have transmitted it to A.? And *could* A. have somehow dreamed all this? Everything is so familiar. She should get up, call the doctor, get antibiotics, hot water—but she remains in her chair.

Sitting in the dark kitchen, cradling her injured hand, A. considers the two old women bitten by rabid raccoons. And now at last she understands how wrong she was about that. The real news was not that it happened twice, but that it happened at all, that someone was shocked from a deep sleep in her own bed in the middle of the night and looked up into those dark masked eyes and those spitty razory teeth, and almost, almost saw something there, something she recognized, in the moment before the pain flared up and burned everything else away.

Charles Wright

Apologia Pro Vita Sua III

June is a migraine above the eyes,
Strict auras and yellow blots,
                                    green screen and tunnel vision,
Slow ripples of otherworldliness,

Humidity's painfall drop by drop.
Next door, high whine of the pest exterminator's blunt
    machine.
Down the street, tide-slap of hammer-and-nail,
                        hammer-and-nail from a neighbor's roof.

I've had these for forty years,
                        light-prints and shifting screed,
Feckless illuminations.
St. John of the Cross, Julian of Norwich, lead me home.

•

It's good to know certain things:
What's departed, in order to know what's left to come;
That water's immeasurable and incomprehensible

And blows in the air
Where all that's fallen and silent becomes invisible;
That fire's the light our names are carved in.

That shame is a garment of sorrow;
That time is the Adversary, and stays sleepless and wants for
    nothing;
That clouds are unequal and words are.

•

I sense a certain uncertainty in the pine trees,
Seasonal discontent,
                    quotidian surliness,
Pre-solstice jitters, that threatens to rattle our equilibrium.

My friend has lost his larynx,
My friend who in the old days, with a sentence or two,
Would easily set things right,

His glasses light-blanks as he quoted a stanza from Stevens
    or Yeats
Behind his cigarette smoke.
Life's hard, our mutual third friend says . . . It is. It is.

                    •

Sundays define me.
                    Born on a back-lit Sunday, like today,
But later, in August,
And elsewhere, in Tennessee, Sundays dismantle me.

There is a solitude about Sunday afternoons
In small towns, surrounded by all that's familiar
And of necessity dear,

That chills us on hot days, like today, unto the grave,
When the sun is a tongued wafer behind the clouds, out of
    sight,
And wind chords work through the loose-roofed yard sheds,
                    a celestial music . . .

                    •

There is forgetfulness in me which makes me descend
Into a great ignorance,
And makes me to walk in mud, though what I remember
    remains.

Some of the things I have forgotten:
Who the Illuminator is, and what he illuminates;
Who will have pity on what needs have pity on it.

What I remember redeems me,
                              strips me and brings me to rest,
An end to what has begun,
A beginning to what is about to be ended.

•

What are the determining moments of our lives?
                              How do we know them?
Are they ends of things or beginnings?
Are we more or less of ourselves once they've come and gone?

I think this is one of mine tonight,
The Turkish moon and its one star
                              crisp as a new flag
Over my hometown street with its dark trash cans looming
    along the curb.

Surely this must be one. And what of me afterwards
When the moon and her sanguine consort
Have slipped the horizon? What will become of me then?

•

Some names are everywhere — they are above and they are
    below,
They are concealed and they are revealed.
We call them wise, for the wisdom of death is called the little
    wisdom.

And my name? And your name?
                              Where will we find them, in what pocket?
Wherever it is, better to keep them there not known —
Words speak for themselves, anonymity speaks for itself.

The Unknown Master of the Pure Poem walks nightly among
    his roses,
The very garden his son laid out.
Every so often he sits down. Every so often he stands back up . . .

•

Heavy, heavy, heavy hangs over our heads. June heat.
How many lives does it take to fabricate this one?
Aluminium pie pan bird frightener
                            dazzles and feints in a desultory breeze

Across the road, vegetable garden mojo, evil eye.
That's one life I know for sure.
Others, like insects in amber,
                            lie golden and lurking and hidden from us.

Ninety-four in the shade, humidity huge and inseparable,
Noon sun like a laser disc.
The grackle waddles forth in his suit of lights,
                            the crucifixion on his back.

•

Affection's the absolute
                            everything rises to,
Devotion's detail, the sum of all our scatterings,
Bright imprint our lives unshadow on.

Easy enough to say that now, the hush of late spring
Hung like an after-echo
Over the neighborhood,
                            devolving and disappearing.

Easy enough, perhaps, but still true,
Honeysuckle and poison ivy jumbling out of the hedge,
Magnolia beak and white tongue, landscape's off-load, love's
    lisp.

Katharine Coles

Pantoum in which Time Equals Space

for Jack Droitcourt
and for Eugene Gudaitis, 1992

Eugene would say, "Someone died. Time to redecorate."
Everything we owned was secondhand.
We needed to move. We were running out of space.
He cruised the Goodwill every weekend, collecting

anything he could find secondhand.
Suphlatus, angel of dust, was his guardian—
a sort of cosmic Goodwill queen, cruising, collecting
the dead like artifacts going to dust. First, strangers

made Suphlatus, angel of dust, their guardian.
Then he collected, one by one, our friends.
Dead as artifacts, they turned to dust, to strangers.
Joseph left a couch. Ted, a table. Odd chairs

collected one-by-one replaced our friends.
Hooked rugs, cookie jars shaped like dogs,
a couch left by Joseph, Ted's table, odd chairs.
When his last lover died, he told me, Eugene gave away

all the hooked rugs and cookie jars shaped like dogs
and checked into the Ritz, stripped to nothing.
His lover had died at last. Eugene gave way:
he threw off his clothes, his shoes, even his eyeglasses

and his checkbook; at the Ritz, he stripped to nothing
and scattered all he owned on the sidewalk below,
threw out his clothes, his shoes, even his eyeglasses.
Then he lay down on the king-sized bed and swallowed pills.

38

Some scattered. All he owned on the sidewalk below—
he planned not to need it. Doomed anyway, naked as death,
he lay down on the king-sized bed. He swallowed pills,
but not enough to do the trick. He was found in the stairwell.

He'd planned to need nothing, doomed anyway. Naked as
    death,
he let them take him. All he had left was grief.
It was not enough. Tricked out of the stairwell
where he'd carried the urn, full of his lover's ashes,

he let them take him. All he had left was grief.
When he got out, he burned up the asphalt west,
carrying the urn, full of his lover's ashes.
At the truck stop in Little America, the car burst into flame.

He got out, but the car burned down to asphalt.
He said, "Who can tell one ash from another?
At any little truck stop in America, flame is flame,
and ash is ash, no matter how it began."

Who can tell? One ash *is* much like another.
Eugene said of his lover, "He was always a little dense.
Ash is ash." No matter. How it began—
the waitress gave him a mason jar, and he scooped it full.

Later, Eugene said of his lover, "He was a little dense,"
and he touched me. That was him: gallows humor all over.
A mason jar, scooped full and labeled "lover"
for Suphlatus to guard, dust of flesh and metal.

It always touched me, his gallows humor. All over.
Eugene was no Einstein. He's left me empty-handed,
while Suphlatus guards his dust. He was flesh and mettle.
Now, his jar's packed in a living room full of boxes.

Eugene was no Einstein. He left me with time on my hands.
Someone died. Eugene would redecorate,
but everything's packed. The living room's full of boxes,
and I'm on the move. I've almost run out of space.

Gwyneth Lewis

Pentecost

The Lord wants me to go to Florida.
I shall cross the border with the mercury thieves,
as foretold in the faxes and prophecies,
and the checkpoint angel of Estonia
will have alerted the uniformed birds
to act unnatural and distract the guards

so I pass unhindered. My glossolalia
shall be my passport — I shall taste the tang
of travel on the atlas of my tongue —
salt Poland, sour Denmark and sweet Vienna
and all men in the Spirit shall understand
that, in His wisdom, the Lord has sent

a slip of a girl to save great Florida.
I shall tear through Europe like a standing flame,
not pausing for long, except to rename
the occasional city; in Sofia
thousands converted and hundreds slain
in the Holy Spirit along the Seine.

My life is your chronicle; O Florida
revived, look forward to your past,
and prepare your perpetual Pentecost
of golf course and freeway, shopping mall and car
so the fires that are burning in the orange groves
turn light into sweetness and the huddled graves

are the hives of the future — an America
spelt plainly, translated in the Everglades
where palm fruit hang like hand grenades

ready to rip whole treatises of air.
Then the S in the tail of the crocodile
will make perfect sense to the bibliophile

who will study this land, his second Torah.
All this was revealed. Now I wait for the Lord
to move heaven and earth to send me abroad
and fulfill His bold promise to Florida.
As I stay put, He shifts His continent:
Atlantic closes, the sheet of time is rent.

Peter Sacks

Halo for Marianne Moore

> *"Astronomy or pale paint?"*

Imagine starting with that option
(a deistic turn of faith, or generosity?)
each lens minutely tinted a petition-
blue, the color of restrained impetuosity
that keeps the eye from pitching through
the angled telescope of view,

or, put more accurately, desire,
since blue's the color both of atmospheric distance
and of residues: against a peeling spire,
beneath more superficial layers of preference,
the paint gives back the dying light
as blue, the last to fade at night.

Precipitate beyond solution
to our question of which one it is (perceive/create,
reflect/project?), the semblance of invention
yet of loyalty and faith—for centuries, the weight
of lapis in the dye alone
ensured the worth of Mary's gown;

the only wavelength long or true
enough to climb back from the glacier's otherwise
insatiable white jaws, thus crevice-blue;
or here the complementary gleam undazzled eyes
could find beneath the sun-dyed spell
binding scholar and lion in one cell

42

of gold reserved only for gods,
or for the sovereign disks approaching crosswise
through old fresco walls above the heads
of saints—who, were they looking upward, would surmise
neither astronomy nor painter's trace,
since these, however blessed, can only mock that grace.

Maureen Seaton

The Sculpture Garden

Deirdre was almost ebony. She washed your boxers
and folded them neatly inside your backpack.
When I came home from the Cape, you'd painted our
   bedroom
black. A black box, you said. You lay down in the black box
and cried until your legs spun out around you, kicking me
hard like a dancer's. *Melissa's* skin was chocolate mousse—

gorgeous, you said, and your voice hunkered down
as if she were your fur coat. She took you
to a dungeon on Thanksgiving. You both ate turkey
then she invited you to remove her blouse and hurt her.
The last time you saw her she said, "You're bald!"
And you flushed beneath your glossy scalp.

Martha the Carpenter was a buddy of yours.
You told me she came to you naked once
but you turned her down. I imagine her white matte shoulders
on an island in the Atlantic, how she taught you stars
are real and nothing is more sacred than wood. She said
you needed someone like me, and I felt proud.

The Ivory-Soap Girl was a quick study.
I heard her call your name from Dojo's and watched you
fly inside the How Club, smirking. As she walked away
she looked back and shrugged, red hair singeing in the sun.
She was an actress, off-Broadway, semi-famous.
You said you'd done nothing but sketch her. And *Ina*

posed between *The Woman in Kente Cloth with Extensions*
and *Kat*, who was your first Chicago sculpture,
an accountant by day who gave us her phone number
as a gesture of welcome. *Ina* had enormous freckled breasts
and liked to rub them against you. You held your cupped
hands out in front of you to demonstrate their size.

It's true—I'd always loved the delicacy of your hands,
the way they held me as if I were priceless.

Two Poems by Daniel Rifenburgh

Melville / Ishmael

Call it a lack;
Lacking the ability
To stop at a certitude,
To arrive at a plain of comfort,
There to make a substantial abode and
There reside, contented, with pipe and bowl.

All is flux.
The wet wars against the dry,
The cold against the hot,

Manhatten upon the Marquesas,
Fiji upon the widows' walks
Of Bedford and Nantuckett.

So Heraclitus would have it said,
But not so Jehovah, nor
His righteous folk. Still,

The way into the valley
Of the shadow of doubt
Is the way out
And back in, as from everlasting.

Or a floated plank,
Trimmed for a coffin,
Is the way,

Where a man looks for days at the sun
Overhead, and keeps the seas at their work.

He is an orphan, or a god,
And a bible would do him
Little good.

A trade good, he would call it;
So much calico, so many unchapleted, ruby-like
Beads.

The board he clings to
Turns by turns
Under sun and stars.

"No!"
In thunder he declares,
Adrift in his disconsolate declaration, working
Out the grammar of it, exploring the fine
Largess of it,

As the swells pass over and under
And Rachael madly,
Vainly searches out
Her lost children.

Hawthorne

This quill is a wand;
I wave it about

And box all doubt
In a high, storied redoubt.

Thus I re-route
Pandora's rout,

Let it whelm there and riot
To the mad heart's content,

A negative number scouring
Its darkest quadrants,

While my outward life, largely
Undescribed, stays calm, covert, undefiled.

This is the art that is hid:
To wildly write and quietly live,

Loosen romance
In a brazen coffer, where furies

Cascade and rage, conflagrate
Among the mind's night-lumber,

About those frail, fanciful
structures, so weirdly dear to us,

Then, having kicked
Once at the insignificant embers,

To seal the lid
With a period.

Two Poems by Christopher Middleton

Cypress at the Window: A Letter to Lotten

A sort of cypress reached
Halfway up the longer window;
I came to live here, all the same.

Seldom visited by birds,
More often by chameleons,
It fills the window now.

Disheartening any window cleaner,
It filters dust and south light,
A permanent winter dream.

Yet if I go, evenings, to the door
In August, while I cross the room
It's me soaks up the shadow of the tree.

And I remember it was small: on the floor
We sat, if you remember, Lotten,
Watching, flake by flake, the snow

Cascade over, through, and round
The cypress, in a safe place.
The snow was rare and fell thick,

Whitest on the ground, for interposed
Green, like a whisper in the dark, is buoyant.
Now in the wind it sways, dusky thing,

And if hot light still floods the south,
The shadow of it whisks across the wall
Where camels loiter, silhouetted, in a desert.

Camel humps with saddle bows ink the dunes,
Alongside the shadows of their drivers.
The shadow of the cypress, waving, also

Includes my skin, now a sort of cloak;
I feel it in the desert for the first time
Lightly rustle round the shadow's tree.

Supposing, Lotten, you can catch
In Stockholm shadows that prolong,
Northward, articulating it, the violet

South, to swivel east,
As fold on fold, reversed,
The desert veers away

And forges west, through snow, remember
How lightly for an hour you felt
The shadow rise, the growing tree.

On a Photograph of Chekhov

for Katharina Wagenbach

While the rain comes pouring down,
Chekhov, in his white peaked hunting cap,
And prone beside a rick of hay, surveys
The scene behind the camera, narrow-eyed.

While in Berlin the rain comes pouring down
And will refresh the yellowed centenarian
Blossomer in the courtyard, Chekhov has
Anchored his umbrella, gone to earth.

Ivory handle of the slim umbrella shaft atilt
To birch trunks in the background, has a curve;
Eyesight arching clean across the image
Divines, in the cap's white crown, a twin to it.

Chekhov's brother, meanwhile, props his head—
Summer rain, phenomenally somber—
On Chekov's hip; from his blubber mouth
A howl escapes, the sockets of his eyes

Are black, as if he wore, beneath his bowler,
Smoked eyeglasses; as if he were, perhaps,
A horror Chekhov carried on his back, and still
The rain comes pouring down, and the umbrella,

Hulk become a dome to shelter Chekhovs, both,
Can float across a century, be put to use.
O perishable hayrick! —and its fringe,
Where Chekhov tucks his knees up, will be damp.

Yet Chekhov's massive cap, laundered a day ago—
Intent beneath its peak his eyes are watching
How people make their gestures through the rain,
Set dishes on a table, turn

Vacant faces to the window, wring their hands,
Cling, so predisposed, to their fatal fictions,
Or stroke the living air, to make it hum
With all they mean to talk about today.

Sandra McPherson

Lessons Learned from a Small Drawing
by Victor Joseph Gatto, Self-Taught Artist

If you cannot make a living from your art,
double the art, double any part

(but not the whole)
of the body of a woman,

multiply eyes in every head.
She'll never view you in a simple way.

If you cannot make a living from your art,
the freak is yours.

Think of your lady's two heads on your shoulder.
Make only what you cannot bear to part with.

Because you will not make a living from your art.

> My poems are my age, X'd out on their hanging
> calendar, where the pretty picture
>
> is not mine — mine's the gargoylish deadline
> (I hold my pen wrong too).
>
> And while the populace reads make-believe
> I swear to all true language
>
> each pate's an equal citizen, willing to work.
> One will perform the chore in fact you hired her for
>
> if you just let her other wit
> (the one that's made of poetry)
>
> come along.

she ~~switched it on~~ pulled it down. There was no response; obviously

the bulb had gone. And then, as she stood there irresolute,

she was aware of the sound of gentle breathing, the ~~sense~~ knowledge, immediate

and terrifying that someone was standing there in the darkness. And

at that moment the noose of ~~rope~~ leather came down over her head

and tightened round her neck. It jerked violently, she was precluded

and she ~~fell to the floor, her~~ felt the crack of the concrete momentarily stunning her hands scrabbling on the rough

concrete. and then it scrape against the back of her skull.

It was a long ~~rope~~ strap. She tried to reach ~~over to~~ but there was no strength in her arm

struggle with whoever was holding it, but ~~he~~ was out of

reach, and every time she moved tried to the noose tightened and her mind

She thrashed on its end like a hooked fish. feebly and dying the

feet hands scrabbling ineffectively on the rough concrete for a hold

And then she heard his voice. 'Lie still, Claudia, and turned into

Lie still and listen. Nothing will happen while you lie still. brief unconsciousness

She ceased her struggles and at once the dreadful

throttling stopped. ~~The noose was eased.~~ ceased His voice was

speaking quietly, persuasively. She heard what he said and

~~but fear had numbed her brain~~ she or half understood He was telling her that

she had to die, and why. She wanted to shout out that

it was a terrible mistake, that it wasn't true, but only her voice was

by lying totally motionless ~~not attempting~~ to speak, throttled and she

could she stay alive. He was explaining now that it would listened my

look like suicide. The ~~rope~~ strap would be tied to the fixed

wheel of the car, the ~~exhaust~~ engine would be left running. She would

be dead by then but it was increasing important to him.

that the garage should be full of a total jass.

He explained this to her patiently, as if it was

important to him that she should understand.

or don't kindly

A P.D. James manuscript page.

P.D. James
The Art of Fiction CXLI

P.D. James is one of Britain's most admired and best loved writers. Long considered the "Queen of Crime" and the doyenne of detective novelists, she has a large and varied readership beyond the confines of the genre and is praised by critics in such literary journals as the Times Literary Supplement *and the* Literary Review.

James was born in 1920 in Oxford and educated at The High School for Girls in Cambridge, where her family settled when she was eleven. Upon leaving school at sixteen, she

*started work, and in 1941 married Dr. Connor Bantry White
with whom she had two daughters, Clare and Jane. Her husband returned from World War II mentally damaged and
unable to work, and James was forced to earn a living for her
family. She started working in the National Health Service
and later moved to the Home Office, where she ended up as
a principal in the Police Department. She published her first
novel,* Cover Her Face, *in 1962, at the age of forty-two.*

*In the three decades that followed, James wrote eleven more
novels, achieving critical acclaim and increasing popularity.
She "hit the jackpot" with her eighth novel,* Innocent Blood,
*which shot to number one on the American best-seller list
and brought her worldwide fame and fortune. To date she
has sold over 10 million copies of her books in the U.S. and
tours regularly, to publicize her novels and to give lectures.*

P.D. James's first mainstream novel, Children of Men, *a
futuristic moral parable set in England in 2007, also gained
considerable success. Her thirteenth and most recent novel,*
Original Sin, *is set in the London publishing world and features detective Commander Adam Dalgliesh, the most famous
detective since Sherlock Holmes and a protagonist of many
previous novels.*

*James was awarded the Cartier Diamond Dagger in 1987
for her lifetime achievement, and the Silver Dagger of the
Crime Writers' Association for her fourth novel,* Shroud for
a Nightingale. *In the United States she has won the Edgar
Allan Poe Scroll for the same novel, as well as for* An Unsuitable Job for A Woman. *Eight of her novels have been serialized
on television. She is an Associate Fellow of Downing College,
Cambridge, has won honorary degrees from four universities,
and is a fellow of the Royal Society of Arts and of The Royal
Society of Literature. In addition, James has served as the chairman of the literature panel of the Arts Council and as a governor
of the BBC. In 1991 she was ennobled by the Queen and sits
in the House of Lords as Baroness James of Holland Park.*

*P.D. James lives in an elegant Regency house in Holland
Park, London, where this interview took place in April, 1994.*

Her drawing room is furnished with comfortable armchairs and sofas, gilt mirrors, Staffordshire figures, and a fine bookcase containing the complete bound volume of Notable British Trials, "fascinating to read."

INTERVIEWER

You did not start writing until you were in your forties, yet you say that you always wanted to be a writer. How did you know and how did you think you would go about it?

P.D. JAMES

I think I was born knowing it. From an early age I used to tell imaginative stories to my younger brother and sister. I lived in the world of the imagination, and I did something which other writers have told me they did as children: I described myself inwardly in the third person: "She brushed her hair and washed her face, then she put on her nightdress . . ." as if I were standing outside myself and observing myself. I don't know whether this is significant, but I think writing was what I wanted to do, almost as soon as I knew what a book was.

INTERVIEWER

Were your parents interested in literature? Did they read a lot? What books did you have in the house?

JAMES

I was the eldest of three children, and my father was a middle-grade Inland Revenue tax official. My parents' marriage wasn't particularly happy, partly, I think, because of their very different characters. My father was essentially reserved, highly intelligent and unemotional; my mother was warm-hearted, impulsive and much less intellectual. I was rather frightened of my father in childhood, as, I think, were my younger sister and brother, but when he reached old age I grew greatly to value his qualities of courage, intelligence and humor. I think I have inherited characteristics from both my parents, and I remember both with love. Neither of my parents wrote or was particularly interested in literature, but they took great pleasure in my success.

What did you read at school? Was English your best subject?

JAMES

Yes. I was educated in the state system at an old-fashioned grammar school in Cambridge. In those days state education was very good, but I had to leave at sixteen because university was not free, and my family could not afford to pay for me. I would have loved to have gone to university, but I don't think I would necessarily have been a better writer, indeed perhaps the reverse. Looking back I feel I was fortunate: we had dedicated teachers who were attracted to Cambridge which is a very beautiful and stimulating city, and stayed. They were women who would have been married but for the slaughter of men in the First World War. Only one had been married, and she was a widow. They gave us all their dedicated attention. When I left school I had read more Shakespeare and other major poets than many a university graduate today. It astounds me how narrow and limited their reading is compared to ours.

INTERVIEWER

What about novels, did you read the major novelists as well?

JAMES

We didn't have many books at home, so I got most of my books from the Cambridge Public Library. I read widely — from adventure stories to Jane Austen. I came under her spell early on, though she usually appeals to older people. One of my first loves was the Book of Common Prayer — I loved its beautiful language and the sense of history, of timelessness it gave me.

INTERVIEWER
What in particular attracted you to Jane Austen?

JAMES
Her irony and control of structure. One's response to literature is like one's response to human beings — if you asked me
what appeals to me in a certain person, I might say his courage,
or humor, or intelligence. In Jane Austen it was her style and
her irony, the way she creates so distinctive a world in which
I feel at home. I called my second daughter after her. She
was born during some of the worst bombing in London. I went
from Queen Charlotte's Maternity Hospital to a basement flat
in Hampstead because I thought it was safer being underground, and we could hear the flying bombs overhead and
the guns trying to shoot them down, and I just read Jane
Austen for the hundredth time!

INTERVIEWER
Did you read George Eliot as well, and with the same relish?

JAMES
I came to her later. Like most people I believe *Middlemarch*
to be one of the greatest English novels, but I don't have the
same affection for George Eliot as for Jane Austen. I read
Dickens and recognized his genius, but he is not my favorite.
I find many of his female characters unsuccessful — wonderful
caricatures, wicked, odd, grotesque, evil, but not true. There
isn't the subtlety of characterization you get, say, in Trollope,
whose understanding and description of women is astonishing.
Jane Austen never described two men talking together if a
woman was not present — she would have thought that was
outside her experience. In Trollope, by contrast, you get continual conversations between women — for example Alice Vav-
asor and Lady Glencora Palliser in *Can You Forgive Her* —
without a man there, and he gets it absolutely right. This
plain, grumpy looking man had obviously an astonishing
knowledge of women's psychology.

INTERVIEWER

Trollope has become a hero of the feminists, especially his *The Way We Live Now* in which he proclaims women's rights before anyone else did.

JAMES

I tend not to think of books in terms of contemporary issues and passions; it diminishes them. But that particular book is a kind of contemporary novel. The main character was a sort of Robert Maxwell, a monster. Trollope describes women's lives at a time when marriage was the only possibility for personal fulfillment.

INTERVIEWER

Did you read foreign novelists, the great Russians, the French?

JAMES

I read the obvious ones, *War and Peace*, *Anna Karenina*. I didn't have time to read enough writers of my own language as I went to work after school and kept working. I read some American novelists: Hemingway, Fitzgerald, John O'Hara and the crime writers like Dashiell Hammett and Ross MacDonald. I think American crime writers have had a profound influence, not only on the genre but on the course of the novel as a whole.

INTERVIEWER

In what way?

JAMES

By the vigor of their language, its imaginative use—the wisecracks, the one-liners. It is a distinctive style which has influenced the mainstream American novel.

INTERVIEWER

This brings us to the genre you chose for yourself. Did you choose it because you were aware of having a talent for it?

JAMES

I don't make a distinction between the so-called "serious" or "literary" novel and the crime novel. I suppose one could say mainstream novel. But I didn't hesitate long before I decided to try to write a detective story, because I so much enjoyed reading them myself. And I thought I could probably do it successfully, and the detective story being a popular genre, it would have a better chance of being accepted for publication. I didn't want to use the traumatic experiences of my own life in an autobiographical book, which would have been another option for a first attempt. But there were two other reasons. First, I like structured fiction, with a beginning, a middle and an end. I like a novel to have narrative drive, pace, resolution, which a detective novel has. Second, I was setting out at last on the path of becoming a writer, which I had longed for all my life, and I thought writing a detective story would be a wonderful apprenticeship for a "serious" novelist, because a detective story is very easy to write badly but difficult to write well. There is so much you have to fit into eighty or ninety-thousand words — not just creating a puzzle, but an atmosphere, a setting, characters . . . Then, when the first one worked, I continued, and I came to believe that it is perfectly possible to remain within the constraints and conventions of the genre *and* be a serious writer, saying something true about men and women and their relationships and the society in which they live.

INTERVIEWER

Alain Robbe-Grillet once quoted Borges saying that all great novels are detective stories from *Crime and Punishment* down to Robbe-Grillet's own *Jalousie*. Do you agree?

JAMES

I hadn't thought of it that way, but now you mention it, I think there is some truth in that; it is an interesting observation. It is true because the novel is an artificial form, and the detective novel especially so, as the writer has to select events and arrange them in a certain order, making use of his or her experience to reveal a view of reality. The problem-solving too is characteristic of both genres. For example, Jane Austen's *Emma* is a remarkable detective story in which the truth of human relationships are inserted into the narrative in a very cunning way—for instance, Frank Churchill arriving in Highbury already secretly engaged to Jane Fairfax. She needs a piano, and Frank goes to London to have his hair cut and a few days later a piano arrives. The novel is full of this kind of clue to the truth of relationships. There is no murder or death in the book, yet it is a novel of deceit and detection.

INTERVIEWER

That makes the definition of the detective novel too general. What we understand by the term is a specific genre, with its conventions and rules, and it requires a special talent, a particular cast of mind; there is usually a corpse, and the corpse has come to be there in mysterious circumstances which the novel sets out to discover. It sounds a bit morbid, yet most detective novelists I have met are perfectly sane! Was your experience of working in the Health Service influential in your choice of material?

JAMES

No. I didn't come across corpses because I was an administrator, a bureaucrat, not a doctor or a nurse. But I had an interest in death from an early age. It fascinated me. When I heard, "Humpty Dumpty sat on a wall," I thought, "Did he fall or was he pushed?" But if I could get back to what you first said, that a detective story needs a corpse, I don't think it necessarily does. For example Dorothy L. Sayers's *Gaudy Night* is without a corpse. But you are right, it is rare. On the whole the story is centered around a mysterious death, which gives it an extra emotional punch—who-killed-the-canon has more impact than who-stole-the-diamond-ring. Perhaps the people who write these stories have a human interest in death, and they feel that by fictionalizing and intellectualizing it, turning it into a puzzle, they can diffuse their atavistic fear of death and violence.

INTERVIEWER
Do you find the corpse first, and build the story around it?

JAMES
No, although that is one way of doing it. A naked body wearing a pince-nez started Dorothy L. Sayers's *Whose Body?* Certainly one of my books, *Shroud for a Nightingale*, started with a particular idea for killing somebody. It came to me when I saw a patient being fed through a tube into the stomach, and I thought you could use the same method to kill somebody — by pouring in poison instead of milk. And I did — in the story I mean! But usually what sparks off my imagination is the setting.

INTERVIEWER
How do you get the setting? By chance or by imagining it? Do you ever go and look for it the way a film director looks around for possible locations?

JAMES
I never deliberately look for it. I have never taken the view that as soon as I have finished a book I have to start a new one. I wait, however long it takes, for inspiration. Of course I keep my mind and my imagination open to receive inspiration, but I don't rush around looking for places in the hope that they can provide me with a setting. It is always fortuitous. To give an example: *Devices and Desires* is set on the east coast of England, in Norfolk. I was visiting Suffolk, the county to the south, and one day I was standing on a shingly beach looking out over the cold, dangerous North Sea. I saw two boats pulled up, with a few nets drying, and I thought I could have stood there for a thousand years and seen the same things — boats, nets, shoreline. Then I turned my gaze to the north, and towering over the whole headland was the stark

outline of a nuclear power station. I thought of the ruined abbeys I had been visiting in the area, which were the symbol of a decaying faith, the ancient windmills turned into houses, and the other artifacts of today which were a sharp contrast to that timeless scene. I decided that my next book would be set on a lonely stretch of the East Anglian coast under the shadow of a nuclear power station, and that I would deal with some of the issues of nuclear power. That spring of inspiration is a very exciting moment, because it is then that I know I have a book, however long it takes to produce it.

INTERVIEWER

A number of modern novelists and playwrights admit that they have trouble inventing plots. I remember Tom Stoppard saying this one day. Many dispense with plot altogether and write novels in which nothing in particular happens. In the detective story the plot is all. How do you plot your stories after you have got the setting? Do you start writing immediately?

JAMES

No. Not for months. I think many people don't know how to plot, and can't tell stories anymore. Some writers could do it but don't want to, they wish to be different. But there is a tradition of strong narrative thrust in English fiction, and all our great novelists of the past have had it. For myself I believe plot is necessary, although it would be easy to write a book without it. In the thirties, the so-called golden age of the detective story, plot was everything. Indeed what people wanted was ingenuity of plot. You couldn't have an ordinary murder, it had to be done with exceptional cunning. It was the age when corpses were found in locked rooms with locked windows, and a look of horror on their faces. With Agatha Christie ingenuity of plot was paramount — no one looked for subtlety of characterization, motivation, good writing. It was rather like a literary card trick. Today we've moved closer to the mainstream novel, but nevertheless we need plot. It takes me as long to develop the plot and work out the characters as to write the book. Sometimes longer. So once I've got the setting, I begin to get in touch with the people, as it were, and last of all the clues. With *Devices and Desires* I had fifteen notebooks—I went back to the original setting and took notes about the sky, the landscape, the architecture, the local people . . . It is a curious process—I feel that the characters in the story already exist in a limbo outside my control, and what I'm doing over the months of gestation is getting in touch with them and learning about them.

INTERVIEWER

For that reason novelists say they don't know what the ending will be. With the detective novel you *must* know, since it is there at the beginning—the corpse.

JAMES

That is true, but there is a distinction between a crime novel and a detective novel. The latter has a very ordered form, as it depends on ratiocination and logical clues for solving the mystery. It is a cerebral form of literature. Since your solution must be logical, you must know the ending at the beginning.

INTERVIEWER

Can you elaborate on the difference between the crime novel and the detective novel? Since in both cases a crime, usually a murder, has been committed?

JAMES

The crime novel covers a wide spectrum, from the cozy certainties of Agatha Christie and her little English village, which despite its above average homicide rate never really loses its innocence, through Wilkie Collins and Trollope (*The Eustace Diamonds*), Dickens (*The Mystery of Edwin Drood*), Graham Greene, to novels of espionage and Dostoyevsky's *Crime and Punishment* and *Brothers Karamazov*. So I see the detective novel as a sub-species of the crime novel. The Americans call it the mystery novel, which I think is an apt description. In the crime novel you might know from the start who committed the crime, but the interest is in whether the criminal will be caught and in the effect of the crime on him, the people around him and the society in which he lives. You can say Graham Greene's *Brighton Rock* is a crime novel, but it contains no mystery. It is the relationship between Pinkie and his mistress, and the theological aspect that matter. So the detective story is more limited.

INTERVIEWER

Once you start the story, do you go from alpha to omega? Or do you write the murder scene first?

JAMES

It depends. I sometimes write the major, decisive scenes first, then fill in the rest. You could get into trouble with continuity, but I usually get it right.

INTERVIEWER

We come to the central character, the detective. He returns in novel after novel, which is rather handy, since having created him, you can watch him change, age, fall in love. Your detective is Commander Adam Dalgliesh of Scotland Yard. How did you find him? Where did you get his name? Is he a male version of you?

JAMES

My English teacher was a Scottish lady called Maisie Dalgliesh. I wanted a name that was not too unusual and yet not too common. What is interesting is that I called him Adam, and years later my teacher said that her father was also called Adam Dalgliesh. But I don't think he is a male version of me. Certainly he has characteristics I admire in a human being, because if you create a character who is to come back in subsequent books you have to like him and be able to live with him over the years. Then there is a lesson for all of us in the novels of the thirties: Agatha Christie must have regretted

"The Paris Review remains the single most important little magazine this country has produced."

— T. Coraghessan Boyle

THE
PARIS
REVIEW

Enclosed is my check for:

☐ $34 for 1 year (4 issues)
☐ $1,000 for a lifetime subscription
(All payment must be in U.S. funds. Postal surcharge of $8 per 4 issues outside USA)

☐ Send me information on becoming a *Paris Review* Associate.
Bill this to my Visa/MasterCard:

_____
Card number   Exp. date

☐ New subscription   ☐ Renewal subscription
☐ New address

Name _____

Address _____

City _____ State _____ Zip code _____

Please send gift subscription to:

Name _____

Address _____

City _____ State _____ Zip code _____

Gift announcement signature _____

Please send me the following:

☐ The Paris Review T-Shirt ($15.00)
    Color _____ Size _____ Quantity _____
☐ The following back issues: Nos. _____

    See listing at back of book for availability.

☐ The Paris Review Print Series catalogue ($1.00)

Name _____

Address _____

City _____ State _____ Zip code _____

☐ Enclosed is my check for $ _____
☐ Bill this to my Visa/MasterCard:

_____
Card number   Exp. date

BUSINESS REPLY MAIL

FIRST CLASS   PERMIT NO. 3119   FLUSHING, N.Y.

POSTAGE WILL BE PAID BY ADDRESSEE

THE PARIS REVIEW
45-39 171 Place
FLUSHING NY   11358-9892

No postage
stamp necessary
if mailed in the
United States

BUSINESS REPLY MAIL

FIRST CLASS   PERMIT NO. 3119   FLUSHING, N.Y.

POSTAGE WILL BE PAID BY ADDRESSEE

THE PARIS REVIEW
45-39 171 Place
FLUSHING NY   11358-9892

this funny little Belgian with his waxed mustaches. But she was stuck with him. Dorothy L. Sayers had the same trouble with Peter Wimsey, who began as somewhat a silly young man-about-town in *Whose Body?*, but is a very different Lord Peter Wimsey in *Gaudy Night*. So I thought I would create someone who has the qualities I respect—generosity, compassion, intelligence.

INTERVIEWER

The very qualities everyone ascribes to yourself! Then one day you dropped Dalgliesh and brought in a woman detective—Cordelia Gray. Was it the feminist wave catching up with the detective novel?

JAMES

No. It was the need of that particular story. I wanted to set the book in Cambridge, a city I love. A particularly horrible murder of a student had taken place, which looked like suicide, and it required a young detective. Suddenly I thought it could be a woman. It is a mystery how these ideas suddenly occur to one. Cordelia is lovely, courageous, independent. She inherits a run-down agency from her boss, which she has to build up again, hence the title, *An Unsuitable Job for a Woman*. The first case she gets is the death of an eminent Cambridge scientist's son. The inquest gives a verdict of suicide, but the father feels it is murder and wants to know why. So in comes Cordelia, and she finds that the suicide was faked, and that the death was indeed a murder.

INTERVIEWER

There are a number of other famous women detectives, particularly in America. Unlike Agatha Christie's Miss Marple, they are not amateurs but highly professional—they carry guns, eat take-out food and are not domesticated—not an awful lot of anima around them!

JAMES

It is true, particularly with the American women writers, you get professional private eyes. They operate in a violent

world and they carry guns just as men do. But in this country
private eyes are not allowed guns, and, anyway, Cordelia is
an older creation—I wrote her twenty years ago. In Dashiell
Hammett and Raymond Chandler the detective is a loner,
often working against the police. Indeed the police are as
much of a danger to him as the criminal, since if they don't
approve of him he might lose his license to practice. But in
my book it would have been unrealistic if Cordelia were a
gun-toting licensed private eye.

INTERVIEWER

Do you suppose feminism has something to do with the
emergence of the female detective?

JAMES

Probably. But also these are realistic novels, and private
eyes have to be professional if they are to work successfully
in that society.

INTERVIEWER

You are, as you say, of an older generation. Would you
describe yourself as a feminist?

JAMES

Oh well . . . that is just a label. I am a feminist in so far
as I want a fairer deal for women, equal opportunity, equal
pay, a more just society. And I have a great affection for members of my own sex. But it seems to me that some radical
feminists today are against men, and they dislike being
women, and I can't go along with that. The truth is that there
are no easy answers to some fundamental questions: we are
biologically designed to bear children, and the children have
great need of us, especially in their early years. This makes it
more difficult for women to pursue careers on equal terms
with men. Paradoxically women today have a much harder
life than had our mothers and grandmothers, although there
is more equality between the sexes. In the past, women had

extended families, and good reliable nannies. Today we don't have such help, and careers are open to women at the very time when it is difficult to pursue them without risk of damage to their children. As a result women are stretched physically and emotionally, working hard to hold down a job and have a family. Somebody has to run a household, and the woman is the heart of the family, however good the husband may be at sharing the chores. It may be that women have to make difficult choices, give up work and stay at home for a few years until the children go to school. So often this so-called independence means that you are paying someone else to do your work — you go out to work in order to earn money to pay the woman who is looking after your children. She is enjoying your children instead of you!

INTERVIEWER

Do you find it hard to air such views in the politically correct atmosphere of certain establishments, such as universities where you often lecture?

JAMES

I went to Somerville College, Oxford the other day, and in the cloakrooms there were notices about a help-line for this and a help-line for that, the harrasment help-line and the date-rape help-line . . . I thought of those splendid women who were the first to graduate from the college and whose portraits are hung on the walls, and I thought life could not have been easy for them. If they came back today, they would be horrified to see what kind of society we live in. I believe that political correctness can be a form of linguistic fascism, and it sends shivers down the spine of my generation who went to war against fascism. The only way to react is to get up in the morning and start the day by saying four or five vastly politically *in*correct things before breakfast!

INTERVIEWER

To go back to your work: which detective novelists did you relish most before you started writing?

JAMES

I read mostly women detective writers: Dorothy L. Sayers, Ngaio Marsh, Josephine Tey, well, the sisterhood. I don't read many crime novels now, they are not my favorite reading.

INTERVIEWER

What about contemporaries, like Ruth Rendell? And younger ones, of whom quite a few have achieved success?

JAMES

I like them. Ruth Rendell writes detective stories under her own name and crime novels under the pseudonym Barbara Vine. I admire and prefer the latter.

INTERVIEWER

You have already alluded to several predecessors—Agatha Christie, Dorothy L. Sayers, Hammet, Chandler . . . I would like to ask you about two of the all time greats. Let us start with Sherlock Holmes, Sir Arthur Conan Doyle's detective.

JAMES

Every crime writer has been influenced by Sir Arthur Conan Doyle, even if only subconsciously. He bequeathed to crime writing a respect for reason and a non-abstract intellectualism, the capacity to tell a story and the ability to create a specific and distinctive world. He is also, of course, the creator of one of the first and certainly the most famous of all amateur detectives, Sherlock Holmes. Probably his greatest contribution to crime writing was that he made the genre popular, a popularity which it was never subsequently to lose.

INTERVIEWER

And Georges Simenon? Did you read him much?

JAMES

I have a great admiration for his work; he is a very good novelist by any criteria, with a remarkable understanding of human psychology, particularly that of the criminal mind. He worked in what I think must be a unique way for the crime novelist in that he has told us that his books weren't carefully plotted in advance. What he did was to choose the names of his characters from the international telephone directory and then put them in a certain situation and let them take over. This, of course, would not be a reasonable method of working for a detective novelist, since it isn't really comparable with the careful clue-making which classical detection requires. Georges Simenon, in my view, was a crime writer and a very fine one, not primarily a writer of detective stories.

INTERVIEWER

It is often said that women are particularly good at detective stories. Why do you think that is? Are they more intuitive, or observant of details, or sympathetic?

JAMES

It is certainly true that women do excel at the carefully clued, traditional detective story, although less successful with the hard-boiled, fast-action and violent crime novel, which is still largely the domain of male writers. One reason why women are good at writing detective stories may be our feminine eye for detail; clue-making demands attention to the detail of everyday life. George Orwell said that murder, the unique crime, should raise only strong emotions, and we are interested in those emotions rather than in weaponry. It may also be that women find that the ordered structure of the form is supportive, enabling us to deal with horrific events which we might find distressing outside the constraints of the genre.

INTERVIEWER

When you finally wrote your first novel, were you surprised it was accepted?

JAMES

No. But I was delighted. I always felt that if I managed to get the book written, it would be published. As it happened, the first publishers to whom I sent my manuscript, Faber & Faber, accepted it. I have been with them ever since. I was lucky; there are very good novelists whose desks are full of rejection slips.

INTERVIEWER

So the success of that first book encouraged you, and you went on. Then after eleven detective stories, last year you produced *Children of Men*, which one could describe as a futuristic moral parable?

JAMES

Yes, that's a fair description, because I don't think of it as science fiction, as some have claimed. I didn't set out to write a moral fable, but it came out that way. This time it was not a setting that inspired it, but the review of a scientific book drawing attention to a dramatic drop in the sperm count of western men: 50 percent in as many years. I asked some scientists about this, and they said that it was perhaps due to pollution. But the article drew attention to another factor: that of all the billions of life-forms that have inhabited this earth, most have already died out, that the natural end of man is to disappear too, and that the time our species has spent on this planet is a mere blink. So I wondered what England would be like, say, twenty-five years after the last baby was born, and then for twenty-five years no one had heard the cry of a baby. I sat down and wrote it. There is murder, but it is not a detective story. As you said, it is a moral parable, very different from my other books.

INTERVIEWER

The greatest problem of the world is overpopulation, not the drop in the sperm count of the Western man. The drop of the sperm count could be a blessing, don't you think?

JAMES

I know. India can't cope. They say the Chinese are curbing their population, but at what price! In Africa AIDS and famine are the main causes of death. But in the West the birthrate is dropping. So either man uses his knowledge to regulate his fertility, or the species is doomed.

INTERVIEWER

What about your new novel, *Original Sin*? Adam Dalgliesh is back. Did you decide to go back to your old genre because some critics said they preferred it? Or did your public reclaim Dalgliesh?

JAMES

Children of Men did well — it reached number six on the best-seller list. People wrote encouragingly about it, but said that they missed Dalgliesh, and hoped I had not discarded him for good. However, that is not why I brought him back. The book is set in London, in the publishing world.

INTERVIEWER

Why did you set it in the publishing world?

JAMES

I decided to set it in London, on the Thames, in a mock Venetian palace, and I thought why not the publishing world?

INTERVIEWER

Can you tell us a little more about it?

JAMES

The river runs as a unifying theme through the novel. Dalgliesh is again helped by my professional woman detective, Kate Miskin, who first appeared in *A Taste For Death*. Henry Peverell has just died and his partner, Jean-Philippe Etienne, has retired. Gerard, Etienne's ruthless son, has taken over as chairman and managing director. He has already made enemies — his discarded mistress, a rejected and humiliated author, his colleagues and threatened members of the Peverell staff. When he is found dead on the premises, his body bizarrely desecrated, there is no shortage of suspects.

INTERVIEWER

Why *Original Sin*? Are titles important to you?

JAMES

They are very important, and it is difficult to find the right one for a book. In my case the title comes either very early on, with no problem, or takes a long time and is found with difficulty.

INTERVIEWER

Does anyone help you if you get stuck for a title? Your editor?

JAMES

No. Except once, for *Innocent Blood*, which was my first best-seller in America, and which is a novel about a girl who has been adopted and is trying to discover her parents. The original title was Blood Relation, but we found that it was the title of another book in America. There is no copyright for titles, but on the whole it is better not to repeat something recent, and we decided to change it. The book was in proof form already, and we were desperate. I thought of Blood Tie, but wasn't very happy with it. Then a Catholic friend of mine told me that if something is lost and you pray to St. Anthony, you find it. I'm not a Catholic, but I did pray to St. Anthony, and the next morning when I woke up the first thing that came to my mind was *Innocent Blood*, which is a very good title.

INTERVIEWER

Are you already thinking of the next book?

JAMES

No. Not yet. It may come or it may not come. As I said, I don't worry; I wait and see what the Good Lord will send me by way of inspiration. Meanwhile I'm busy with proofreading and then with promotion, here and in the United States.

INTERVIEWER

I would like to take up another point, to which you alluded earlier: the preoccupation with death. Apart from your professional interest, so to speak, are you personally concerned with it? I mean some people live with a constant awareness of death—including your interviewer—while others never give it a thought.

JAMES

I always see the skull beneath the skin, which, incidentally, is the title of one of my books. I have always been preoccupied with death, and nowadays I think of my own death often. But as Shakespeare said "the readiness is all." I don't fear death; what I fear is loss of mind and limb, a long protracted painful dying. At seventy-four I have had my biblical three-score-and-ten. I feel I have been privileged with a long life. Those of us who lived through the last war, or have watched younger friends die of cancer or heart attack, are particularly aware of being lucky. My father used to say, "I'm on borrowed time now." I'm grateful for every extra day I have. But I *do* love life, and as long as I stay healthy I hope I'll go on for a long time.

INTERVIEWER

I believe you are religious, so perhaps you believe in an afterlife?

JAMES

I certainly believe in God. As a Christian one is supposed to believe in "the resurrection of the body," but I don't think I do. I *hope* the soul is eternal. I am rather attracted to the Buddhist idea of reincarnation, that we are on the up and up!

INTERVIEWER

Reincarnation is meant to be a process of purification—we get better and better until we achieve Nirvana, which is void, nothingness. I have never understood what is so great about that. I mean isn't it what atheists believe?

JAMES

I rather hope that reincarnation will mean that a future life will get better and better!

INTERVIEWER

Joking apart, the truth is that we don't know, and that we can't know. But we have lost the ability to accept and live with mystery.

JAMES

I absolutely agree. I think we are not meant to know. You are *so* right: religion devoid of mystery and beauty is nothing. One only gets an intimation of something beyond this world, but we are not meant to know more than that. I do believe in redemption through love. That is my religion, and Christ is showing us the way to love. But I don't believe Christianity is the only way, that no one comes to God except through Jesus Christ. Most people on this planet haven't even heard of him! To damn the great majority of the human race is absurd. Perhaps I have a simplistic view of these things, but I think different spiritual disciplines are like so many paths all leading to the summit of the mountain, where God is. We each choose our own way. The scenery and the track which is the Christian faith and which I have chosen is quite different from a Buddhist's or a Muslim's, but I hope we will all get there, eventually.

INTERVIEWER

Let us talk about your method: when do you write?

JAMES

When I first started writing, I got up early and wrote from six to eight, as I had to go to work. The habit has stuck, and I still get up early and write in the morning. When I'm writing a book, I get up before seven, go down to the kitchen and make tea, listen to the news on the radio, and have a bath, then I settle down to work. I find that after a few hours I can't go on, and I stop around twelve. The rest of the day is given to all other matters.

INTERVIEWER

Where do you write?

JAMES

I don't write in a particular place, and I can, in fact, write anywhere provided I have absolute peace and privacy. A favorite place is here (in the kitchen of my London house), since I can easily walk out into the garden when I feel inclined to a break in the fresh air, or make myself a coffee. It also has the advantage that the kitchen table is large enough to spread out my notes, dictionary and reference books. When I am writing a novel I never go anywhere without carrying a notebook in which I can jot down descriptions of places, impressions of the people I may meet, snatches of dialogue or a new sophistication of plot. I prefer writing by hand but my handwriting is so bad, particularly when I am writing quickly, that I can barely decipher it myself the next day. What I do is almost immediately to transfer the handwriting to tape, which my secretary types out to provide the first draft. I write the books out of order, rather as if I were shooting a film, and then put the story together at the end before sending the manuscript to a professional word-processing agency where it is put on disc. Then it is done.

— Shusha Guppy

Adrienne Rich

Sending Love

Voice
from the grain

of the forest bought
and condemned

sketched bond
in the rockmass

the earthquake sought
and threw

●

Sending love: Molly sends it
Ivan sends it, Kaori

sends it to Brian, Irina sends it
on pale green aerograms Abena sends it

to Charlie and to Joséphine
Arturo sends it, Naomi sends it

Lourdes sends it to Naoual
Walter sends it to Arlene

Habib sends it, Vashti
floats it to Eqbal in a paper plane

Bored in the meeting, on a postcard
Yoel scribbles it to Gerhard

Reza on his e-mail
finds it waiting from Patricia

Mario and Elsie
send it to Francísco

Karolina sends it monthly
home with a money order

June seals it with a kiss to Dahlia
Mai sends it, Montserrat

scrawls it to Faíz on a memo
Lenny wires it with roses

to Lew who takes it on his
whispery breath, Julia sends it

loud and clear, Dagmar brailles it
to Maureen, María Christina

sends it, Meena and Moshe send it
Patrick and Max are always

sending it back and forth
and even Shirley, even George

are found late after closing
sending it, sending it

•

Sending love is harmless
doesn't bind you   can't make you sick

sending love's expected
precipitous and wary

sending love can be carefree
Joaquín knew it, Eira knows it

sending love without heart
—well, people do that daily

         ●

Terrence years ago
closed the window, silent

Grace who always laughed is leaning
her cheek against bulletproof glass

her tears enlarged
like scars on a planet

Vivian hangs her raincoat
on a hook, turns to the classroom

her love entirely
there, supreme

Victor fixes his lens
on disappearing faces

—caught now or who will ever
see them again?

Two Poems by Stephen Dobyns

Then What Is the Question

It is hard to think of the people of Thebes
as being fortunate (so much time has gone by),
but they possessed a machine of exact measure:
a monster with the head and breasts of a woman,
body of a lion, wings of a bird, serpent's tail,
a lion's paws and a sweet human voice: the sphinx,
a sort of savage bureaucrat who kept life on track,

asking questions of the passersby. Those unable
to guess the answer became lunch. Functional
Darwinism. Who knows what strains of stupidity
were deleted from the Theban populace when some
cheerful dummy rubbed his jaw and said, "Beat's me."
Only Oedipus got the answer right. "What goes
on four feet, on two feet, on three. But the more

feet it goes on the weaker it be." The point is
the Sphinx was a fixed spot on the road. Tourists
could take her picture had there been cameras.
Sad to say, these days the Sphinx is invisible,
but even more ravenous. The young, the pretty,
the ugly, the old—the Sphinx eats them all. Victims
of Violence, reads the newspaper, Unknown Assailants,

Mysterious Motives. The cops scratch their heads.
Not only is the Sphinx hidden from us, but also
we don't know the riddle—a new one this time.
You ask why poets stand at the crossroads shouting
single words: Hypotenuse, Zebra, Waffle Iron!
These are potential answers to a question which
remains secret or has yet to be asked. A foolish

endeavor, you suggest. But imagine the feather
in the cap of the poet who gets it right. Snow
Flake, Radish, Goose Drop! Abruptly the killing stops:
a feeling of bouyancy, the sense that it is OK
to go outdoors. No more drive-by shootings, no more
murder in the night. One can argue the death
of the Theban Sphinx led to the flowering of the arts

in ancient Greece. Be that as it may, all we know
for sure is that our Sphinx is like a pane of glass
between us and the sun, or perhaps a gossamer web
in the clouds above us, or a single vicious drop
of water in an otherwise kindly sea. Perhaps someday
she will tire of life incognito and reveal herself.
Perhaps she will articulate the riddle and we can

put the computers to work. Poets will stop shouting:
Rutabaga, Doorstop! We can join together in a kindly
manner to discover the answer. Those Thebans: how we
should envy them! Their Sphinx was three-dimensional.
Her claws sparkled in the sunlight. Her laughter woke
babies in their cribs. For good or ill, you always
knew what questions to answer, what roads to avoid.

Garden Bouquet

For today at least the snow has gone
and the backyard is awash with daffodils.
See how the sun has come to court you? Quick,
take a snapshot, just to remind yourself
when the weather skulks back to normal.

Between the sun and yellow flowers exists
a silent chatter as the daffodils push
through the matted leaves and detritus
of winter. You try to think the flowers
and blue sky offer an essential worth

beyond any you impose on them. Fragile stems,
frail blossoms: how muscular they must be
to bear your devotion. For the cat they form
a decorative cover in her constant quest
for creatures small and briefly inattentive.

Across your eyes today is also a picture
from the paper: a man with a cigar and his legs
spread apart shooting his rifle at another man
collapsed on the ground. There is nothing special
about this photograph. Yesterday had a picture;

tomorrow will have another. These scenes
are the tinted glasses that human beings
learn to look through. No wonder the flowers
seem fragile. Most days are neatly divided —
flowers on one side, violence on the other.

Too bad, you say, about the victims of Monday,
and you turn away to whatever you call pretty.
But today something has broken in your eyes.
Today across the daffodils and blue violets
sprawls the figure of Tuesday's corpse. This one

is Moslem, yesterday's was Texan or German.
Where can one go to get one's eyes fixed?
You would like to apologize to your wife
for the ugliness you have spread across
the flowers she has personally tended.

You have put blood on the blossoms and it won't
wash off. If beauty is a human valuation, then
is the ugliness of murder equally subjective?
This corpse between the flowers and your eyes,
perhaps it's wrong to think it wrong, just

as it is foolish to think the flowers beautiful.
Some days all the answers are bad ones.
Some days there is only the word Stop
and you try to make a wall of it and repeatedly
beat your head against it. But of course

nothing stops and it is foolish to think so.
There is only this constant ongoingness
until your own private light blinks out:
the cruel variety, the savage bouquet,
the world's victims interspersed with flowers.

Two Poems by Cynthia Kraman

King Solomon and Dame Julian
in the Nut Garden

Through the veiled hush of the nut garden, God
was walking in the cool of the day; He
felt like talking again to a mortal
being, someone bright, maybe a king, who
might listen for once, but that would be too

wonderful, really, by a long shot, yet
he sought one of them out, Solomon, who
was wise and kind and a very fair man.
Later Solomon would say he began
"descending" in order to understand—

going down, "penetrating" the garden.
Impatiently peeling the layered shells
of the nuts, he would claim to know new things
about the cosmos, how the soul of light
lay deep at the core of the mystic night.

Then much later, an eyeblink later, God
wanted to speak again with a mortal
being, someone bright, maybe a woman
off on the side somewhere who'd understand
the nuts in the garden, how it began

with a nut and ended up as a
universe, although nothing had changed much
except size. And He handed Julian
the nut. She said, "It is all that is made.
Love keeps it safe." And God paused as she prayed.

Semiramis

Lascivis penitus lex est ablata deabus (When goddesses yield to voluptuousness, law is wholly overcome.)

—from "Semiramis", an 11th century manuscript found in Northern France, translated by Peter Dronke

In the time it takes for a hummingbird
to scratch his subtle ear, Semiramis
was not "the woman who took Babylon"
but the one who opened her thighs and stretched
for Jove to take his pleasure in the vetch.

See how the god mounts her powerful back
and clasps the warrior thighs in his great loins,
smelling of dung and wild carrots. Rejoice
in the mutual lowing, the mad voice
of interspecies love untethered, moist,

flinging off its used shame like a snakeskin
and pressing flesh to flesh—"Who comes back chaste
from the garden, if Jove wills otherwise?"
She shivers. He shudders down. They both breathe,
unoriginal as Adam and Eve.

A woman's honor stained by a bull's loins?
Semiramis laughs from her funeral urn.
But her brother isn't laughing. Her hips
have set tongues against him like cruel whips;
"O Sister, bring me your tragic lips!"

he weeps weakly, being a weak, nice boy.
"This is no tragedy," she says, "to love
a god, to be embraced, caressed, inspired
into the urn. Catch on now, or never . . .
the dead are not granted speech forever."

John Harvey

Angelus Novus

> *As an angel of illness I have Kafka at my bedside.*
>
> —Walter Benjamin to Gershom Scholem

I do not make phone calls, talk to anyone,
    let alone write. Even this letter
is mailed reluctantly. I move without cause,
    living with one friend, then for a time

with myself. They say I climb down from one cross
    to another. A voice whispers, *cry*
against it. I think this means words, all of them.
    I lie on the sofa, forget to

turn a page. Jonah drops off to sleep: casting
    for and into a dark ocean.
In this kind of apartment, the bed is my

    shadow and on certain nights my fingers
trace a dove at the window. Announcements like
    this are frequent, and at times I watch

a coat of arms pass through chambers and hallways
    toward a room, a book, a fable.
I sing hymns to comfort all that mourn, to hold
    and swallow death. I admit the time

has come to tell you about these things. I see
    a mass of flowers, a bridge, statues,
a laughing couple moving past trees. I feel
    light-headed, a bout of nausea.

Their smiling doesn't make it any better.
  The man stops and asks me if I live
around here. (They come upon you as if they

  have the right.) I frown and pretend not
to understand. It was in my letter from
  Povermo that I closed doors, burned lamps.

Now I sit here without seeing any of my
  attempts to afford food and clothing
(at least to pay a bill) succeed. I may move
  backwards come morning. In this way,

I become a gloss. As that one can hide, then
  escape. I take to my bed and leave
telegrams offering help unread. The world
  becomes an illness tonight, a sign

enunciated by holy mouths praying
  over blankets thin as frayed pages.
This is where I collect dark times, boxes piled

  in a corner of the room. I pull
back one flap, reach inside, and touch a road through
  the Pyrenees. I am confused by

its turns and sometimes have to crawl on all fours.
  In the evening I arrive at
the police station; my papers are reviewed,
  commented on, then returned to me

with a request for more. I have no stamp nor
  signature. The police, in despair,
beg for a name. They suggest I spend a night
  at the hotel—under guard, which means

they will return me to my room. I cannot.
  The room spins, nothing but color now,
pink or melon, and collapses into life,

    phrases like "silent and upright" or
"from each of them a head, two arms, and two feet
    protruded." The road, the papers, police

spill out on the floor. Rumors begin
  to circulate about Palestine,
about my son. This obnoxious mess riots
  to the door, pounds and yells, while the world's

lights flick on. Everyone looks. Something fumbles
  with the lock, calls out for a key, a
toothpick, and the much apprehended mass groans
  until the landlord shouts up for me to

quiet down and go to bed. Someone must need
  this room without its being here. I
look through the floor: a man in overalls shakes

    his fist (meat, just meat) at the boiler,
which menacingly shrugs its shoulders and laughs,
    a sound which uncouples its mouth, smears

an eye into a chin, lolls a useless tongue,
  a sound which carries me toward sleep as
a snuffer spoons away a candle's glow. All
  of this happens without my knowing

what the next hour will bring. I gather my night
  and place it back in its box. I close
the flaps like a child's hand closing on a toy.
  Make room. I sweep fresh air, stronger than

any hatred, into closets and behind
    bookshelves. The only illness here by
morning will be a spider's thread, the velvet

    imprint of an old day. This letter
may arrive without me. When I fall asleep
    I still dream of unimportant things.

Three Poems by Cathy Stern

Generation

Inside the picture it is 1903 — late spring or early summer.
The three women sit on the front porch steps,
a potted fern to their right on the middle stair,
another pot of what looks like vinca higher up
on the porch itself. Delicate ivy vines fall
from the low railing; a profusion of blurred leaves
moves up the turned wooden column at the porch's edge
and disappears at the top of the picture.
The woman in the middle, sitting highest,
holds a baby of three months or more,
who wears a bright white dress and smiles.
The baby is my father, and my young grandmother,
her hair piled high and caught with a ribbon,
her high-necked, dotted-swiss dress trimmed with ruffles
and appliquéd lace, looks quietly down
on her first born, her face so beautiful
I catch my breath. Her mother sits to her left,
gray and aging at forty-eight, unfrivolous
in her tailored skirt, blouse, and jacket;
her grandmother sits to her right, plump and white-haired,
serene in gingham and a long lace collar.
I can't take my eyes from their faces, their clothes.
I want to enter the picture, slip myself
into 1903, climb into the dresses and sit on the porch,
become each woman, touch the baby,
find the unborn daughter I will be.

Desert Storm

U.S. Helicopter Reconnaissance Photo, February 1991
Road North From Kuwait City To Basra

Like sandbox toys abandoned in mid-play
when mothers finally call the children home,
cars, trucks, and tanks lie strewn along the highway,
twisted, smashed, and burned—mile after mile—
receding into the desert as far as the eye can see.

All motion ceased abruptly—as if a spell
halted a thousand vehicles at once
spinning in panic toward the unbroken sand.
The world here ended in mid-breath. But there are
no bodies. The unnumbered dead have disappeared
into the vanishing point of the Road to Basra.

Domestic Archeology

In old movies they searched the mummy's tomb
with flashlights, on tiptoe—as if the dead
were listening, numbered the catacombs
skull by silent skull, hacked through unbounded
jungle brush to crumbling temples and ball
courts. But *National Geographics* show
pick, trowel, brush, and impenetrable
layers of earth with who knows what below.
Half heroine, half laborer last spring
I excavated long-forgotten sites—
den, attic, closet, cupboard—everything
piled up for years, and one dig brought to light
tracks, trestles, station, farmhouse, church—the boys'
electric train beneath my many Troys.

Two Poems by Dan Quick

Study for La Vie

Later, we will notice a vast communication
between separate selves. We will learn
in the colors of our lover's body
there are sullen blues darker than shadows,
whites whispering of absence, and grays
that join soundlessly into bedroom walls.

Later, we will listen to our own voices
speaking back to us. We will hear
words told to a lover in bed,
promises taken flight by their own shape,
sentences through which our future was named.

We will realize how tomorrow judges us today
for its position, how apparitions form
in every room to remind us
that every moment chains itself to another,
that every choice, though slightly made, changes destiny
into something else: a concrete slab,
or a silence that gathers terribly in the mouth.

La Vie

"I did not think my posing for him
would reveal anything not already known.
After all, we are passionate lovers
and share many intimacies. But I was not prepared
for the unexplained blue of my breasts,

or how he has drawn me twice, one self
consoling the other, as one does after loss.

No, I thought nothing of it. And must not think
anything of this new presence in the room, to whom
he raises one hand, as if to say 'Not yet.'
A presence called forth in the paintings,
a woman with my own eyes, draped in dark robes,
a child at her breast. I must not think of it.
I would rather remember, how after making love,
he once said to me: 'The delicate rose
of your nipple, it is something I must paint.'

How much that means to me. I will think only of it."

James McManus

Preludes

August Insomnia

Hunkered, totally

spaced, in the half-open door of the fridge
with my trifocals fogging, scanning the five

wrinkled grapes, tuna

casserole, hoping for pudding, banana
bread—which would, of course, be in the breadbox

I've already searched

three, four times, ignoring the caramel-corn
rice cakes—although whatever I find will

require an extra

few units of insulin—but so why not some
Equal with cornflakes, now that the finches are

dicking and cheeping?

Downward Rapture

I saw it.
A thing that was shivering, wet.
It was me.

Sapphire

I would like to avoid going through with it late
of a Monday evening, three or four hours before
the cure gets announced in the Science Times pages

of the newspaper down in my hallway, immaculate
inside its sapphire and black plastic tube, inky
fragrance, just waiting for me to *damn* read it and go

get my islet-cell implant, my bad genes unspliced
or resequenced. Whatever. Instead, there'd be viscous
beige drool caking up on my cheek. Or whatever.

Opus 28

I now understand

I will not get better, so as much gulping pleasure
—them too!—as I get from a Claudio Arrau and

or Tzimon Barto

rehearsing the sleeted-on drill and daily unhappy
surprise—still not in love? where's the sun?—of

George Sand and Chopin

biding their time, and he staying sick, on Majorca,
I still would've loved to hear Glenn or Thelonious,

out of time, try them.

Amulets

Silicon sludge from my bicycle's chain keeps tattooing my calf
with pewtery crescents of linked, half-inch-long figure eights.
I scrub them away in my afternoon shower and smudge myself
fresh ones each morning. Perhaps if I left them unscrubbed
through the evening they'd ward off bad luck: female
mosquitoes,
insulin reactions, the adolescent banshees of Down . . .
My calves are among my best features — aside from good noses
and cheekbones, they're the last things to go with most women
— especially when I have on my clogs or suede pumps, heel
perpendicular to opposite insole, toes lightly tapping . . .
So they might not look much less intriguing — at functions,
in
French class, glimpsed from four tables away as I sit with
Molloy
in a Wicklow cafe — crossed at the knees, neatly shaved, with
the mark of the chain on the steep inner curve of the right
one.

Chabela del Río y de la Fuente Contreras,

Thrice Married (Once Divorced), Reflects on
Her Relationship with Her Mother While
Lying on Her Bed, Mexico City, 1990

C.M. Mayo

Mother rescued the three zebras that escaped from the London Zoo.

For years, I didn't believe it.

When I was really little, she would tell me the Luftwaffe's bombs were as loud as a sweet potato man's steamer, like a jet engine on the runway. When I was a year or so older, she let me know that the bombs were far-off whistles, exploding out in the suburbs. Then, when I was too old to be bounced on her knee, she said the bombs were hitting the flats next door, the bandstand in the park, the bridge over the Thames. One flattened the neighbor's coach house; blood dripped from baby Victor's left ear.

Every time Mother told the story, she said she had run out

to the street in her blue silk bathrobe and Moroccan slippers, a cigar jammed into the side of her mouth like Mr. Churchill. When I was little, she said the zebras had been so frightened, she only had to grab one's mane with her left hand, the other's with her right, and the third zebra followed along like a tired old sheepdog.

But when I was older, she let me know that the zebras reared up and neighed. She lassoed one of them with an old dog leash, another with her belt. The third she wrestled down and tied up with twine, like they did on the ranch in Sonora. She told me one of the zebras kicked her, gave her a gash that needed six stitches.

Mother had a white quarter-moon-shaped scar on her thigh. One day, when we were all swimming at Eden Roc, I asked Victor, "Is that Mother's zebra scar?" When Victor wants to be nasty, he still says, "Is that Mother's zebra scar?" in a high, whiny little voice.

Mother got that scar in 1953. She misjudged a mogul and went flying into a pine tree at Gstaad.

*

I call my maid: bring me a cucumber and a knife.
On each eyelid, I place a slice of cool.

*

Mother died last month. Last week I cleaned out her closets. In a cardboard box, underneath a sheaf of letters tied with ribbon, I found a brittle newspaper clipping, so old it had turned orange. It had a picture of Mother in front of the zebra pen at the London Zoo. The caption said:

WIFE OF MEXICAN AMBASSADOR BRAVES NAZI BOMBS
FOR LONDON ZOO

She was bundled up in a bulky coat, arms akimbo, her bobbed hair disarranged in a wind. She was squinting, in that funny way she did, her eyes very black, but bright.

*

I have an eiderdown quilt. The duvet is Pierre Deux. The ceiling over my bed is a dome made of lightweight bricks which are staggered precisely, row upon curving row, spliced with triangular wedges. When I told the architect I wanted a brick dome for the bedroom, he said it would be difficult: he knew only one man in all the Republic who could make one properly. He was an old Chichimeca who lived in a village on the northern foothills.

Weeks passed.

The Chichimeca arrived in Mexico City without notice, on a third-class bus. I did not visit the construction site, but I knew he was there, balancing the bricks in my sky. He would have a wizened brown face and thick white hair. He would know only a few words of Spanish, which he would pronounce strangely, in a high, quavering voice. He would be wearing huaraches, the soles made from a bald car tire, and his toes would be splayed, blackened, twisted.

The dome is beautiful.

Wen Pao, my pug, lies next to me. I stroke her little head. Wen Pao has soft apricot fur. She snores, lightly.

*

Three months after the war ended, Mother, Papi, Victor and the staff were packed off to Buenos Aires. Then Rio de Janeiro, then Bogotá, I think, and then Paris, where I was born. I grew up in Grandfather's apartments near the Place des Vosges.

Victor is much older than I. He was thirty when we came back to Mexico in 1968. I was nineteen. I say came back to Mexico, but we had never actually lived there. When I was ten, Grandfather died and we left his apartments on the Place des Vosges and moved to the suburbs, St. Cloud, dreadful. Then the government changed, and Papi was posted to Jamaica, Kingston, blistering filth, smells of rotting fruit and butchered animals. Quito, cold and filthy. Tunis: hellhole on the Mediterranean.

Then Papi died.

Nineteen sixty-eight was a terrible year to be in Mexico, a terrible year to be nineteen. At the time, I thought it was wonderful. Every day was a clean vista, crash of energy and spume.

*

Wen Pao leaps to the carpet, barking furiously. My maid shouts through the door, Señora! A boy is selling blackberries from Puebla, 35,000 pesos the kilo. I tell her no—(a reflex)—I saw them for 28,000 at the market yesterday—(pure invention)—but she cannot hear me over Wen Pao's staccato. I stretch. I toss the cucumber slices onto the bedside table.

*

Mother promised me the Aubusson carpets. She said that when she died I could have the blue one, the one with the festoons and the gold urns on a robin's-egg blue, a blue (one of the few things I remember Papi saying) like a spring sky over Provence. Mother said I could also have the red Aubusson, which is unevenly faded, and frayed in the center. Knowing Mother, I thought that meant she would leave me the red Aubusson and Victor the blue one. But he got both.

*

What did I say? Yes to the blackberries? Would I make a cheesecake with blackberry sauce? Goose stuffed with blackberries? Blackberries served in a crystal bowl with powdered sugar, a pitcher of cream on the side? They would be spooned

out into Mother's French porcelain bowls — the white ones with
the swirling patterns and the little black stars.

No; I said no.

*

We came back to Mexico in 1968. I was nineteen, which
is to say I was nothing. Victor had a job with a French invest-
ment bank in the Colonia Centro. He also had a wife, a baby,
a station wagon, a set of left-handed golf clubs, a cocker spaniel
named Tartuffe.

*

Papi was on his deathbed in Tunis. He had gone on a three
week trek to see the Roman ruins at Dougga, and had suffered
an attack of appendicitis in the last week. Mother cried when
she read the telegram. That same morning, Papi was carried
into the embassy red-faced, screaming. His bed was brought
down to the receiving room, which had a marble floor, cooler
in the Mediterranean summer. He was sedated. A servant
fanned away the flies with an enormous sheaf of palm leaves.

I remember the ceiling there, in the receiving room: it was a
frieze with *rinceaux* of acanthus leaves, made of cream-colored
plaster. In its corners and center, there were putti with tiny
wings and monkeyish faces, all pointing to something out the
window: a cinderblock wall. *Belle epoque à la tunisienne.*

All afternoon, Papi lay with his eyes squeezed shut, sweat-
ing. Sometimes he groaned, or let out a sharp breath. The
boy with the palm fronds wove his arms over the bed like an
automaton, hour after hour, his features registering nothing
but concentration, rhythm.

I tried to mop Papi's brow with a hand towel I had soaked
in lemon water. He flicked open his eyes and waved me away.

Later that same afternoon, Mother said, "Well, you are not
his child." Just like that.

*

There is an ear-splitting whistle: the sweet potato man's steamer. He sounds it every day at about this time. Chabelita is home from school, the dishes from lunch have been washed, and dried. The traffic has lost the energy of morning, or even early afternoon; now there is only a soft, tired droning. If I were to walk downstairs, I might hear the steamer clattering over the cobblestones.

Wen Pao sighs, and rolls over onto her side. She splays her paws, like a cat.

Once, when I was small, we came to Mexico City for Holy Week. My nanny bought me a sweet potato. She gave it to me in a dish, with a spoon. We poured honey over it, and heavy cream. Mother came into the kitchen while I was eating it. She said it was a filthy thing, and if I got sick, *ni modo*. Nothing to be done about it.

*

We packed our things in Tunis and came to live in Mexico City in 1968. Within a month I'd developed an interest in literature (a crush on Carlos Fuentes), in art history (a yearning to travel in Italy), and in whatever my new boyfriend Esteban might suggest (Asian philosophy, Jimi Hendrix, cannabis, batik wraparound miniskirts).

Mother loved Esteban. She cried more than I did when he was arrested. And it crushed her that when he was released, he had changed, become practical.

*

So whose child was I? My mother's and only my mother's. I have her curly chestnut hair, her mouth with the puffy upper lip. I have her owlish black eyes. Her thick waist, her ample chest, her tapered fingers, the second toes longer than the big toes. I have her light spray of freckles across the bridge of my nose. And her skin so white, my veins show greenish-blue.

And now: I am just beginning to suffer her snowy hairs, that shock of white over my left temple. And too, the crow's

feet, the double chin, the age spots on the backs of my hands.
I have had affairs.
But would I have rescued the zebras from the London Zoo?

*

The army occupied the university in mid-September 1968.
Esteban was picked up in the basement of Philosophy as he
was cranking out handbills. He was held incommunicado.

I didn't know what I was doing. I went crazy, shouting at
people on the street, the newspaper vendor on the corner,
housewives at the supermarket—especially the well-dressed
ones, matrons in below-the-knee skirts and big gold Virgin
of Guadalupe medals hanging down the middle of their buttoned-up blouses. They'd reach for the Campbell's soup and
I'd say, "The students' six demands are perfectly reasonable!"

There was Mother: she wore below-the-knee skirts and had
a Virgin of Guadalupe medal hanging down the middle of
her buttoned-up blouse. But when I said, "The students' six
demands are perfectly reasonable!" she would say, "Yes, of
course they are."

The day after Esteban was picked up I took the bus to Victor's
office. All the way into the Colonia Centro, the bus lurched
and rattled. It smelled of greasy food, and of bodies that have
been washed, but without soap. I found Victor's office on the
fourth floor of a colonial mansion on the Avenida Madero.
The secretary showed me a leather couch. I sat there for a long
time, crossing and uncrossing my legs.

I curled my lip at the hunting prints, framed in burlwood
and black lacquer. I flipped through the annual reports that
had been neatly stacked on the coffee table. Their thick glossy
paper made me angry. Their photographs of fat men in pin-
stripe suits made me think of Papi.

I can't remember what I said to Victor. I know I had wanted
him to help find out where Esteban was being held. I know
I must have cried, said awful things. It was before the massacre
at Tlatelolco. He ran an index finger around his little beige

hearing aid and took a sip of coffee from his cup, a delicate Limoges.

"Long before you were born," he said, "we had to sleep in the underground, deep down, deeper than any metro in New York, or Paris, or Mexico. The air-raid wardens would sound the sirens, and we would gather up water and blankets, playing cards and a good supply of candles and hurricane lamps. We huddled together for warmth, Mother with me and Papi, the servants and the guards from the embassy in their olive-green coats. I don't actually remember this," he went on, "nor the drone of the Luftwaffe, the smells in the underground, nor even the whistling sound of the bombs. I just remember how everything was being destroyed. Every day was going to be the end."

He coughed and set his cup on his desk. "One morning Mother was walking me to my school on the other side of St. James's. A German pilot had come down without his parachute. There was a tree branch as thick as your waist on the sidewalk next to him. He was nude."

"Victor," I said, "get to the point."

"I kicked his head with my shoe is the point."

I crossed my arms over my chest and looked at him with disgust. "Mother slapped you of course."

"Of course. So I kicked it again."

*

Victor was useless. I was unable to rescue Esteban. I remember Mother playing hour after hour of dominoes in the library. She and her friends would nibble chocolates, and she began to spread. The wicker sofa groaned when she got up or sat down. She cried often, and kept a linen handkerchief in her pocket to dab at her eyes.

There was nothing to be done.

They let Esteban out a few days before Christmas. He said the police had lined them up, and beat them with their rifle butts. And herded them into a tiny cell without a lavatory.

I was so terribly impressed.

*

I married Esteban in 1970; I divorced him in 1972. I have lived as one lives without him since then (marrying twice more, moving to La Jolla once, and back). Mutual friends tell me his management consulting business is doing well, despite his drinking. His second wife is an American, from Dallas, and she was a nationally ranked golf player. Or a tennis player, I don't recall. Esteban has just made the down payment on a condominium in Cabo San Lucas, overlooking the harbor.

I believe whatever I am in the mood to believe.

*

I had a daughter with my second husband, Sebastian. Her name is also Chabela, so I called her Chabelita. Sebastian was killed on the Cuernavaca highway eight and a half months before Chabelita was born. He was changing a tire when a cement truck hit a slick of water and swerved into him.

Mother hated Sebastian. Sebastian owned a chain of American-style steak restaurants. He wore Countess Mara ties and on weekends, white loafers. He played golf with Victor, and he actually liked the cocker spaniel, Tartuffe. He would stroke Tartuffe's silky muzzle, and whisper things in its ears.

"What in God's name are you telling that dog?" Mother thought Sebastian was ridiculous.

When Chabelita was small, Mother would sing her funny songs.

Up above the world you fly,
Like a teatray in the sky.

She would ask her riddles: "Why is a raven like a writing desk?" Once, Mother asked Chabelita the riddle of the Sphinx. Mother searched her little face, and tucked her curls behind her ears. "Why it's woman!" she said, and kissed Chabelita's fat baby cheeks.

*

When I was five years old, and Victor sixteen, we were left alone for a weekend in the apartment in Paris. My nanny had left without her pay, I cannot remember why; Papi was in Mexico, Mother had gone to ski in Gstaad. Victor tried to entertain me with his jigsaw puzzle collection, unsuccessfully, because when I couldn't fit the pieces together, I would force them. When he took my work apart, I cried and punched him. Then he shut me up in my bedroom, but I howled until the neighbors in the opposite building called to complain.

Then Victor got the idea that we should dig up the tiny garden out back, searching for treasure. We dug around and under every single bush and plant, and even poked a spade in between the roots of an old tree. It was a cold and dirty business, but we worked all afternoon Saturday, and the greater part of Sunday. The amazing thing is, Victor actually found something. Behind a pruned rosebush, he unearthed a rotted leather bag of silver coins.

When Mother returned on Monday morning, we found her hunched over a steaming cup of Turkish coffee, her eyes squeezed shut. Victor emptied the coins out on the breakfast table. They made sharp clicks and thuds on the blackened oak surface, and Mother's eyes opened very bloodshot, very wide. She almost spit out her coffee.

"You've stolen them," she said flatly. Victor was indignant. He kicked a leg of the table, too hard. He hopped away biting his lip.

I said, "Mother! We dug them up in the garden!" And suddenly, she smiled at me so warmly. "The war," she whispered, as if to herself, and began to laugh. I think that was the last moment I loved her without reserve: I climbed on her lap and clasped my arms around her neck. Her face was tanned, her cheeks windburned. She smelled of calamine lotion and hot coffee.

From the corner by the sideboard, Victor said, "They are *my* coins."

"Why?" Mother said, and she scooped them off the table into her purse.

*

After Sebastian's funeral I went back to our apartment and sat on the bed. I should have thrown the curtains open; perhaps that simple gesture would have saved me. But I sat on the bed, weighted down as if by stones, and as the afternoon slipped by I could no longer recall his face, or his voice. I knew his features by rote — the curve of his chin, the tufts of coarse hair on his earlobes, the oblong mole on his cheek. But they were like scattered pieces of a puzzle; they didn't fit, they didn't make a whole. I remembered that he liked to sing along with his Lucha Villa records; I remembered that as he went out the door to work, he always winked and said, "Ciao, Baby." But his words ran through my mind in my own voice, as if I were reading aloud from strips of paper. And somehow it chilled me that his clothes were still hanging next to mine in the closet, that his credit cards and cuff links were lying in a box under my shoes.

Mother had to come take care of me. She plumped the pillows and made me lemongrass tea. She brought glossy magazines and she turned the pages for me. She brushed my hair with slow gentle strokes.

Days later, when I was well enough to get up and put on my bathrobe, I saw that Mother had taken all of Sebastian's things from the closet. And when I went to brush my teeth, I found that she had removed all the medicines, even the aspirin.

*

On Chabelita's tenth birthday, Mother gave her a leather pouch. It was new and supple, and quite heavy. Chabelita untied the strings and emptied it over the carpet: out tumbled ten silver coins the size of sand dollars.

I bent down and picked one up. It was a Mexican coin, with a sunburst and a lumpy cap. LIBERTAD, it said. Liberty. On the obverse was the eagle perched on a cactus, a snake writhing in its beak — but with a Chinese character crudely stamped into its wing.

Mother was beaming at Chabelita. "You see those Chinese stamps? There was a time when the peso was worth something."

"Now pesos are for spending," I said. I thought that was terrifically witty.

"You must hide them in a safe place," Mother was telling Chabelita, "but in a place where you won't forget them."

Suddenly I realized: these were the coins Victor and I had dug up in that garden.

Chabelita held one of the coins in her palm, rotating it as she read the minute lettering. "Why would I forget them, Grandma?"

She looked exactly like I did at that age.

*

Sebastian was killed eight and a half months before Chabelita was born. I had been seeing his brother. He was a politician with the PAN, always running, always losing. He made his money in plastic tubing. We met on Tuesdays at the Camino Real. We ordered room service.

After the funeral, his brother wouldn't speak to me. Later, Mother told me he'd given his house to the Opus Dei.

Que pendejo, she said. What an ass.

*

The week before Mother died, I was in New York with my lover, Karl. My husband, my third husband, my current husband, Juventino, was in London with Victor, on business. I told him I had to shop.

"Shop till you drop," Juventino said.

*

I bought this eiderdown quilt there, at a boutique on East 63rd Street. I had a devil of a time getting it into my suitcase. Karl and I jumped up and down on the suitcase to flatten the feathers.

The Pierre Deux duvet, I bought in New York as well.

My robin's egg-blue Aubusson, at auction.

And Wen Pao, my furry baby. She was the smallest in a litter of pugs we saw in a pet-shop window on East 78th Street. When she saw us walking by, she stood up on her hind legs, her front paws pressed against the glass.

Karl gave me her red ostrich leather Hermès collar.

We walked Wen Pao in Central Park, every day for a week. It was early November and the leaves were still brilliant orange, burnt sienna, the red of Wen Pao's collar. The air was sharp and clean, and bittersweet with the smell of pretzels and roasting chestnuts. *"Liebling,"* Karl would whisper into my ear, and nudge the nape of my neck, brush his chill lips across my cheek, *"Steh Kopf,"* *stand on your head*. Nonsense. *Dance the mambo. Make me a frog leg sandwich with this American ketchup*. But I would return his kiss, his clear-eyed gaze, that satisfied laugh that will always make me think of salted chestnuts shaken in a newspaper cone. We held hands as we shuffled through the brittle leaves, my buttery deerskin glove against his, rough and black. When Wen Pao tired, Karl would pick her up and carry her in his coat.

On the last day, we were walking behind the band shell when I thought I saw Mother with a black man, Rollerblading down East Drive. Her snowy hair, thick waist and ample chest, her back still strong though curved with years. She was wearing striped stretch pants and a white sweatshirt that said FREE THE — I could not read the rest; she disappeared around a bend.

"Das bist du," Karl said, pointing at her, laughing. Just like you.

*

Mother died of a stroke in Mexico City the following week. I found her suitcases piled in the foyer, still packed. I tore off all the luggage tags. Kennedy, Orly, Gatwick, and two others I didn't recognize.

Victor asked me where she was going; I said I had no idea.

*

Those letters I found in her closet, tied with silk ribbon: I burned them, one by one. Postmarked Rangoon, postmarked Berlin, London, Lugano. 1927, 1987. Brittle ivory foolscap, red block-letter stamps, browned fountain-pen ink, a black wax seal, cracked through the center. Words floated out at me: Rue, dear, raining very hard since Easter, love, will you? have you? Gstaad, this damn, war. I stared at the flame and let my eyes water. Had I read them?

I might have.

*

I see my life in leopard print: spotted with black spots. Tan background, tan like the Sahara desert, like butterscotch pudding, the color of my maid's face.

I bury my face in the fur of Wen Pao's scruff.

Victor looks old now. He has a wattle under his chin. His hair is white, running around the rim of his scalp like a stripe. His bald spot has grown.

"Is that Mother's zebra scar?"

I wish I had never asked him.

*

Out my bedroom window, the sky is electric orange. If I could see through my brick dome, the sky would be a starless indigo. I have to do my nails, crimson. I have to set my hair. I will wear my gray wool Louis Ferraud, my faux pearls, my Chanel wristwatch, a few daubs of Joy de Patou. Juventino will pick me up for a dinner at the German Embassy, where they will serve us canapés and champagne next to the Christmas tree. There will be a quartet playing Haydn and Handel, and everywhere, the sweet musky perfume of beribboned swags and beeswax candles. Then we will sit in the dining room, for goose with blackberry sauce, Black Forest cake, coffee and liqueurs. Karl is the Ambassador. I think I'll tell his wife about the London Zoo.

Chapter VII

apart from a little attack of ~~tricolour~~ calm
aboard, & the omnipresent smell,
by stealth

Bombay: fresh fruit for the invalids, to be sure; enormous meals for those
who had time to tame them; but, the wonders of the East, the marble palaces,
remained distant, half-guessed at objects for the Surprises people, for she was
taken into the ~~dockyard~~ naval straight ~~discharged~~ stripped her to the bone; they also
~~emptied~~ took out her guns & ~~emptied her~~ cleared the hold to come at her steps &
what they found there made them clear the dry-dock as fast as they could
& warp her in. before she sank at her moorings.

The Admiral, having visited them in state & having ~~said~~ the kindest things
about the frigate's appearance, instantly deprived Jack of his first lieutenant
giving ~~him~~ Mr Hervey his commission as master & commander and appointing him to an
eighteen-gun sloop.   This threw all the work of refitting on to Jack's shoulders
and the Admiral, touched in his conscience, ~~spoke~~ aware of Mr Stanhope's importance,
~~& well disposed towards~~ spoke the good word to the master-attendant, and all the
resources of a well-equipped yard were freely at the frigate's disposal ~~Jack flung himself~~
~~into the harvest with this Tom Tiddlers ground~~ The daughter of the horse leech was
nothing to Captain Aubrey let loose in a T. Tiddlers ground strewn with tar
hemp, iron, spars, cordage, sailcloth by the acre, even new copper, and he kept
the ship's company to their task by night & day, while gangs of native caulkers
made her thunder like a great deep grumbling ~~distant~~ drum.

Stephen left him caressing a massive teak stem-knee, a piece of timber
that would outlast the centuries & the malice of the deathwatch beetle, & quilted
the ship with an artfully ~~vague~~ word about 'seeing him ~~presently~~ at a convenient time
'reviewing the local ?   What patients

should have no objection, he was sure, to his   'Taking the sense of the inhabitants
~~profiting~~ by the present situation   in the matter of Kampong

Patrick O'Brian

The Art of Fiction CXLII

*The serious American publication of Patrick O'Brian's Au-
brey-Maturin novels began in 1987. They were greeted with
yelps and growls of satisfaction rising rapidly to a thunderous
ovation as deserved as it was belated. But the earliest brilliant
flicker of lightning dates back to 1952, when his first novel,
Testimonies, appeared. Delmore Schwartz, in an omnibus
review (which has lately become famous along with O'Brian)
including novels by Hemingway, Steinbeck, Waugh and Angus Wilson, gave O'Brian pride of place and praise.*

Testimonies *had been preceded by a collection of short sto-*
ries, and was followed by novels, more stories, several poems
(three of which we are privileged to reprint here), many trans-
lations from the French (including Papillon *and most of Si-*
mone de Beauvoir's books), more lately biographies of Joseph
Banks and Picasso, a constant flow of book reviews, and of
course the Aubrey-Maturin series, beginning with Master and
Commander *in 1969. Fifteen years earlier O'Brian had written*
The Golden Ocean, *a cheerful fiction based on Anson's expedi-*
tion to the Pacific in 1740. ("I had been reading naval history
for years and years, and I knew a fair amount about the sea:
I wrote the tale in little more than a month, laughing most
of the time.") The novel is a lark, and had, as its author later
noted, "pleasant consequences." Among those are the now
seventeen volumes of the Aubrey-Maturin series, which are
in many languages, including Japanese, and are justly famed.
O'Brian's eloquent admirers include not merely distinguished
critics and reviewers but noted novelists (Mary Renault wrote,
"Master and Commander *raised almost dangerously high ex-*
pectations; Post Captain *triumphantly surpasses them. Mr.*
O'Brian does not just have the chief qualifications of a first-class
historical novelist, he has them all"), actors, judges, professors,
reporters — and thousands upon thousands of fervent readers
who thank the gods for him, quote him, thrust him confidently
upon friends, and give whole sets for Christmas.

The young O'Brian spent long periods in England, "but it
was Ireland and France that educated and formed me, in so
far as I was educated and formed." The reservation is too
modest; he studied philosophy and the classics formally, and
certainly has a way with languages. The young man met the
sea, and canvas, with delight (". . . although I never became
much of a topman, after a while I could hand, reef and steer
without disgrace, which allowed more ambitious sailoring later
on"). During the war he and his wife drove ambulances and
served in intelligence together. Afterward they lived briefly
in Wales, but presently "sun and wine came to seem essential,"
and they settled in a little fishing village in the Roussillon.
O'Brian knew early that he was a writer, and seems never to

have been tempted by other vocations. He is also a reader,
of course, and the range of his knowledge is rather daunting,
but the tact and skill with which he uses that knowledge are
remarkable. He values privacy and dignity, loves his work and
his home, resents interruptions but is unfailingly courteous.
In our bizarre age of masquerade and mammon, of footlights
and flashbulbs, of tabloids and television, O'Brian seems ex-
traordinary: he is his own man, he does his work, he values
history, the arts and sciences, morality. He lives on good terms
with his neighbor and with Homer, with the birds in his garden
and with Mozart, with his readers and with Linnaeus. He is
surely "one of the best storytellers of the age," as one eminent
admirer put it, and his work accomplishes nobly the three
grand purposes of art: to entertain, to edify and to awe.

This interview took place by correspondence over a period
of months in 1994.

INTERVIEWER

Delmore Schwartz wrote of *Testimonies*, "In O'Brian, as in
Yeats, the most studied cultivation and knowledge bring into
being literary works which read as if they were prior to literature
and conscious literary technique." Homer and Hesiod come
to mind. Are your "influences" all classical, or are there mod-
erns as well among them?

PATRICK O'BRIAN

Before I comment on "influences" may I first take up Delmore Schwartz's "conscious literary technique"? Since I grew
up I have never deliberately used any technique at all other
than the physical shaping of my tale so that it more or less
resembles what has been thought of as a novel for these last
two hundred years. Earlier, in the wicious pride of my youth,
I sometimes threw myself into postures, imitating writers I
admired and producing a certain amount of Proust and water
(the recipe for the Avignon lark pâté comes to mind: one lark,
one horse) to Joyce and very small beer; but none of this
survived the war, and by the time I was writing *Testimonies*,

for example, I was setting down what I had to say in the words and with the rhythm that seemed right to what might perhaps be called my inner ear, and doing so without any immediate debt to anyone.

INTERVIEWER

Which does not mean that you were unaffected by literary predecessors. Just how do these influences operate? Can they teach you morality, or elegance, or plotting? Do you feel a special kinship to Smollett?

O'BRIAN

Of course deeper formative influences were there by the hundred, barely touching the conscious level: the obvious classics, together with a fair amount of Vulgate and later Latin, and people like Chaucer, the Elizabethans, Dryden, Pope, Johnson, Fielding, Jane Austen, as well as quantities of dear, somewhat out-of-the-way writers such as Camden, Selden, Burton, Isaac Disraeli; and, by means of Waley, the Chinese poets. You mention Smollett. No, I feel little or no kinship with him. For although the influences that I have mentioned did not, as far as I know, teach me morality or elegance (can either be taught?) they did perhaps make me dislike a certain variety of coarseness that Smollett shares on occasion with Sterne, a kind of sniggering that calls for a complicity that I am unwilling to give, though I find Rabelais excellent company and laugh wholeheartedly with Chaucer when he is bawdy. " 'Te-hee!' quod she, and clapt the window to" seems to me a splendid line.

INTERVIEWER

Along the same lines: your erudition, plotting and style (to say nothing of Maturin's quotations from a hundred classical authors, some indeed "out-of-the-way") seem not sudden ingenuities or laboriously prepared effects, but the products of habits of mind formed by long and serious reading. Which great literatures, which great writers, have taught you most?

Do you reread them continually? Or is the past wholly incorporated, so to speak, so that rereading ceases to be a joy?

O'BRIAN

As for the point about prepared effects, they do not exist. Effects, in so far as there are any, either present themselves or they do not come at all. And if they do present themselves it is because they rise from a fairly copious stirabout of reading in which countless books and pieces of books are merged, oddments coming to the surface either of their own volition or in response to some computer whose working is far beyond my reach.

Which great literature, which great writers, have taught me most? An earnest and a solemn question, and it seems odiously flippant to say that all they have taught me is that writing (as Picasso said of painting) is not *only* but *also*. The eighteenth century had the notion that literature's function was to encourage virtue and to lash vice; but that is scarcely a view shared by those who read for delight (or for pity and terror) rather than instruction, and although a man like Shakespeare may teach one respect, admiration and humility to the point of putting down one's pen, at least for a while, I do not believe he teaches anything else. Indeed, apart from the mechanical trades and the exact sciences, what of value can be taught? Taught directly? And where the heart of writing is concerned, if you have to ask, surely it ain't no good.

Yet there are many who have certainly and directly taught me admiration and yes, I do read them again and again. I have a Horace upstairs and a Horace down: last summer I read Homer right through in the warm evenings out of doors, with a female black redstart fluttering angrily about my head because I read under the light that was her usual perch; and indoors I have a set of Jane Austen, all early editions for the added delight of immediacy, that I very often consult and rarely put down in less than an hour. In all these and in the more glorious parts of Dickens, Boswell, Gibbon and many more I continually find new joys. The same applies to very good painting: less so, alas, to top music other than plainchant.

INTERVIEWER

The Aubrey-Maturin series is shot through with the blissful sort of humor that cannot be invented or learned but must spring from deep within. Until *The Golden Ocean* your work was not at all playful. Was it the sea that brought out your sunny side?

O'BRIAN

What you say about humor that "cannot be invented or learned but must spring from deep within" really applies to the rest of writing: *le style c'est l'homme même*, said Buffon, taking style in the broadest possible sense. But where the rest of your question is concerned fun came into my writing on the shores of the Mediterranean, with sea, wine, sun and a happy marriage.

INTERVIEWER

Had you any formal training as a naturalist, biologist, taxonomist, or have you learned all that for the sheer joy of it? And medicine?

O'BRIAN

Science? What little I have was mostly acquired by osmosis: one relative was a bacteriologist, another a physicist who worked on radium with Rutherford and Louis de Broglie, another a geologist. Yet I was taught a certain amount of biology; and being very sick I necessarily learned a certain amount about medicine.

INTERVIEWER

Every now and then a Frenchly phrase pops up, e.g., "entered into the line of count." Do you also read widely in French and hop from one language to the other all day?

O'BRIAN

Gallicisms: yes, they exist. My wife and I have spent most of our lives in France and we are both pretty well bilingual, my wife more purely than I, since as a little girl she went to school in French Switzerland. At one time we used them for fun, saying, for example, "Foute it in the poubelle," and insensibly this has come to taint my English idiom. If I am suddenly asked my telephone number I am sadly puzzled to say it in anything but French. Yet a slightly shaky idiom is a small price to pay for having the whole of French literature open to one; and French translations too, for the great Russians, and how astonishingly good they are, are splendid in French, often ludicrous in English.

INTERVIEWER

The Russians: *War and Peace* is a "historical novel" (though Russia had not altered much in the interval), and many of its leading characters — even Platon — are aspects of Tolstoy or people he knew. Are Jack and Stephen aspects of you? Or do you think of them as friends? Or are they your creatures only?

O'BRIAN

I do not think they are. I am fond of them both, but I am in no way identified with either.

INTERVIEWER

Do you agree with Maturin that Napoleon was a tyrant, an unmitigated disaster? Buonaparte did, after all, reform French law, politics, taxes — doesn't much of his *code civil* endure today? He also restored French national identity after the Revolution and the Terror. Wellington and Metternich, not to mention Louis XVIII and Charles X, were unreconstructed reactionaries. Yet Maturin sees Napoleon as a kind of early Stalin.

O'BRIAN

Yes, I do agree with Maturin. I think Buonaparte did France — a country that he hated as a youth — very great harm indeed, not only because he brought about the death of vast numbers of Frenchmen, far more than even Louis XIV, but because he left the country with a curiously vulgar notion of glory, which Louis did not. I do not think he restored French national identity at all, but superimposed upon it a trashy chauvinism that is still sadly active, particularly in the army. One cannot blame him entirely for the miserable decline in music, painting, architecture and furniture-making that coincided with his altogether regrettable existence, for zeitgeist had a great deal to answer for; but there is no doubt that he was devoid of taste (he admired Ossian) and his manners were as indifferent as his French. His utterly unscrupulous rapacity in Italy, Switzerland, Malta and Spain, to say nothing of his treatment of the Pope, may not quite qualify him as a rival to Stalin, but it seems to me quite enough to justify Maturin's opinion.

As for the *Code Napoléon*, I am not scholar enough to know how much Buonaparte had to do with it, but from what I have seen of the system, or of what remains of it, I do not think it reflects much credit on the authors. It is shockingly authoritarian and misogynistic; and since according to its provisions all the children have equal rights in their parents' property it has a disruptive influence on both family life and the cohesion of an estate. I have often seen the miserable results of this among our friends in the remote provincial corner of France where we live and where many people still depend entirely on the land. The children soon learn — it is a matter of common knowledge — that apart from the small proportion that can be left according to the wishes of the leaver the whole of the rest is theirs as a certain, wholly dependable legacy, however badly they may behave. I will not say that the prospect of being cut off with a shilling in the traditional English way necessarily turns all born under that law into models of filial piety, but I believe it has some effect. And in passing I may observe that parricide is back-page news in this neck of the woods.

As for the rest of the code that is associated with Buonaparte's name, it is so slow, and often so harsh to the accused, that one might almost prefer the English jungle, which does at least preserve some ancient customary law: though indeed

Isaiah dismisses all human systems in a line that the Vulgate renders *et quasi pannum menstruate universae justitiae nostrae* and the Douay Version *all our justices as the rag of a menstruous woman.*

No event in your series seems arbitrary or unmotivated, and even your most labyrinthine plotting seems not merely reasonable but inevitable: you have a Shakespearean talent for establishing and foreshadowing. Think of Admiral Byron's warning about shipwrecked seamen early in *Desolation Island*, or the three (at least) perfectly integrated mentions of the newfangled sternpost. The horrible old *Leopard* is the heroine of that book, but she is introduced briefly midway through the previous volume, *The Mauritius Command*. Do you habitually go back into a completed manuscript to insert delayed charges, signposts, booby traps? (Mary Renault called that "plugging" an event or theme to come.) In *H.M.S. Surprise*, for example, the experiment with madder is not only exhilarating but instructive, as are the fates of the rats and rattivores. But very early on, Stephen shops for madder; did you insert that afterward? You introduced Richard Canning in *Post Captain*, and made us like him immensely: had you already planned the dramatic sequel? Andrew Wray maneuvers through several volumes before his final contribution to medical science; how much of his tale did you know when?

There are many, many such instances—perhaps a doctoral candidate will one day have fun with them. In general, how far ahead have you been able to plot these volumes?

Let me just say that I never go back and insert booby traps into a manuscript: yet on the other hand I rarely work out any of those detailed sequences that constitute a plot. My usual way is to fix upon one central idea—a given voyage or campaign or whatever, a vehicle—and then to envisage a mass of potentialities, often loosely related; and among them I roam about in an often opportunist fashion, either when I lie awake, which I do, often quite peacefully, for hours, or when I walk on a well-known mountain road by night, easy going and generally silent. Then dialogue runs in my head, situations, all the matter of a book, or of several books, since in these naval tales given incidents can be moved in time and space.

On reflection I find this a far from satisfactory answer: but I scarcely know how to make it much better. Where some of the particular instances you mention are concerned, I just do not remember what was in my mind at that juncture. Does it sound pretentious to say that even some quite simple books are the result of tension, of a series of tensions; and that once the book is written, once the tensions are resolved, the whole drifts into oblivion? Sometimes I look into an earlier novel or tale and I am astonished, favorably or unfavorably, that I should have written it: I do not even know what happens next. A freewheeling mind can conceive a virtually infinite number of sequences; but just how that mind picks out and stores those that may perhaps be used later to deal with a given tension, a given situation, is far beyond my understanding. Yet there is a certain analogy with conversation. When one is with friends, talking hard, maintaining a point against severe and well-informed opposition, one draws on resources scarcely to be imagined at ordinary times; and when they are exhausted — all hope gone — fresh reserves come to cheer one's heart, apt quotations forgotten these forty years and more, fine strokes of scurrility. And after all a book can be represented as a conversation with one's daemon.

INTERVIEWER

A related question: how far has your plotting been altered, even superseded, by the very course of events you set in train? This is similar to the question, Do your characters take on a life of their own and force your hand from time to time? (Nabokov said his were his "galley slaves.") But plot is a more protean beast.

O'BRIAN

I do not think my plot has ever turned upon me in this way, though sometimes fresh developments suddenly appear, and if they seem to lead in the right direction I often follow them. As for characters taking on a life of their own, I have heard writers assert that for them this is the case — an assertion sometimes accompanied by a modest simper or a rueful shrug — but I have never experienced it.

INTERVIEWER

How do you name your characters? I note that a Plimpton turns up — a seaman flogged for drunkenness.

O'BRIAN

Names just float up, often with some remote suitability. Sometimes I go through the DNB, the Directory of National Biographies.

INTERVIEWER

You have remarked that it's important not to put important statements in the mouths of celebrated people, Lord Nelson, say, and that one is pretty much limited to having him say such things as, "Please pass the salt."

O'BRIAN

Yes, I think that's so. I don't really think you should. It's horrible when important characters pontificate.

INTERVIEWER

Do you think Nelson really said, "Kiss me, Hardy?"

O'BRIAN

I don't know. I very much doubt it. It probably came out of Robert Southey, hardly to be trusted. I don't think it's the sort of thing admirals say whatever the circumstances.

INTERVIEWER

One theory is that he may have said, "Kismet" . . . fate.

O'BRIAN

Much more sense there. But, alas, the OED quotes no *kismet* before 1849.

INTERVIEWER

You've mentioned your need for intercalary years—there just aren't enough 1813s to hold all your stories—but sooner or later you will arrive at 1814 (will we see Lord Keith aboard the *Bellerophon*, I wonder?) and Waterloo in 1815. Is the grand climax, the termination of the series, already in your mind, or written in outline? There are alarming hints (as near the end of *The Nutmeg of Consolation*: "swirling without pause: or as you might say without an end, an organized end. And there is at least one Mozart quartet that stops without the slightest ceremony: most satisfying when you get used to it") that you may leave your readers desolated by a subtle and inconclusive stroke of high art. Can you say anything now about the story's future?

O'BRIAN

The intercalary years: yes. I do like a fairly high degree of historical accuracy—even the chronological exactness to which I adhered in *The Mauritius Command*—but it is historical credibility and what I might call poetic truth that matter most. Then again, as I think I have said before, it seems to me that for the English-speaking people this war against France has assumed something of the character of the Troy Tale, which, ranging in all its countless variations and embroideries from Homer to Boccaccio and well beyond, never took much notice of the calendar; and therefore the writer concerned with this more recent epic struggle is not to be strictly confined by dates.

As for the end of my tale, at present I have two themes in mind, but which I shall follow depends on how well I seem to be lasting. The other day I fell off a ladder, and although I just avoided a harpoon hanging on the wall I nevertheless broke a vertebra (the third lumbar, to be exact) and now I feel rather more mortal than before.

INTERVIEWER

What is it like to fall into the past?

O'BRIAN

The sensation of falling into the past is not unlike that of coming home for the holidays from a new, strenuous, unpleasant school, and finding oneself back in wholly familiar surroundings with kind, gentle people and dogs — inconveniences of course, such as candlelight in one's bedroom (hard to read by) but nothing that one was not deeply used to.

INTERVIEWER

Your love of music shows often. Do you play an instrument? Good listeners are essential too; is that what you are? One thinks of the opening Corelli; Jack's shocked discovery of old Bach, and his later metaphor for the chaconne, in *The Ionian Mission*; and the triumphant concluding quotation of Mozart in *Letter of Marque*.

O'BRIAN

Alas, I play no instrument at all. If I were capable of playing a cello, I feel, like Dr. Johnson, that I should do nothing else at all. By the way, I have not been able to check that quotation. My edition of Boswell, the first octavo of 1793, is a very beautiful set and it has been so much read that the pages are limp and the opened volumes will lie flat; but its index, strangely placed in the front of the book, is sadly imperfect.

INTERVIEWER

Like good listeners, good readers are essential. You credit readers with high intelligence, and vast numbers of them seem delighted, even vindicated, by your recent great public success. Have you been much aware of your audience, or have you simply written the sort of book you'd want to read yourself? (Gide once reproached Malraux because all his characters were intelligent; Malraux replied, "Je n'écris pas pour m'embêter.")

O'BRIAN

I have never written for an audience. On the other hand I
do not write merely to please myself. When words are flowing
faster than one's pen can catch them, writing is a strong though
wearing delight; but these splendid bursts are rare and they
are paid for by many, many days of only a thousand words
or so, and long periods of silent reflection. And for me the
process works best with no interruption, no breaks in the steady
application, no letters to be answered, very little social life,
no holidays; it is therefore a form of happy imprisonment to
which no man would submit without at least the hope of
publication and its rewards, often dimly seen, often illusory.

INTERVIEWER

Do you still work with pencil (or pen) and paper, and write
all morning? Do you often talk to yourself, or laugh aloud,
or utter cries of satisfaction, while at work?

O'BRIAN

Yes, pen, ink and paper (generally the back of proof sheets,
for the surface) are my tools. I have occasionally beaten out
an unimportant letter on a typewriter; and some people with
quicker minds than I can use a word processor with great speed;
but upon the whole there is much to be said for the reflective
pen. Many capital books have been written with it, and then
it is comparatively economical—Dr. Lodge is said to have completed his famous translation of Josephus (812 folio pages)
with one single goose quill.

Talking to myself? No, not at all: I will admit to an occasional laugh, particularly by night. No cries of satisfaction,
alas.

INTERVIEWER

You once complained about the blocks of dialogue that
come to you in the night and force you to take notes. Does
it happen often?

O'BRIAN

Dialogue still comes to me, usually about three in the morning, but I no longer try to note it down. Instead I do my best
to seize upon a key word that will release the rest next day.
Sometimes it works.

INTERVIEWER

Do readers ever find errors?

O'BRIAN

A Cambridge don who interviewed me for the *Times* diffi-
dently suggested in later conversation that I might be mistaken
in having Sir Joseph Blaine attending a performance of *Figaro*
at Covent Garden, for, said he, there was no Mozart opera
to be heard in London until (I think) 1832.

INTERVIEWER

There's nothing you can do about this?

O'BRIAN

Wriggle.

INTERVIEWER

How about the material about the sea. Have you ever had
that wrong?

O'BRIAN

No.

INTERVIEWER

Well, that's remarkable, isn't it?

O'BRIAN

Fairly remarkable, but I have observed a great deal and read
an enormous amount.

INTERVIEWER

You have total recall?

O'BRIAN

Absolutely not. I'm always forgetting where I've put keys to various padlocks.

INTERVIEWER

How important is a reference library?

O'BRIAN

Although I have encyclopedias and dictionaries on either hand and behind me, a place like the London library, which will send almost any book that you can think of, is of the very first importance.

INTERVIEWER

Would you describe where you write.

O'BRIAN

Our house is built on the side of a steep slope: the terrace and the balcony therefore jut out, providing two long, low, sheltered rooms. In one, which is lined with bookshelves, I do work that requires continual reference: in the other, which I try to keep clear, I make my attempts at purely creative writing. There is also a small stone house in the mountain vineyard to which I can retire when there is too much noise in the village. I write or sit at my desk with paper before me just after breakfast and work or ponder until lunch. Unless writing is flowing very well, the afternoon is usually free — garden, mountain vineyard, lagoon, or seeing friends. Then after tea I go on until about dinnertime.

INTERVIEWER

For each volume you must have studied intensively the geography, ethnography, zoology, etc., of the region; the climate, the holidays, the food, the social structure and business practices. Your Bombay, with Dil and the Parsee and the ecstatic Stephen, is startlingly vivid; so is your Greek-Albanian coast with its Mirdite Ghegs, the tournaji-bashi, etc.; so are your

Cape Town, your Malta, your Sydney. You are at home throughout the world, yet you are a private man, and you love your farm and its seasons — much more Hesiod than Odysseus. How many of your locales have you visited? Are there places other than your farm that you have loved? or detested?

O'BRIAN

Of course, when I come to a new piece of the world I study it with close attention. But I have traveled fairly widely, both physically and even more in books. In my younger days I read vast quantities of voyages and I still possess the great eighteenth-century collections: Churchill, Harris, and the abbé Prévost in sixteen splendid quartos, most abundantly illustrated. A fair amount of the knowledge derived from this desultory but very happy and extensive reading lingers in my memory, and it is rare that the ad hoc study is not superimposed upon earlier acquaintance.

Do you know about the abbé Prévost? He was intended for the Church and indeed after a spell with the Jesuits he became a Benedictine (the most amiable of orders); but for a while he either lost or mislaid his vocation and wandered about the world gathering the kind of knowledge that enabled him to write *Manon Lescaut*. In time however he was recalled and, becoming almoner to the Prince de Conti, he set himself to this prodigious work, a true *travail de Bénédictin*, assembling, arranging and often translating countless books of travel for his *Histoire générale des voyages*. The first volume has a charming frontispiece of the author looking as cheerful and benign as ever his best friends could wish, and it contains about 328,000 words: all the other volumes are on the same scale or even larger, and the whole, filled with plates and maps, amounts to some five million words, ending with a capital index. Could any modern publisher contemplate such an undertaking?

INTERVIEWER

Your series is in several languages. Are any of them odd, landlocked, unlikely? Do you know any of your translators, and do you — with French, perhaps — often lend them a hand?

O'BRIAN

I doubt there are more than a dozen, if as many; none of them very odd so far. Certainly I have helped the translators who have turned to me, French, Spanish, Italian and German; and for the Dutch and Scandinavian whose languages I do not know I rephrase the passages they find incomprehensible.

INTERVIEWER

Do you care to comment on current fiction? Do you read much of it? Current criticism?

O'BRIAN

My comments on current fiction would not be worth much, since I read so little: but I find Iris Murdoch at her best very good indeed, while A.S. Byatt's *Possession* seems to me an admirable tour de force, and Alan Judd's *A Breed of Heroes* is to my knowledge the only sound, objective account of the hideous situation in Northern Ireland. At the moment I am entranced by Jeannette Haien's *The All of It* in spite of some initial reserves. As for literary criticism, I see even less; though occasionally a lively and incisive piece comes my way, usually written by Linda Colley.

INTERVIEWER

Some think we have arrived at a true discontinuity in history, rendering much of it obsolete by an astonishing acceleration in the technological rate of change. Do you "view with alarm" or do you trust the race's resilience?

O'BRIAN

Most people who have been to school have heard the master declare that this is the worst fifth form in all his experience: most people who have been to the university have heard their tutor sigh and observe that in his youth undergraduates used to read hard, very hard, much harder than they do now. It seems to me that humanity has always been tottering on the edge of an abyss, perpetually looking back to happier genera-

tions, when people knew how to build, paint and write, when
children sat up at table, mute and never touching the back
of their chairs. I view the present with distress, but not with
despair.

INTERVIEWER

The historical novelist has at least one advantage: he has
already answered the question, "Did anything at all happen
before World War II?" That may sound like a cheap joke,
but increasingly writers, critics and readers insist that novels
be timely (that is, reflect or outdo the *faits divers* and *crimes
passionels* that we read of every morning) or "relevant" (that
is, wring our guilty hearts about current social and political
inequities). Have you had to contend with charges of irrelevance?

O'BRIAN

I do not remember having been accused of irrelevance, but
it would not grieve me if I were, since I could point to the
equally irrelevant Homer, Virgil, Lydgate and a host of other
eminent hands, including Madame de La Fayette.

INTERVIEWER

Is there any limit to the liberties one can take writing historical fiction? I mean can you invent a substantial naval battle?

O'BRIAN

The limits seem to me the boundaries of historical verisimili-
tude. I very much doubt that one could invent a fleet action —
certainly I could not, in my period.

INTERVIEWER

Historians are often so scornful of historical fiction.

O'BRIAN

Perhaps because so much historical fiction is poor history
and worse prose.

Did you come away from your recent tour of the United States—a triumphant progress, really—with any sharper impression of your audience? Are they older? Mostly white-collar, or plenty of blue as well? Preponderantly male? What note do your fan letters most often strike, questions ask, complaints lodge? Do you answer them all?

Yes, I did. I had almost never spoken in public before, and most of the time my eyes were fixed upon my text; but now and then I did look up and I was charmed to see such amiable, friendly, attentive faces—faces, moreover, that laughed when laughter was called for. They were, upon the whole, younger than I had expected; men and women in about equal numbers—perhaps rather more women—but whether white-collar or blue I cannot say. It is very difficult for a European to place an American by his appearance or even by his accent. At the book-signing sessions people always said something civil, but there was no time to exchange anything more than smiles. One of the few occasions I had to see my audience in greater depth was in Washington, where I spoke at the National Archives, and the archivists very kindly entertained me to luncheon—they also loaded me with gifts: books and reproductions of documents that might give me pleasure. There was time for real contact and among the many people whose conversation I enjoyed was a tall, cheerful young lawyer, so black that it was a joy to contemplate him, who talked to me, as I remember, about the Quasi-War of 1798. And later, when I told him that I had spent the morning with Mr. Justice Kennedy of the Supreme Court and that I had watched the bench in action, he said "That is where I shall be presently" with a flash of brilliant teeth and a friendly smile. Indeed friendliness was the overriding impression that my wife and I carried away from the United States, and we look forward eagerly to our next visit.

The writers of fan letters: they fall into four main classes:
1. Those who say "I love your books and I wish to thank you."

2. Poor lonely souls who just want to write to someone.
3. Those whose ancestors went to sea and who would like
information about their careers, and 4. those who point out
my errors, sometimes real (I am a left-handed man and when
I am writing I easily confuse right and left, east and west: this
does not happen aboard, however) but more often, I am glad
to say, imaginary. All four classes have grown so numerous
these last years that I have had to beg my publishers to sieve
them, because I am a slow, indifferent letter-writer and even
half a dozen eat all the cream of my morning work, the best
time by far. Yet they are sometimes extraordinarily encourag-
ing: I think primarily of sick people who have found some
relief in my books, but also of that splendid admiral who,
dating his letter from the North Atlantic, told me that after
a strenuous day of exercising his submarines he would sub-
merge, sinking to the calmness of deep water, and there, in
the ocean's bosom unespied, he would turn to my naval tales:
or of that other gentleman whose thank you took the form of
a wholly gratuitous offer of his 154-foot yacht with a numerous
crew (including an excellent chef) and room for ourselves and
six of our friends, to cruise for a fortnight in the Mediterranean
or the Caribbean this coming spring or summer, himself making no appearance whatever. And if you do not call that hand-
some you must be very, very hard to please.

INTERVIEWER

Do you still write poetry? You have kindly allowed us to
print some here; are there many more, published or unpub-
lished? Have you translated poetry? Which modern poets have
moved you most?

O'BRIAN

Yes, there are more poems, some published in *Poetry Ireland* and the like, but many more in obscure heaps, most of
which I cannot find without sorting through great masses of
paper. But yesterday I did put my hand on one folder in which
most of the verse went on far too long; still, here is a piece
from it which at least has the merit of brevity.

Old Men

We are old bald ugly
impotent and fat or horribly lean
unarmed disarmed often unspeakably silly
Nobody wants us
least of all ourselves

Our wives are short thick and spectacled
with elaborate hair
nobody wants them
least of all ourselves

It is a crime against humanity
that old people
racked with ignominies, weak
should be made to pay pay pay
and then pay
for a life that has already been lived

And yes, I have translated poetry, but without much poetic success. Modern poets: does Eliot still count? He moved me deeply. And of recent years I have been stirred by one poem of Larkin's and another by Fiona Pitt-Kethley on the nature of unrequited love.

INTERVIEWER

Your tribute to Mary Renault is moving and elegant, but too few of us these days know Greek. Will you tell us about it?

O'BRIAN

Do you mean the dedication in *The Mauritius Command*? It was a proverbial Greek saying that meant "owls to Athens," much as the English say "coals to Newcastle" and conceivably the Americans "cod to Boston" — a delivery of things to a place already overflowing with them. An owl (usually the little-eared scops owl, which haunts Greek temples) is usually to be seen on Athena's shoulder and on Athenian coins.

INTERVIEWER

Why do *you* think the series has roused so much fervent admiration? Do you step back occasionally and wonder, "Who is this Patrick O'Brian they are all talking about"? In brief, how do you like fame? *Beatus ille*, wrote the poet, but also *aere perennius*.

O'BRIAN

I have no idea whatsoever of the reason so many people have taken to reading my books. Years ago the books, the selfsame books, were there: the people were there. But the two sides did not come together until some quite unexplained catalyst came into play. As for "fame," I quite like what I have of it, though at the same time it makes me feel uneasy, vaguely fraudulent; and then its consequences have a way of shattering old frugal values, making them artificial. I do not think it touches me much, or affects my self-esteem. When I sit down at this desk I am still as bashful before the virgin page as I was sixty years ago—perhaps more so, for in the interval I have acquired some notion of what very good writing can be.

—Stephen Becker

Two Poems by Patrick O'Brian

The Deep Gold of a Pomegranate-Tree

The deep gold of a pomegranate-tree
glowing in the clipped frame of cypresses
on an almond-branch
a robin whistling quietly to itself
light flooding down from the high autumnal sky.
In the Massane wood blue mushrooms are pushing through
    the fallen leaves.

A T'ang Landscape Remembered

Mists after mountain rain
Sun slanting through the pines that cling
to the walls of this
improbable chasm.
Feathery waterfalls drifting:
the unseen river sends up another mist of spray
It is all much the same, even to the twisted pine-tree overhead and the feeling of detached unearthly height.

In this remembered landscape
only the sage is missing, the ancient happy man
leaning on a staff. The ancient man (obedient ears
attained long since) and his attendant boy.

I fill that place upon the mountain-path.
I do not fill it well: I have
no visible companions, no staff;
and when I bend, the face that stares back from the pool
    dismayed
has nothing of his wisdom: no trace of happiness.

Judy Glantzman

Drawings

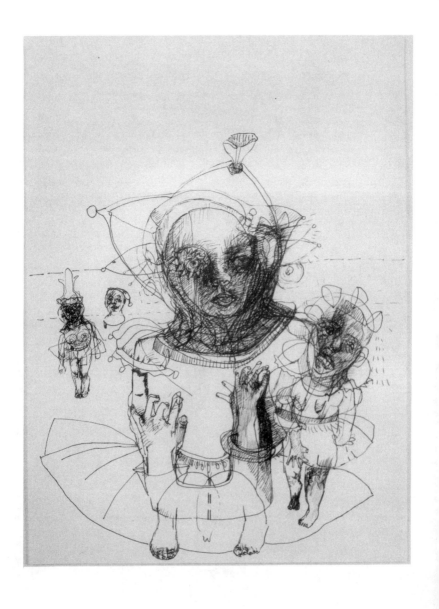

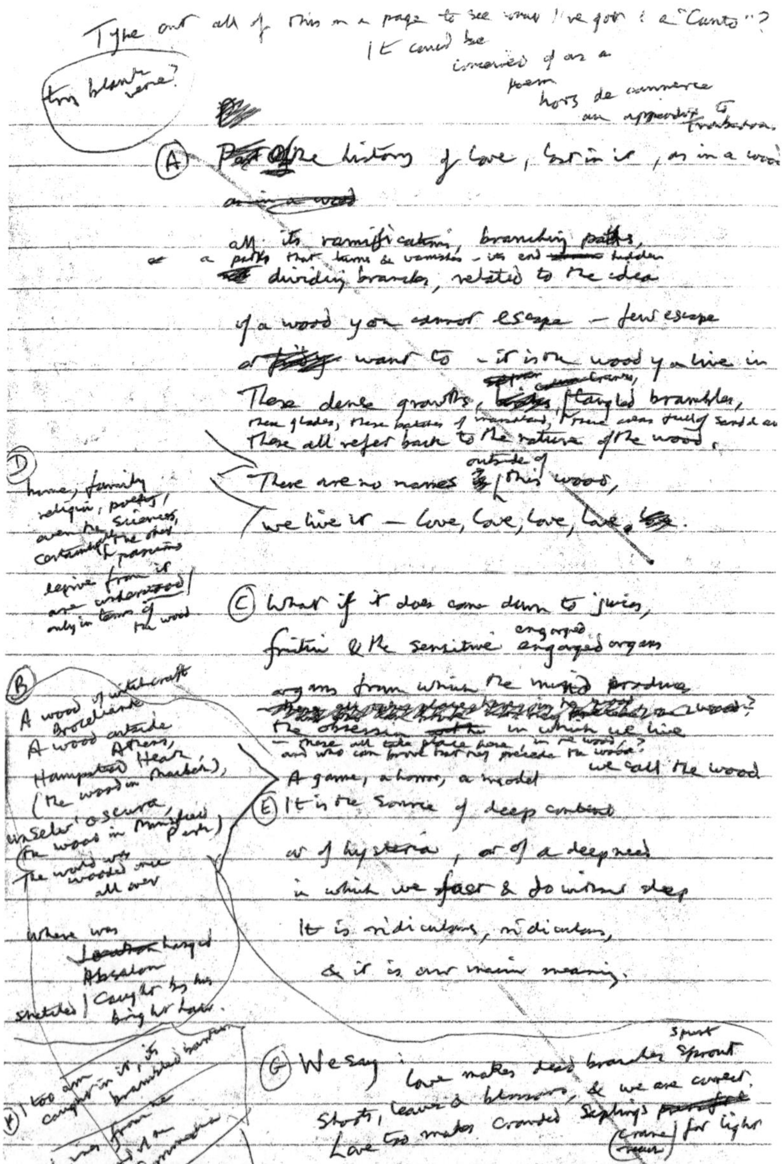

A manuscript page from Thom Gunn's poem "A Wood Near Athens."

Thom Gunn
The Art of Poetry LXXII

Thom Gunn was born in Gravesend, on the southern bank of the Thames estuary, in 1929. His childhood was spent mostly in that county, Kent, and in the affluent suburb of Hampstead in northwest London. A relatively happy boyhood was overshadowed, first by his parents' divorce when he was ten, and then by his mother's suicide when he was fifteen. In 1950, after two years' national service in the army, he went up to Trinity College, Cambridge, to study English. This was during the heyday of F.R. Leavis, whose lectures had a profound effect on Gunn's early poetry.

It was in Cambridge that he discovered his homosexuality, falling in love with his lifelong partner, an American student named Mike Kitay. The wish to stay with Kitay led him to apply for American scholarships, and in 1954 he took up a creative writing fellowship at Stanford, where he studied with Yvor Winters. In 1960 he settled with Kitay in San Francisco and has lived there ever since, though longish spells have been passed in other places, notably London, where he lived on a travel grant from 1964 to 1965. For most of his time in California he has earned at least part of his income from the English Department at Berkeley, where he now teaches one semester a year.

His first book of poetry, Fighting Terms, *written while he was at Cambridge, was published in 1954. Seven major collections have followed:* The Sense of Movement *(1957),* My Sad Captains *(1961),* Touch *(1967),* Moly *(1971),* Jack Straw's Castle *(1976),* The Passages of Joy *(1982) and* The Man with Night Sweats *(1992). Other publications have included* Positives *(1967), a collection of verse captions to photographs by his brother Ander; an edition of the work of Fulke Greville (1968) and Ben Jonson (1974); and a volume of critical and autobiographical prose,* The Occasions of Poetry *(1982). At the time of this interview he was assembling his* Collected Poems *(1994) and another volume of prose,* Shelf Life *(1993).*

As a poet who lives in the United States yet is still thought of as an Englishman, Gunn is probably less widely read and discussed than his striking talent deserves. Nevertheless, he is much anthologized and has been the recipient of several literary prizes, the most recent being, in Britain, the first Forward Prize for Poetry (1992) and, in the U.S., a fellowship or "genius grant" from the MacArthur Foundation (1993).

There has always been a heroic edge to Thom Gunn's poetry. That being the case, his appearance does not disappoint. He is tall and, for a man in his early sixties, remarkably lean and youthful. Tattooed arms and a single earring give him a faintly piratical air. In one of his poems he confesses to a liking for "loud music, bars and boisterous men," *and a certain boisterous charm is one of his own most pleasing characteristics: as we talk, he laughs a great deal, very loudly, with rumbustious pleasure. He enjoys any hint of the vulgar or the tasteless, yet he is also a man of considerable refinement. Modest, considerate and softly spoken, he was once described to me by one of his American friends as "the perfect English gentleman."*

Such complexities, even ambiguities, run deep. One of the most deeply erotic poets of our time, his style has often been praised for "chastity." A celebrator of "the sense of movement," he is strongly attached to his home and his routine. The occasion of this interview, for instance, is his first visit to his native country in thirteen years.

He was staying in his old university city of Cambridge, and he visited my house every morning for three days. In all, we recorded three hours of conversation: we chatted with the tape on and stopped when we felt the talk beginning to flag. He was a relaxed interviewee, amusing and informative. He didn't mind talking about personal matters, but he stopped well short of narcissism. What he said came across as spontaneous and yet one felt he was also well prepared. One was left with a sense of experience not easily translated into words.

INTERVIEWER

I wonder if we could begin with a brief description of how you live? I get the feeling, for instance, that you're quite fond of routine.

THOM GUNN

Well, if you haven't got a routine in your life by the age of sixty-two, you're never going to get it. I spend half the year teaching and half the year on my own. I like the idea of scheduling my own life for half the year, but by the end of that time I'm really ready to teach again and have somebody else's timetable imposed on me, because I'm chaotic enough that I just couldn't be master of myself for the entire year. It would leave me too loose and unregulated. As I say, I'm eager to teach again in January and then, during the term, very often I'll think of ideas for writing on but I usually don't have time to work them out. By the time I can work them out at the end of the term, I've either lost them or else I've got them much more complex and intense, so that's good too. I like the way my life has worked out very well. I live with some other men in a house in San Francisco. Somebody once said: "Oh, you've got a gay commune." I said: "No, it's a queer household!"—which I think was a satisfactory answer. Right now there's only three of us there. There *were* five: one of them left and one of them died of AIDS. But we really fit in well together. We really do work as a family: we cook in turn—stuff like that—we do a lot of things together.

INTERVIEWER

Do you have a writing routine?

GUNN

When anybody says, "Do you have a routine?," I always say piously it's very important to have one, but in fact I don't. I write poetry when I can and when I can't, I write reviews, which I figure at least is keeping my hand in, doing some kind of writing. Finally, however difficult it is, it does make me happy in some weird way to do the writing. It's hard labor but it does satisfy something in me very deeply. Sometimes when I haven't written in some time, I really decide I'm going to work toward getting the requisite fever, and this would involve, oh, reading a few favorite poets intensively: Hardy, for example, John Donne, Herbert, Basil Bunting—any one of a number of my favorites. I try to get their tunes going in my head so I get a tune of my own. Then I write lots of notes on possible subjects for poetry. Sometimes that works, sometimes it doesn't. It's been my experience that sometimes about ten poems will all come in about two months; other times it will be that one poem will take ages and ages to write.

Do you tend to work very hard on poems — revising and so
on?

GUNN
It depends on the poem. Some poems come out almost
right on the first draft — you really have to make very few small
alterations. Others you have to pull to pieces and put together
again. Those are two extremes: it might be anything between
them. For instance, I have a poem called "Nasturtium." I
worked at it for ages and then decided it was just terrible. I
only kept about one line, but then I rewrote the poem from
a slightly different idea — I don't remember the difference between the two, but it was a completely different poem from
the first draft, and I think it only has about one or two lines
in common with it. Only the last two lines, I think.

INTERVIEWER
When you start writing a poem, do you ever have a form
in your head before you write, or do you always discover the
form in writing?

GUNN
Again, sometimes I do, sometimes I don't. For example,
a poem called "Street Song." Part of the idea of that poem
was to write a modern version of an Elizabethan or Jacobean
street song. So of course I knew it was going to rhyme, that
it might have some kind of refrain, it was going to be a particular kind of poem. Other poems I don't really know what they're
going to be like, and I will jot down my notes for them kind
of higgledy-piggledy all over the page, so that when I look
at what I've got maybe the form will be suggested by what I
have there. That's *mostly* what happens with me. I don't start
by writing a couplet or something, knowing the whole thing's
going to be in couplets — though even *that* has happened.

INTERVIEWER
I know that you quite consciously and deliberately draw on
other writers and writings in your poems. Could you describe

that process a little? Do you quite ruthlessly plagiarize or pilfer?

GUNN

Yes, yes, yes. Well, T.S. Eliot gave us a pleasing example, didn't he, quoting from people without acknowledgment? I remember a line in *Ash Wednesday* which was an adaptation of "Desiring this man's art and that man's scope." When I was twenty, I thought that was the most terrific line I'd read in Eliot! I didn't know that it was a line from Shakespeare's sonnets. I don't resent that in Eliot and I hope people don't resent it in me. I don't make such extensive use of unacknowledged quotation as Eliot does, but every now and again I'll make a little reference. This is the kind of thing that poets have always done. On the first page of *The Prelude*, Wordsworth slightly rewrites a line from the end of *Paradise Lost*: "The earth is all before me" instead of "The world was all before them." He was aware that many an educated reader would recognize that as being both a theft and an adaptation. He was also aware, I'm sure, that a great many of his readers wouldn't know it was and would just think it was original. That's part of the process of reading: you read a poem for what you can get out of it.

INTERVIEWER

Actually, though, what you do much more often is model your poems on other poems.

GUNN

Well, I grew up when the New Criticism was at its height, and I took some of the things the New Critics said very literally. When I read (let's say) George Herbert, I really do think of him as being a kind of contemporary of mine. I don't think of him as being separated from me by an impossible four hundred years of history. I feel that in an essential way this is a man with a very different mind-cast from mine, but I don't feel myself badly separated from him. I feel that we're like totally different people with different interests writing in the same room. And I feel that way of all the poets I like.

INTERVIEWER

Donald Davie says of you in *Under Briggflatts* that you don't use literary reference, as Eliot does, "to judge the tawdry present." He finds that refreshing.

GUNN

I don't regret the present. I don't feel it's cheap and tawdry compared with the past. I think the past was cheap and tawdry too. One of the things I noticed very early on — and I probably got it from an essay by Eliot — was that the beginning of Pope's "Verses to the Memory of an Unfortunate Lady" is virtually taken from the beginning of the "Elegie on the Lady Jane Pawlet" by Ben Jonson. Now I don't think most of Pope's readers would have realized that. I don't think Jonson was that much read in Pope's time. I may be wrong . . . So I figured that was a very interesting thing to be able to do. But no, I don't do it in the way Eliot and Pound do — to show up the present. I do it much more in the way I've described Wordsworth or Pope as doing it.

INTERVIEWER

Are there any particular influences that have been consistently — or intermittently — important for you?

GUNN

The first poet who influenced me in a big way — in poems that never got into print — was W.H. Auden. I'm speaking about when I was about nineteen or twenty. He's someone I'm profoundly grateful to for giving me by his example the feeling that I could write about my experience. Anne Ridler, I think, said this many years ago: that his example enabled her to write. That's what his example did for me: it made things seem easy, and the poetry I wrote then — I doubt if any of it exists any longer — was riddled with Audenesque

mannerisms. But he was tremendously helpful to me. He's
not been an influence I've gone back to, however. The biggest
two influences after him were, in my first year as an undergrad-
uate, John Donne and Shakespeare. I read Donne en masse
and understood him for the first time. I had tried reading
him in my teens and I guess I just wasn't mature enough to
know what to do with it. Suddenly I could see, and it was
tremendously exciting. Then, that summer vacation, I read
all of Shakespeare. I read everything by Shakespeare and doing
that adds a cubit to your stature. He's so inventive with language. It's the idea of concepts and experience going into
language, and going into *exciting* language — of *creating* the
language for your poem as you're writing it. Of course, both
of those influences have returned. Who has not been influenced by Shakespeare? Even somebody who doesn't like the
influence, somebody like Pound, is influenced ultimately.
Then, of course, Yeats was an influence . . .

INTERVIEWER

Let me put a more specific question. Could you name anybody who has extended your sensibility — opened you up to
things in experience that you were not sufficiently aware of?

GUNN

Anybody I enjoy reading has always done this. A literary
influence is never just a literary influence. It's also an influence
in the way you see everything — in the way you feel your life.
I'm not sure that this affected my poetry, but I read Proust
when I was about twenty, just before I went to Cambridge.
(We went to university rather late in those days. We had to
do national service first, you should remember.) Of course,
when you read all of Proust, you live in a Proustian world for
a moment. You know, that bus conductor may be homosexual! So may your grandfather — or anybody maybe! I remember when I went to Chartres for the first time, I was all set
to have a Proustian disappointment and I didn't! Instead I
had absolute delight; it was even better than I expected it to

be. But every writer does this to you to some extent. Auden, Donne, Shakespeare, Yeats — I was about to say Yvor Winters: all of these modified the way in which I see the whole of my experience. I don't think there's any one person more than others. And I don't lose them: I never lost Donne, I never lost Yeats really. William Carlos Williams came later on.

INTERVIEWER

Can we take Williams as an example? You got interested in his work in — what? — the late fifties. Shortly afterwards your poetry began changing a lot and started including things from the world which it hadn't included before.

GUNN

It's very interesting you should say "things from the world." Up to about halfway through *My Sad Captains* — that is, my first two-and-a-half books — I was trying to write heroic poetry. There are interesting reasons for this. When I was at Cambridge, as I've said, I was very much influenced by Shakespeare, and of course much of Shakespeare deals with the heroic of a certain kind. This was emphasized by the fact that I was at Cambridge with a particular generation of talented actors and directors. Some of them went on to become famous — people like Peter Wood, Peter Hall and John Barton, who directed remarkable productions of *Coriolanus*, of *The Alchemist*, of *Love's Labour's Lost*, of *Edward II*: all sorts of Elizabethan and Jacobean plays. My great friend Tony White was an actor in many of those. I was in some sense trying to write, with Sartre's help, a modern equivalent to heroic poetry. The influence of Williams altered everything. I'd been reading him a bit, but I couldn't incorporate that influence until I started to write in syllabics, and that was about 1959 perhaps — the poems from the second half of *My Sad Captains*. There I found a way, with Williams's help, of incorporating the more casual aspects of life, the non-heroic things in life, that are of course a part of daily experience and infinitely valuable. I suppose I could have learned that from Hardy too but I wasn't very influenced by him at that time. I'd read and liked some Hardy, but you can't always incorporate your learning from a poet at the time when you first start admiring that poet. Then I got into rather a mess with my next book, *Touch*, and some of that book seems to me distinctly inferior in that I really wasn't quite sure how to connect the poetry of everyday life and the heroic poetry (which is greatly to oversimplify the two kinds). But I wanted to make some kind of connection. I maybe started to do so when I wrote a longish poem called "Misanthropos," which is included in that book.

INTERVIEWER

Let's go back to the beginning. When did you first realize that this business of writing poetry was going to be the main activity of your life?

GUNN

I started writing poetry, as many people do, in my teens. I was also trying to write novels, none of which I ever finished. I also wrote short stories and plays. I wanted to be a *writer* and, if I had succeeded in any of these, that might have shaped my future. However, I only succeeded in poetry. The first poem I published was at the end of my first year at Cambridge. A graduate student editing *The Cambridge Review*, whom I did not personally know, said something very nice about it in print—a man called Peter Green, who's now famous for his books about Greece, Macedonia and Alexander the Great. That gave me a tremendous amount of confidence. I don't know whether I said I was going to be a poet but I wanted to write a lot of poetry. During that summer, when I read all of Shakespeare, I also set myself to write a poem a week, and I carried on doing that for the next two years. Of course, a lot of them were really worthless, imitative junk, but it was wonderful the way that a poem turned up just about every week. Then of course it all slackened, but I suppose that happens when a lot of people start. You have everything to try out, you have to find out who you are. Your poetry has no

identity at first. *You* don't have much identity at that age —
I was twenty-one to twenty-two.

INTERVIEWER

Your first two books seem very unhappy in comparison with
the later ones . . .

GUNN

All young men are unhappy. That's why they identify so
strongly with Hamlet. They're unhappy in a formless kind of
way, partly because they don't have an identity, they don't
know where they're going, they don't know who they are.
You're a pretty unusual person — something slightly sinister —
if at the age of twenty or twenty-two you really know exactly
who you are and what you're going to do. More likely you're
undefined, and being undefined is rather painful. I don't know
that I was more sorry for myself than anybody else was. I was
trying to be brave about it too. Of course, I was striking postures
. . . It was also sexual identity. There was such duplicity in
my mind about the whole sexual question: I was not terribly
willing to be a homosexual but it did seem that I was. I really
can't trace the convolutions in my mind until in fact I fell in
love. That made up my mind and that, I should think, made
me a good deal happier, though the whole of my second book
was written after that . . . so maybe it didn't make my *poetry*
that much happier! It certainly made me happier as a person.
I guess I was so used to writing unhappy poetry that I just
went on writing it!

INTERVIEWER

Do you think the problems of your own childhood contrib-
uted to the *need* to write? The compensation theory . . .

GUNN

Quite possibly, but I don't know. How is one to find out?
I had, I think, a very happy childhood until about the age
of fifteen, perhaps, when my mother killed herself. Then I

was devastated for about four years. I very much retired into
myself. I read an enormous number of Victorian novels and
eighteenth-century ones too. I read them very much as an
escape, and it was an escape into another time when I didn't
have to face this problem of a suicided mother. I gradually
came out of it, but it was a difficult four years or so. I don't
think I knew how difficult they were at the time—luckily—
so maybe originally I wrote as a way of getting out of that,
but I can't tell.

INTERVIEWER

This aspiration towards the heroic in the early books: was
it part of the escape or part of the opening up?

GUNN

Part of the opening up. That was a way of asserting my
strength. One of my favorite words was *energy*—in my conversation and probably in my poetry as well. When I felt really
good, there was a wonderful feeling of the physical energy of
the body *and* the energy of the mind too. They went in tan-
dem. Sometimes I felt physically an almost unlimited energy.
It was extraordinary. Like a young tree feeling the sap going
through its branches. That was a great cause for rejoicing and
that comes into my early poetry. It was probably why I har-
nessed so much on to a Sartrean idea of the *will*, because the
will for me seemed to be a way of channelling the energy. I
obviously use that word far too much in those early poems—
it becomes monotonous.

INTERVIEWER

How conscious were you when you used the word *will* that
it also means the penis?

GUNN

Not at all. I didn't find out till years later that when Shakespeare uses the word *will* it means the penis. I don't think we
had very adequately footnoted editions of the sonnets in those

days, because I read through all the footnotes in my edition:
I had to study it for my exams. But I never came across it!

INTERVIEWER

But do you think it's significant none the less?

GUNN

Yes, I do. So I was getting it unconsciously. But I don't
think I found out until my thirties. I was astonished when I
did!

INTERVIEWER

In those early books you establish almost a kind of map of
terms and conceptions which stay with you all through, though
they get more ghostly and more complex later on. They're
things like the will and energy, and the figure of the soldier,
and the concept of self, and posing, and this whole idea of
risk as something which helps to define the self. Is that something that you're conscious of as you work — that you have this
structure, almost, that you build on?

GUNN

Well, I don't think conceptually about my poetry very
much. I try not to think as a critic, I try not to think of key
words: otherwise I would start being overly self-conscious
about using them. But some of them I just can't avoid noticing,
and of course they're also life-images. Now the idea of the
soldier: my childhood was full of soldiers. I tried to write
about this in a poem called "The Corporal." I was ten at the
beginning of World War Two and sixteen when it ended, so
my visual landscape was full of soldiers. Of course, I became
a soldier for two years of national service and so that was
another kind of soldier. It was a strange kind of role I had to
measure myself against. And the idea of the will: there's a
poem in *The Man with Night Sweats* called "The Differences"
and in the last two lines I say that I

think back on that night in January,
When casually distinct we shared the most

And lay upon a bed of clarity
In luminous half-sleep where the will *was lost.*

So that is not *willed* love at all. This was a very conscious
reference back to my over-use of the word *will* in my early
books. I'm saying in a sense that I'm no longer the same person
as I was then, and I'm pleased that I'm not the same person.
So there is a certain consciousness of themes but, at the same
time, there's a certain blessed unconsciousness. There was a
review, for which I was profoundly grateful, in the *Times
Literary Supplement* by Hugh Haughton: he was reviewing
my recent book, *The Man with Night Sweats*, and he traced
the imagery of embracing and touching and holding hands —
and even embracing oneself at one point. That was extraordinary: it was all there. That was not planned, it was due to
the consistency of my own mind. We all have that kind of
consistency of course. It's a question of opening yourself up
to what you really want to say, to what for you is the truth,
and you come out with consistent images in that way. I've
not been aware of that, I've really not been aware of that,
and of course the embrace is in half the poems in the book.
I was glad I didn't find that out till the book was finished!
So one does not operate in complete rational awareness of
what one's doing all the time, and I don't want to. I seem to
write awfully rational poetry, but I want there to be a considerable amount of strength given from what is not conscious into
the consciousness there — that kind of energy. (I won't talk
about the unconscious.) I've noticed recently I've been particularly attracted by various things in visual art or in poetry that
I explain to myself as being a mixture of the extremely sophisticated and the primitive. I was just pointing out this morning
some lines from Spenser's "Epithalamion." They're the ones
about who is it "which at my window peeps." It is the moon,
who "walks about high heaven all the night." It's a wonderfully
sophisticated and ornate kind of poetry, and suddenly this
tremendously physical, almost anthropomorphic image of the

© Martin Rosen

moon walking around the sky. It's so magnificent! I find them
wonderfully beautiful lines! I think that kind of thing happens
in some way in all the art I like. I'd like that to happen in
my poetry. I think that sometimes when my poetry comes
off—anybody's poetry when it comes off—it's making use of
two strengths at once: a very conscious arranging strength,
keeping things in schematic form, but also the stuff you can
call primitive or unconscious.

INTERVIEWER

So you have the controlling mind or intellect, but it's a
control that's prepared to allow things to slip in . . .

Yes, *allowing*, very good word, yes. It's a control that will
still allow things to slip under. Welcomes them in fact.

INTERVIEWER
Going back to the soldier for a minute, one rather striking
thing about that figure is the way it establishes an atmosphere
for those early books. At the time there was a lot of talk,
much of it rather vacuous, about violence in those poems. I
remember Ted Hughes saying somewhere that he thought this
emphasis on violence superficial and what was much more
important in your work was tenderness. Don't the two things
go together?

GUNN
Of course, of course. I can quote from "The Missing," a
passage in which I'm speaking about a sense of "the gay community" (a phrase I always thought was bullshit, until the thing
was vanishing). In "The Missing" I speak about the "Image
of an unlimited embrace," and I mean partly friends, partly
sexual partners, partly even the vaguest of acquaintances, with
the sense of being in some way part of a community.

> *I did not just feel ease, though comfortable:*
> *Aggressive as in some ideal of sport,*
> *With ceaseless movement thrilling through the whole,*
> *Their push kept me as firm as their support.*

Take that image of sport. (Somebody pointed out that I constantly use the word *play* in *The Man with Night Sweats*, which
is—again—something I wasn't completely aware of.) If you
use the idea of sport, you think of the violence of the push,
yes, but there's an ambiguity: an embrace can be a wrestler's
embrace or it can be the embrace of love. There's tremendous
doubleness in that image, which I have used elsewhere in fact:
the idea of the embrace which can be violent or tender. But
if you look at it at any one moment, if it's frozen, it could

be either, and maybe the two figures swaying in that embrace are not even quite sure which it is. Like Aufidius and Coriolanus: they embrace, they're enemies. They embrace in admiration at one point. It's ambiguous because the two things are connected. It could turn, at any moment, from the one to the other, I suppose.

INTERVIEWER

When you first went to America, you studied at Stanford under Yvor Winters. What you're saying at the moment reminds me of Winters's emphasis on rigor and discipline. So the idea that when you're writing you're up against some sort of resistance all the time: there's an element of masculine struggle in it.

GUNN

Yes.

INTERVIEWER

Was Winters very important to you?

GUNN

Tremendously important, yes. I underplayed his importance for many years because I was afraid of it — because he was such a strong person. I was afraid he might suck me into his own personality and I would simply be a disciple. I now feel I'm a strong enough son to be able to acknowledge my father figure fully! He was important to me in ways I'm not even sure I can completely identify or speak about. I mean, I can speak about things that have some importance but are obviously not the whole story, like matters of meter. I do think, as he did, that a meter should be correct. I don't like a sloppy meter, which is what most people write nowadays. But the extent of Winters's influence on me I find myself unable to assess. He would have been *appalled* at the idea that I was queer. But he *was* a friend and was very good to me. I liked him very much — I loved him. And I feel a huge debt of gratitude towards him. I'm not sure I would have been able to admit this twenty years ago, but I think it would be fair enough to say that his definition of a poem is essentially my definition of a poem: "a statement in words about a human experience" — which is rather large, but he meant "with moral import." Well, I once showed a poem of mine to a friend to see what he thought of it and I said: "Do you think it's too didactic?" And he said — giving me a pitying look — "Thom, your poetry is *always* didactic!" And it's true! It is! So I certainly take morality as part of my poetry, as in that poem "The Missing" for example. I make moral evaluations of a life that many people would consider totally immoral.

INTERVIEWER

You didn't quite finish what you were saying about meter. You said sloppy meter is what most people write nowadays . . .

GUNN

Well, it is. If you look at most of my contemporaries and most new poems, they write something that's not quite free verse and not quite meter. I would say that it comes ultimately from the example of Eliot and, because *The Waste Land* was *so* wonderful (and I must say it's a poem I find more wonderful as I get older), they have an example of how it can be treated at its best. By "it" I mean basically an iambic pentameter kind of broken up, made uneven. We know that he made it uneven on Jacobean precedents: people like Webster and Tourneur. There is a little genuine free verse in *The Waste Land*. On the whole it *can* be scanned iambically and mostly it's iambic pentameter. There are whole passages of perfect iambic pentameter; there are also passages of very much broken-up pentameter. Many of the people who write in this way do so with a sense that it's okay to bring in a few extra syllables: you're just making things more casual. Actually, I think you're making things more indefinite and sloppier and less memorable. Metrical poetry is ultimately allied to song, and I like the connection. Free verse is ultimately allied to conversation, and

I like that connection too. Not many people can mix the two.
Eliot could, obviously, and the great shining modern example
of somebody who could, too, is Basil Bunting. If you go
through "Briggflatts," for example, it is very difficult to define
what is happening metrically, but whatever is is happening
wonderfully. He would have used a musical analogy. If you
just take that first part of "Briggflatts," you can't scan it. There
is obviously some kind of meter at work there — it's not free
verse — but you don't really know when it's trimeter, when it's
tetrameter, or when it's varying between the two. Certain lines
could be read either as trimeter or tetrameter in light of what
went before. The first line is

Brág,| swěet tén-|ǒr búll,

which one would be inclined to read as a trimeter, but the
next line is

Déscǎnt| ǒn Ráw-|thěy's mád-|rigál,

which is clearly a tetrameter. In that case, going back, you
might choose to read the first line as a tetrameter too:

Brág,| swéet| tén-|ǒr búll.

That's the kind of ambiguity I'm speaking about. It occurs
constantly. It's not a particularly modernist ambiguity in the
meter of a single line. For years, for example, I read Shakespeare's line

Whěn íc-|iclés| hǎng bý| the wáll

as

Whěn íc-|iclěs háng| by the wáll

as a three-foot line. But it's not: it's a tetrameter line, because the rest of the poem is in tetrameter. You can go back to Shakespeare's line because you know the whole of the rest of the poem is in tetrameter, so you just read it incorrectly. There's much greater ambiguity in Bunting because you don't know what the basic norm is. This is possibly a pedantic question, because it works so well that it's just a question of analysis. But it's something very few people are able to do.

INTERVIEWER

You once said to me that free verse and metrical verse are different in *kind*. Did you mean by that that, from your point of view as a writer, to write in free verse is almost as different from writing in meter as it is again from writing in prose?

GUNN

Yes, as a form, given the essential difference that prose is enormously expansive and that most good poetry tends to be condensed. That makes for the major difference. But otherwise, yes, I think there is as much difference. You know, I've been reading for the first time a bit of Glyn Maxwell, whom I like very much. I originally got his book because I read a terrific poem of his called "Dream but a Door." That poem and a great many of the other poems I've read so far seem to be in what I would call proper meter, as opposed to sloppy meter.

INTERVIEWER

In 1961 you published a book, *My Sad Captains*, in which this difference in kind was acknowledged by the structure of the book and, except for your last collection, you've followed that pattern ever since. However, in *My Sad Captains* the non-metrical section is in syllabics, not free verse. How did you start writing in syllabics?

GUNN

I admired a lot of American poetry in free verse but I couldn't write free verse. The free verse I tried to write was

chopped-up prose, and I could see that was no good. Then
I thought of ways in which I could learn how to write in
something that was not metrical, that did not have the tune
of meter going through it. Once you've got the tune in your
head it's very difficult to get it out. Then, somehow or other
I heard about syllabics and discussed them a bit with Winters,
and I found a terrific example in some poems by Donald Hall
about Charlotte Corday. Donald Hall, as opposed to (let's
say) Robert Bridges or Marianne Moore, was not using a long
syllabic line. His was a short line and the great virtue of this,
for me, was that it was not in what we understand as a meter,
which involves combinations of stressed and unstressed syllables. It was virtually in free verse or prose, arranged in lines,
but each line simply depended on a mechanical count. I found
the short line adaptable and interesting. After a while, when
I was writing in (for example) the seven-syllable line, which
was my favorite, I found that I could recognize or could think
up a line of that length without counting the number of syllables. I'd check on it — yes, there were seven — but it had a kind
of tune of its own. This was interesting. Anyway, I was halfway
to writing in free verse and then I did, later on, in my next
book, go into free verse itself. I don't think I have written
any syllabics since the poems in "Misanthropos" in *Touch*.

INTERVIEWER

Was there anything you could do in syllabics that you can't
do in free verse?

GUNN

I'm not sure. I must say I'm quite pleased with the poem
called "My Sad Captains." I think I hit on something there but
it's not something I've been able to repeat. There's something
going on there with the sounds that I'm amazed I was able
to achieve. I don't think I've ever done that in free verse. I
don't think I could do it in syllabics again. I certainly couldn't
do it in meter: it's not a metrical effect.

INTERVIEWER
It's sometimes struck me that, in syllabic verse, you get closer to prose than you do in free verse.

GUNN
I don't know. It seems to me that a good deal of D.H. Lawrence's free verse is very close to prose. I like it for that. Some is more incantatory, some is more biblical, but some of it is not. It depends which poet you're speaking about: there are so many different *kinds* of free verse. There's a different kind for every poet using it in fact.

INTERVIEWER
As if each writer had to invent his or her own?

GUNN
Yes, though of course Pound invented several kinds. Williams invented one kind in his youth and another kind — I don't think so good — in his old age. Stevens invented one amazingly subtle kind. Winters invented a kind all of his own.

INTERVIEWER
Do you think yours is a different kind again?

GUNN
I try to make it so. I hope it is.

INTERVIEWER
But is there a principle that you follow?

GUNN
No, it just depends on my ear.

INTERVIEWER
We're about to touch on the point where form and content relate to one another. When you look at *My Sad Captains*, it's not just a formal difference between the first and second halves of the book, but a difference in the kind of content.

GUNN

It seems to me that the freer forms—and that includes syllabics—are hospitable to improvisation or the feel of improvisation. Lawrence puts this wonderfully in his famous essay
"Poetry of the Present." He speaks of free verse as poetry of
the present: that is, it grabs in the details and these are probably very casual details of the present, of whatever is floating
through the air, whatever is on the table at the time, whatever
is underfoot, however trivial—trivial but meaningful. Whereas
metrical verse, he says—I think rightly—metrical verse has
the greater finish, because in a sense it deals with events or
experience or thinking that are more finished. "Finished" in
both senses: in a punning sense, it's also more over and done
with. He calls it "poetry of the past." (He also calls it "poetry
of the future" but I've never understood what he means by
that.) But there is the idea of the completed thought; there
is what we nowadays call the idea of closure. So the freer forms
invite improvisation and are hospitable to the fragmentary
details of one's life, as opposed to the important completed
thoughts and experiences of one's life. The freer forms are
less dramatic, I think, and more casual.

INTERVIEWER

Taking *My Sad Captains* as a whole, it's a much more hu-
manistic book than the previous two.

GUNN

I was less of a fascist. I had been a Shakespearean, Sartrean
fascist! I was growing up a little, I wasn't quite so juvenile.
I was very much influenced by Sartre, as everybody realized
and as I was not sorry for everybody to realize. I was in quest
of the heroic in the modern world—whether I succeeded or
not—and that was a slightly fascistic quest because the heroic
is so often a martial kind of virtue. Well, by the time I got
to *My Sad Captains* I was growing up a bit . . . I suppose I
acknowledge other kinds of life in the first poem in the book,
"In Santa Maria del Popolo," in that I'm speaking about the

old women as well as the heroic gesture that's "Resisting, by embracing, nothingness."

I become very conscious in that book that religion is an option not open to you.

I'm not very spiritual!

Yes, but I'm asking you about a quality of language, I think. There are certain poems in the first part of *My Sad Captains* which are metaphysical in content. They seem to invite inquiry into purpose and meaning in experience, yet the possibility of purpose and meaning seems closed off for you. You know: "Purposeless matter hovers in the dark" and so on.

Oh I agree. Of course, this was somewhat different when I came to write *Moly*, when I took LSD. LSD certainly extends your awareness into other areas. It's chemical: it may be simply that you're not seeing round corners but you just think you are. You tend to think that these other areas are spiritual— and they may be. There's at least one poem, "The Messenger," in which I speak about angels: "Is this man turning angel as he stares / At one red flower . . .?" I was playing with the idea. I don't think I was being irresponsible. It is still a question, and it's not a question that I answer in the poem. The poem where I most overtly take up religious terms—spiritual terms would be better—is a poem called "At the Centre," which I now think is rather a pompous poem. This came out of my biggest acid trip. I took a colossal amount and stood with my friend Don Doody on a roof from which you could see the sign of a brewery, which had on the top of it a magnificent image in neon lights, even during the day, of a huge glass. The outline was permanently there, but it would fill up and drain with yellow lights, as if it were a filling-up glass of beer that would suddenly vanish and then fill up again from the bottom. This of course became a fantastic image for . . . Existence Itself! I think it comes into the poem with all the talk of flowing and stuff. And there I was indeed having, in that experience, a rather defiant conversation with a God whom I did not believe existed! There was one very funny thing happened during that day. I've only been able to admit it in recent years. (This was about 1968.) At one point, in this grandiloquent way that I had, I said to God: "What does it all mean?" Suddenly—this was a genuine hallucination—what seemed like a plastic bubble of shit crossed the sky. I did not admit this to my companion but I do remember saying: "No, oh no, not that. I do not want to believe that life is shit!" And I rejected that hallucination. But of course, the hallucination came from *me* in the first place. I'm not saying that the experiences in *Moly* were not genuine and I wouldn't disown anything in *Moly*. In fact, I still think of it as my best book, though few others have thought so. I think these experiences elicited my best poetry from me.

INTERVIEWER

The last poem in *Moly*, "Sunlight," is in form a kind of religious poem—in a way that "At the Centre" isn't. I mean, it's a sort of hymn.

GUNN

And the sun is like a god. At the same time, I do say in the poem that it has flaws and it's all going to burn out one day. So I'm qualifying it there.

INTERVIEWER

So it's finite.

GUNN

It's finite, yes, but to take a line of Stevens's from "Sunday Morning": "Not as a god, but as a god might be."

INTERVIEWER

The other thing in *Moly*, of course, is metamorphosis, and that reminds one of paganism.

GUNN

Yes, well the whole theme of the book is metamorphosis. Almost every poem I think. That was LSD, of course. It did make you into a different person. The myths of metamorphosis had much more literal meaning for me: the idea that somebody could grow horns, that somebody could turn into a laurel tree, or that somebody could be centaur (in the "Tom-Dobbin" poems — Tom is me of course), or turn into an angel. In the hallucinations — or more likely, distortions — that you saw under the influence of LSD, things did change their shape. You know, you could see bumps on somebody's forehead perhaps — I never did — but that's the kind of thing you could see that might resemble horns. You saw other possibilities.

INTERVIEWER

Was there also a literary source? Were you thinking of Ovid?

GUNN

Of course, yes. But I don't know if I'd read Ovid yet. Where I first got the myths was from Nathaniel Hawthorne's two retellings of them in *Tanglewood Tales* and *A Wonder-Book for Boys and Girls*. Often when people think I'm deriving from Ovid, I'm actually deriving from those books, which I read in my childhood. But he got them from Ovid.

INTERVIEWER

We've skated over your previous book, *Touch*. A lot of that was written during a year's visit to London, wasn't it?

GUNN

It wasn't actually. I'll tell you what I wrote on that year's visit. I wrote a good deal of "Misanthropos," but it was about half written before I came. It was certainly all sketched out, so I was in a sense filling in blanks. I also wrote "Confessions of the Life Artist" and all of *Positives*—but those are just captions, those were easy.

They're quite important though, aren't they? Weren't they your first poems in free verse?

I think they probably were, yes. I remember thinking to myself rather pompously at the time that I was trying to adapt William Carlos Williams for the English—as if Charles Tomlinson had not been doing that for some years before me! I had very great difficulty in the years when I was writing the poems that went into *Touch*. There was a lot of time that went by when I just wasn't able to write . . . I either couldn't write anything or I was writing poetry that got printed but didn't ultimately seem good enough to put in the book. I still wouldn't want to reprint them. They seem melodramatic or phony or something.

The book strikes me as transitional. Would you say it was because around that time—possibly through coming to London—you were becoming more decisively American than British? You lay yourself open to American influences . . .

I suppose that's right. How interesting! Yes. You know, people don't always think of themselves that clearly, so I need someone like you to tell me this kind of thing and I can assent to it. I'm not being ironic when I say this. It's just that we all know how difficult it is to stand back from ourselves and to perceive the pattern in our own lives, which may be perfectly obvious to other people. I do indeed think that's true. Yes.

Was it difficult to accept that you could write that sort of
"open" poetry?

No, though change is always difficult. It's so true what you're
saying. While I was in England I wrote an essay about William
Carlos Williams, which later got into my prose book *The Occasions of Poetry*. So I did a lot of reading of Williams for
that. And I discovered Snyder while I was here in England.
I read *Riprap*, which I found in Foyle's bookshop in London.
It had been out for four or five years but I hadn't yet read it.
Creeley I didn't like at that time. I had to read more of him
and eventually came to like him a very great deal. But he
didn't make sense for me somehow, until I'd read him more
thoroughly.

And Robert Duncan?

Oh yes, and Duncan was all mixed up with my acquaintance
with him of course. The three writers who have influenced
me *personally* — in a combination of their work and their character — in other words through friendship — have been Yvor
Winters, Christopher Isherwood and Robert Duncan. With
two of those, Winters and Duncan, I was really just a listener.
I call myself a friend but I wasn't a friend in that there wasn't
much reciprocation between us. I don't think Winters or Duncan knew me very well. Partly, with Duncan, because he talked
so much! He talked all the time — fascinatingly — and didn't
give you much time to answer. Or when you did have a chance
to answer, it was about ten minutes too late. Duncan was
aware of this and was always making jokes against himself
because of it. He had one very funny story about Olson. He
said: "When I first met Olson, we found there was an immediate problem, because he liked to talk all the time and I liked

to talk all the time, but we solved it at once by talking simultaneously!" But I don't think Duncan knew me very well. I was perfectly happy: I *learned* from him. Having lunch with him or spending an afternoon with him was such an extraordinary experience. I would go away with my head teeming with ideas and images and I'd write them down in my notebook and feel like writing poetry. I usually didn't and I didn't write Duncan-type poetry in fact, but he was a tremendously fertilizing influence. He was that kind of influence on everybody.

INTERVIEWER

Winters and Duncan, though, seems an extraordinary contrast.

GUNN

I have sometimes said to myself: "I am the only person in the world ever to have dedicated poems to both Winters and Duncan." They hated each other. They didn't meet but they hated each other. When they referred to each other it was with contempt, though I must say Duncan was a little more respectful at times of Winters for his sheer consistency. Of course, as I said before, Winters was what we would nowadays call homophobic.

INTERVIEWER

That seems not to have bothered you, though?

GUNN

Well, most people were homophobic; whole departments of English were! You couldn't be honest then. Sometimes young people say to me: "Why were you in the closet in those days?" I was in the closet because I would not only have lost my job, I'd have been kicked out of America and consequently would not have been able to live with my lover. That was a very practical reason for my behavior, dishonest though it may have been. I suppose there was even a danger of going to prison at certain times, because the act of having sex with another man was illegal in many states. So there was no question of my being frank with Winters, though I think latterly he must have realized. He certainly didn't at the period of our greatest contact. I didn't see that much of him once I had left Stanford.

Can we return to the contrast with Duncan?

Yes. Winters tried to be a complete rationalist, though he was in fact a tremendous romantic. Nobody would be that much of a rationalist unless they were really romantic. Duncan was a joyful irrationalist, even liking to write non-syntactical sentences which could be looked at from each end! It could be very irritating: looked at from each end they'd have different meanings. Suddenly the syntax can change . . .

How do you think it is that you absorb such contrasts into your personality without losing the coherence of your writing?

I've never had any trouble with that. When I was reading what they nowadays call the canon of English literature to get a degree here at Cambridge, I had no difficulty in reading Pope with appreciation and Keats with appreciation, though they stood for completely different things. I, in a sense, read them as living writers. They were living in that they were speaking directly to me. I'm aware of all that's wrong with reading unhistorically. Nevertheless, one does read unhistorically. Primarily it's Pope or Keats speaking to me, Thom Gunn. I was aware that they would not have wanted to have anything to do with each other, but I never had difficulty in reconciling people who were in themselves irreconcilable. I'm a very unprincipled person. People like to talk so much about poetics now and theory. I don't have theory. I expect my practice

could be brought down to theory but I'm not interested in
doing that. Maybe if I ever get famous enough, somebody
will do it for me!

INTERVIEWER

Can you summarize what you learned from Duncan? There's
a poem dedicated to him in your next book, *Jack Straw's
Castle*.

GUNN

It's not the best example though. I think the poem where
I used Duncan most was "The Menace." I put on different
voices, I am somewhat dislocated . . . His greatest poem he
speaks of as a mosaic, "A Poem Beginning with a Line by
Pindar." Actually it's something like Pound's way of writing —
by juxtaposition of fragments. "The Menace" is written in this
way: there is free verse, there is even kind of nursery-rhyme
regular verse, there is prose and there is a freedom of form
that I learned from him. It's deeper than just form, of course.
Put it this way: the main difference between Winters and
Duncan was that Winters was deliberately a poet of closure
and Duncan deliberately a poet of process. Duncan spoke of

writing as a process in which, if you were a good boy, things would come to you during the writing. The most interesting parts. Of course, they're both right to some extent, but they were making different emphases. I think in my practice I have become more interested in this idea of writing as a process and being open to things happening to you while you're writing — I mean things coming out of your imagination.

INTERVIEWER

In the second half of your career, you seem to have become preoccupied with those ideas of openness and closure. Somewhere, talking about *Moly*, you refer to "definition" and "flow," which are analogous to openness and closure.

GUNN

They are analogous. I play with these notions particularly in a poem called "Duncan," which is about his death. The last lines of the poem recapitulate the Venerable Bede's famous story about the sparrow flying through the feasting hall. I see the hall as some barns are nowadays, with open gables at each end: that is, both open and closed. It depends whether you're inside or outside. They're inside a building, and Bede's analogy is that this is a man's life. But if you see it under the aspects of eternity — of the whole sky as being what you're in — then you're never inside. I'm playing with the notion of insideness and outsideness.

INTERVIEWER

The subject of that poem, "Duncan," is a writer who takes the view from the outside, but the poem itself is in a strict traditional stanza form. Is that also important, that not only are you preoccupied with openness and closure but that you marry the two in different ways?

GUNN

I've always been trying to, yes. Donald Davie once said that he wanted to combine the influences in himself of Pound and

Winters. I remember rather sarcastically remarking in print that this was like trying to abide by the principles of Hitler and Gandhi at the same time. But Donald was right! One can do this kind of thing; if one believes in the validity of the different poetries, then one can in some way marry or digest whatever is in them. Yes, I feel very much at ease in metrical and rhyming forms. I feel a certain freedom in them. I don't feel that they are constricting. I feel I can play tricks with them that open them up.

INTERVIEWER

There are two moments in your relatively recent writing when you seem to fall back on closure and on meter. One is in *Moly* and the other is in *The Man with Night Sweats*, the elegiac poems about AIDS victims . . .

GUNN

I know why I did that in *Moly*. I've spoken about it so often that I'll simply summarize it by saying that I was trying to deal with what seemed like the experience of the infinite, deliberately using a finite form in dealing with it because I was afraid that it would not be dealt with at all in a form that also partook of the non-finite. I don't know why I've been attracted to it recently. It's not just with the AIDS poems. It's in the poems I was writing for about four years before I started on any of those. The first of the AIDS poems was "Lament" and that's in couplets. It just came to hand, it just seemed to me a useful form, but it was also that because I'd been writing in rhyme and meter so much, so concentratedly, for the previous four years.

INTERVIEWER

Do you think that writing "Lament" in couplets established that as the kind of form you would use for the rest of them?

GUNN

That's probably right.

INTERVIEWER

Let's go back to *Jack Straw's Castle*. A lot of that book, particularly the title poem, seems to me to represent the bad face of the *Moly* experience.

GUNN

That was deliberate. Much of *Moly* was about dreams; this was about nightmares. Maybe I should explain who Jack Straw is. There's one of many songs that I like from the Grateful Dead called "Jack Straw" and I used to wonder what an American could make of the phrase "Jack Straw." There's an English pub called Jack Straw's Castle and an English reader might know that Straw was one of the leaders of the Peasants' Revolt. But Americans couldn't be expected to know that. So I looked "Jack Straw" up in the dictionary and found that it means a worthless person — legally "a man of straw," a person of no account. Also I was reading Dante at the time, so lots of references to the *Inferno* come in. There are heaps of literary references in that poem, but it's absolutely unnecessary for anybody to know. It was just fun doing them. The kittens changing into the Furies came from *Through the Looking Glass*, when the kittens change into the Red Queen and the White Queen and so on. There's a bit from *Kidnapped* when David Balfour's walking up some stairs and suddenly there's a great gap. But yes, you're right, the drug dreams of *Moly* have all gone sour in *Jack Straw* . . .

INTERVIEWER

I suppose I was trying to say that *Jack Straw's Castle* feels less optimistic than *Moly*. Also, Robert Wells was telling me that he'd noticed in a lot of your poems a preoccupation with sequences of rooms, with houses and cellars and so on, which have a somewhat claustrophobic effect.

GUNN

You'd have to ask a shrink about that. It's a common enough metaphor for a person's body or a person's mind. It's like a house and there are rooms, there are half-hidden rooms in it, there are attics where nobody ever goes . . . I expect Freud speaks about it somewhere. You might almost say it was a cultural metaphor rather than an individual one. I do dream a lot about houses and about rooms, but I've always assumed everybody did.

INTERVIEWER

Two other things happen in *Jack Straw's Castle* that hadn't obviously happened in your work before. One is that there's a series of poems which are clearly autobiographical, in which you're looking back mainly on your childhood and adolescence. The other is that it's the book in which you come out as a homosexual. I wondered if there was any connection between that and the secret rooms: you know, the opening-up.

GUNN

Probably, probably. In the following book I use it as a metaphor in a poem called "Talbot Road," where I speak about the canals which are there all over London, but you never know they're there unless you happen to be on the top of a bus: they're hidden behind walls and fences mostly. Yes, it's not unconnected. Of course, I came out sexually because, when everybody came out sexually, it became safe enough legally for the first time. In 1974 I was in New York, and there was the gay parade there. I didn't particularly want to go on it, but I was staying with somebody who was going on it and who would really have felt considerable contempt for me if I hadn't gone. I went on it so that he would think well of me. I was delighted by it! I was walking along in it and I kind of floated forward and backward a bit, so I was sometimes walking with my friend and sometimes not, and there was this wonderful little man who looked like a bank clerk. He was wearing a suit and he said he was from Hartford, Connecticut, and I thought: "Yes, that's terrific. That's what it's all about, isn't it?" I was delighted by it. Or as they nowadays say, "empowered!"

INTERVIEWER

But how did it then come into the poetry?

GUNN

I admitted it in, whereas formerly I had covered it over or disguised it or excluded it. I was now *able* to include it. For one thing, if I'd brought it in when I first started to publish, I don't think periodicals or possibly even book publishers would have found my work publishable. Things were that different in 1954. It was good reasoning; it was not just cowardice. I mean, it was cowardice as well, but there was good reason not to write openly. Only a few very unusual people like Robert Duncan and Angus Wilson did write openly, and even with Angus Wilson I think it was only implicit—nobody could have been that interested in gay behavior without being gay himself. So that's how it happened. The end of "Jack Straw's Castle" where I'm in bed with a man—it would not have ended that way twenty years before. I'd have found some other way of dealing with it. Mind you, I never lied. I never wrote about a woman as a disguise for a man, the way Tennessee Williams in a sense did in his plays.

INTERVIEWER

So the women in *Fighting Terms* . . .

GUNN

The women in *Fighting Terms* were real women, yes. But I was guilty of using the Audenesque *you* to cover both sexes, which is what I think Alan Sinfield means when he speaks about "universality," which we were always taught at school was something we should be finding in our reading. Sinfield says that, when you use *you*, Auden could say it was the universal *you*, which could be applied to anybody, but in fact we are going to think it's a woman—and probably a white woman too! It's something I have a great distaste for, the word *universality*. My attitude to it is slightly different from Alan's—or rather, I come to a dislike of it through a different approach.

Of course, this is something I was taught at school—this is something my students were taught at school. I started to have trouble with it when I would say to a student who was reading (let's say) *Othello*, "What value is this play to us? Why should you be interested in Othello?" And they would say—a little too glibly, I thought—"Oh, it's universal!" Well, one thing the situation of Othello is not is universal! In his position as the black commander of a white army, or in his marriage, or in his very dubious connection with Iago. That's unique. I suppose one might say that there are sentiments voiced in the play that could be universalized. I mean, if we were in that position—though I have certainly never felt jealousy of that sort myself—we could feel "What oft was thought, but ne'er so well expressed." But it seems to me that, in a larger sense, the idea of universality depends on a notion of similarity. That is, people like Hamlet particularly, men like Hamlet, young men like Hamlet, because they identify with Hamlet, because they are similar to Hamlet. But in my own experience, what I get from reading is both similarity and dissimilarity, likeness and difference. I think I probably read more for difference than I do for likeness. Appealing to universality seems to obscure this (for me) rather important mixture. I reached this conclusion quite independently and now I find that it's a very fashionable notion indeed! I find that all the critics nowadays are against universalizing.

INTERVIEWER

There's a review of *The Passages of Joy* by Donald Davie, where he somewhat recants on an earlier statement he had made in which he had praised you for renouncing what he calls "the glibly deprecating ironies" of much modern British poetry and going back to "that phase of English in which the language could register without embarrassment the frankly heroic." He's talking about the influence of Shakespeare and Marlowe on your work. But in this particular review he suggests that something has happened to your poetry which involves your sacrificing that rhetorical force. It's quite clear, though he doesn't directly say so, that what he means is that by admit-

ting to homosexuality in your poems you have somehow given
up a poetic advantage.

GUNN

Yes. I'm terrifically grateful for that essay and for everything
Donald has written about me. I think it has been consistently
insightful. Nevertheless, his particular point there is that coming into the open about homosexuality — not *being* homosexual, but *speaking* about it openly — has been a diminishing
force in my poetry. I don't see that at all and I don't quite
understand how it operates in his mind, as if the subject matter
were so *modern* that there can be no influence from any poet
earlier than (I think he says) Whitman. Well, there *is* Marlowe!
There are others whom one knows were homosexual. There
are also most of Shakespeare's sonnets. We don't know what
Shakespeare's primary sexual preferences were, but he does
rather more than take up the subject. So it's not without precedents. I don't agree with his main assumption there. Nevertheless, he's got a right to his evaluation of that particular book.
It's true that there's probably more free verse in that book
and, if we're dealing with traditions, the tradition of free verse
doesn't go back very far. So, when I'm writing free verse, I'm
writing in a comparatively modern tradition. He connects the
two in a way that I think is wrong, but he does it very intelli-
gently. I don't think he'll any longer be able to make that
connection in light of *The Man with Night Sweats*. Let me
say that I also respect Donald so much that something that
was in my mind the whole time I was writing this new book
was: how can I show him that he's wrong?!

INTERVIEWER

I wonder if I can play devil's advocate at this point? Take
an early poem of yours, "The Allegory of the Wolf Boy" from
The Sense of Movement. It seems to me very clear now —
though it wasn't when I first read it — that that poem is about
being a homosexual.

GUNN
Indeed it is.

INTERVIEWER
The poem is, to use Davie's word, "resonant." It's almost
as if the not-owning-up is precisely what makes it so resonant.
I suppose this is related to what we've just been saying about
the universal: that from the particular experience of being
homosexual, it seems to establish resonances which all of us
can feel as human beings.

GUNN
There's no real answer to this. I think you probably overvalue
that poem a bit, but I'll admit your general point: that sometimes strategies of evasion — that does sound very 1990s,
doesn't it? — may contribute to what makes a poem successful.
In fact, whatever you have going, including the obstacles,
contribute to the making of a poem, even the obstacle of
having to write with some baby yelling in the next room or
something like that. That kind of very obvious difficulty is
something you may have to overcome and it may end with
some benefit to the poem. I'd go further and say that one of
the things that makes for good writing is getting to a certain
point and getting stuck in the elucidation of an idea or whatever you're writing about — the description of a thing, some
imagery, or even choosing a word — and you have to stop and
think maybe for weeks. *That* very likely may be a strength in
the poem. But it doesn't mean that you have to *invite* obstacles. If you did that, you could invite them so successfully
that you'd never write a poem. There are always plenty of
obstacles in writing, and I don't think that being honest about
one's sexuality is something to be avoided because the need
for evasion is a useful obstacle.

INTERVIEWER
There's a splendid phrase on the blurb of one of your books
that comes from a review by Frank Kermode. He calls you "a

chaste and powerful modern poet." You said earlier on that
your poems were moral evaluations of a life some people would
find immoral. There's something paradoxical here. What is
it in your language that invites such a word as *chaste*?

I can't really comment on that because I don't know what
the principles are that make me choose one word rather than
another. I choose a word that seems to me more appropriate,
more meaningful. But we all do that, don't we? And we end
up with different styles. I do know that, extremely unfashion-
ably, I admire the qualities of somebody like Isherwood—of
what I would call a "transparent" style. Now the word *transparent*, as you know, is much frowned on by most critics nowadays. They don't like that at all. I *love* it! I think that's what
it's all about. I certainly think that's what I *want* it to be about.
Obviously I want more than clarity. I'm raising questions all
the way with each of these words, with each questionable
abstraction! But you see what I mean? I'm aiming to get
through—most of the time—on a first reading if possible. I
do not want to be an obscure poet. I do not want even to be
as obscure a poet as Lowell, though I may often be so. That's
in no sense a derogatory comment on Lowell; he's just a little
more difficult at times than I am.

What do you mean exactly by transparency?

Transparent to my meaning. Of course, there is an implied
contradiction with what I was saying before about poetry as
process. There's the whole question raised of how much meaning you have before you sit down to write and how it gets
altered in the process of writing. But you do start with some
knowledge of what you're going to say after all. It may well
not be what you end up saying, but it often is related to what
you say. Yes, transparent . . . as though you're looking through

a glass at an object. That's what the word implies. So the
words are the glass to my mind. My mind is the fish in the
tank behind the glass.

Isn't it also that you want a style that allows something to
come into the poem which has nothing to do with you? You
want the world in the poem. You don't want just Thom Gunn
in it.

Oh, indeed, yes. I see what you're saying: it's not just the
fish but it's all behind the fish as well.

One of the things that happens in *The Passages of Joy* is
that there are lots of other people in the book—there, as far
as I can see, for their own sake.

I liked the idea of a populated book. I've always liked the
idea of a book of poems as a kind of . . . if not a world, a
country in a world. One of my impulses in writing is the desire
to possess my experience and to possess *all* my experiences—
my funny and trivial experiences too. I like to bring in people
on the street. I was thinking that, if the romantics had "effu-
sions" and certain of the modernists had "observations"—*Pru-
frock and Other Observations*, Marianne Moore's book *Observations*—what I'm trying to do is *record*. I'm recording the
past, I'm also recording the present and I'm recording the
world around me and the things that go through my mind.
One of the things I want to record is the street, because the
streets that I move through are part of my life that I enjoy
and want to *possess*. I don't any longer think of a poem as
"loot," but I do think of it as in some sense possessing something.

INTERVIEWER

The streets are very much San Francisco streets, aren't they—particularly in the last few books?

GUNN

Increasingly, yes. This started with *Touch*, though. There are bits of San Francisco in *Touch*: you know, "Pierce Street," "Taylor Street," "The Produce District." And probably more with each book. It thrilled me to write a litany of names in "Night Taxi," the last poem in *The Passages of Joy*. There are two lines where I take four extreme points in the city:

> *China Basin to Twin Peaks,*
> *Harrison Street to the Ocean.*

I loved doing that. It's pure litany, it's not meaningful. But it gave me a feeling of possession or achievement—to have found a place for those names.

INTERVIEWER

This is terribly surprising for an expatriate really, but it makes you almost a regional poet, like Thomas Hardy in "Wessex Heights." It's almost as if you'd invented roots for yourself.

GUNN

I *have* invented roots. There must be some kind of seaweed that's rooted in one place and then floats to another place and puts down the same roots!

INTERVIEWER

The other great theme in *The Passages of Joy* is friendship.

GUNN

That was quite self-conscious too. It must be the greatest value in my life. This is not a literary influence, though I admire Ben Jonson very much and he likes to write about friendship. I write about love, I write about friendship. Unlike

Proust, I think that love and friendship are part of the same spectrum. Proust says that they are absolutely incompatible. I find that they are absolutely intertwined.

INTERVIEWER

Has AIDS had a fundamental effect on your poetry?

GUNN

Anything as big as that must have had some fundamental effect, but I can't measure it and I'm not sure what it would be. I've had to attend at the deathbeds of quite a few friends. On the other hand, what I'm especially focusing on is not the *kind* of death they had. What most of these poems have in common as a subject is the way people face death. It's not the only thing I'm writing about in them but it seems to be one of the main things.

INTERVIEWER

Take "The Man with Night Sweats" itself. You have the image of the flesh as a shield in that, and it reminds me of things you said when you were young and were writing about soldiers. It's as if the invasion of this virus has called into question a lot of assumptions that your poetry had been built on up till then.

GUNN

I suspect the word *shield* is something of a dead metaphor as I use it there, but it certainly calls into question the whole concept of taking risks. The same is true of the following poem, "In Time of Plague." I'm not much of a risk-taker myself but I've always found the taking of risks rather admirable in a wonderful and showy kind of way. And that's exactly one of the things one can't do any longer in one's sexual behavior because taking risks can have mortal consequences now. The worst consequence before would have been a completely curable disease—since the invention of penicillin after all. It was a fruitful kind of risk. I'm also implying what we know about even children taking risks. Children take risks in their games, which ultimately strengthen their bodies. So there's a kind of pattern in our knowledge that active behavior is sometimes a bit physically risky. You know, when you go swimming, you could get drowned. But that is ultimately a strengthening thing and suddenly it isn't any longer. This is something that those two poems have in common: they had to go together in the book, though I don't think I wrote them together.

INTERVIEWER

"In Time of Plague" takes it a bit further . . .

GUNN

That poem is absolutely true. I changed the names.

INTERVIEWER

In that poem the love of risk is also a love of death, isn't it?

GUNN

Yes, and I say "I know it, and do not know it," and "They know it, and do not know it." We know several things at once, and we also don't know each of them. We also sometimes act as if we didn't know.

INTERVIEWER

Another theme, which seems to have grown through your work, and which flourishes in a special way in *The Man with Night Sweats*, is the theme of dereliction. There are a lot of tramps in the book . . .

GUNN

I've always been interested in the life of the street. I suppose it's always seemed to me like a kind of recklessness, a freedom after the confinement of the home or the family. This goes way, way back to my teens even. There was a poem which started with the words "Down and out," that being (I thought romantically) a kind of freedom. In my second book there is a poem called "In Praise of Cities" where I play with this idea in a rather Baudelairean kind of way. There is the promiscuity of the streets, which can hold promise of a sexual promiscuity as well, which is exciting. I love streets. I could stand on the street and look at people all day, in the same way that Wordsworth could walk around the lakes and look at those things all day. As soon as Reagan pushed the nutcases out on to the street in California, turning them back to the "community," which means turning them out on to the streets in fact, the composition of the people on the streets began to change a good deal. So I wrote about that. There's a funny case in my recent book where I wrote about a character I call "Old Meg" — after Keats, who was writing after Scott — and I found that, at about the same time, my friend August Kleinzahler, who lives a few blocks away from me, had written about (we concluded) the same person. He called her Mrs. B, which says something about the difference between him and me I suppose: I make a rather literary antecedent and he makes up a name.

INTERVIEWER

Do you suffer badly from writer's block?

GUNN

Well, everybody does, I suppose. Or there are very few writers who don't. Even Duncan, who I thought wrote continuously and easily: there were two years when he didn't write anything. There are certain times when you are absolutely sterile, that is, when words seem to mean nothing. The words are there, the things in the world are there, you are interested in things in the same way and theoretically you can think up subjects for poems, but you simply can't write. You can sit down at your notebook with a good idea for a poem and nothing will come. It's as though there is a kind of light missing from the world. It's a wordless world, and it's somehow an empty and rather sterile world. I don't know what causes this, but it's very painful.

Do you think that the periods of fecundity are in any way related to these dry periods?

It might be that you have to go through dry periods so as in a sense to store things up. Maybe it's like a pregnancy. Sometimes I think it is and sometimes I don't. It'd be very nice to get up every day and write a new poem. I'm sure every poet would like to do that, but it's not possible. It may be that you've had some imaginative experience that's going to become a poem and it just has to become more a part of you. It has to stew, it has to cook until it's ready, and maybe there's nothing else to write about in-between. You've just got to cook away until it's ready to be taken out of the oven.

T.S. Eliot, when he was interviewed for *The Paris Review*, was asked whether he thought his poetry belonged to the tradition of American rather than British literature. I wonder if I can put the same question to you in reverse?

I call myself an Anglo-American poet. If it's a question of the poets I admire, there's a tremendous number of both British and American poets whom I admire greatly. I think I'm a weird product of both. I'm not like the other products, but then we're none of us like each other. Most American poets at least *know* all the British poets and there's some kind of a relation there. Probably that's a little less true of British poets, though they're pretty well-read in the American modernists and probably Whitman and Dickinson as well. So I'm not sure that it's any longer a particularly meaningful question.

What do you feel about the situation of poetry in the English language at the moment?

GUNN

There's always a lot to be unhappy with at any time. We look back on the best of the romantics or the Elizabethans or any period. We don't remember there was an incredible amount of junk being written too. The Elizabethans seem so good, and there are so many good ones. There were also very many bad ones. At times it seems to me that all the giants have died, but maybe it always seems like that. People like Eliot and Pound and Stevens and Williams and even Yeats were around for part of my life—I suppose I was already reading a bit of poetry at the age of ten, which was when Yeats died. Then the following generation died early. Crane died very early and Winters didn't exactly live into old age. People like Lowell and Berryman destroyed themselves in various ways. But there are a great many youngish poets or poets of my own generation whom I enjoy reading very much and find exciting and like to explore. If I mention a few names, these are no surprise to anybody because I've written about them. In America I very much admire Jim Powell and August Kleinzahler. In Britain I'd like to mention the present interviewer! And I like Robert Wells's poetry a great deal and Tony Harrison's and there are younger people: I mentioned Glyn Maxwell, whom I'm reading right now and who strikes me as very energetic and wonderfully crazy in a really good kind of way. And then there are surprises, of course, like W.S. Graham. I discounted him for so many years. I thought he was just an imitator of Dylan Thomas—and he probably was at first. But meanwhile he was creeping up from behind and, when we all rediscovered him something like twelve years ago, that was quite a revelation. Of course, Basil Bunting only died the other day, and he was a giant. So this isn't altogether a bad time to be living. I've no idea what the time looks like: how it measures up against other times, or even what it's shaped like—who the big ones are and who the small ones. I'd just rather follow my personal interests and enthusiasms.

—Clive Wilmer

Thom Gunn

A Wood Near Athens

1

The traveler struggles through a wood. He is lost.
The traveler is at home. He never left.
He seeks his way on the conflicting trails,
Scribbled with light.
                        I have been this way before.

Think! the land here is wooded still all over.
An oak snatched Absalom by his bright hair.
The various trails of love had led him there,
The people's love, his father's, and self-love.

What if it does indeed come down to juices
And organs from whose friction we have framed
The obsession in which we live, obsession I call
The wood preceding us as we precede it?
We thought we lived in a garden, and looked around
To see that trees had risen on all sides.

2

It is ridiculous, ridiculous,
And it is our main meaning.
                        At some point
A biological necessity
Brought such a pressure on the human mind,
This concept floated from it—of a creator
Who made up matter, an imperfect world
Solely to have an object for his love.

Beautiful and ridiculous. We say:
Love makes the shoots leap from the blunted branches,
Love makes birds call, and maybe we are right.
Love then makes craning saplings crowd for light,
The weak being jostled off to shade and death.
Love makes the cuckoo heave its foster siblings
Out of the nest, to spatter on the ground.
For love has gouged a temporary hollow
Out of its baby-back, to help it kill.

But who did get it right? Ruth and Naomi,
Tearaway Romeo and Juliet,
Alyosha, Catherine Earnshaw, Jeffrey Dahmer?
They struggled through the thickets as they could.

A wedding entertainment about love
Was set one summer in a wood near Athens.
In paintings by Attila Richard Lukacs,
Cadets and skinheads, city-boys, young Spartans
Wait poised like ballet dancers in the wings
To join the balance of the corps in dances
Passion has planned. They that have power, or seem to,
They that have power to hurt, they are the constructs
Of their own longing, born on the edge of sleep,
Imperfectly understood.

                            Once a young man
Told me my panther made him think of one
His mother's boyfriend had on *his* forearm
—The first man he had sex with, at thirteen.
"Did she know about that?" I asked. He paused:
"I think so. Anyway, they were splitting up."
"Were you confused?"—"No, it was great," he said,
"The best thing that had ever happened to me."

And once, one looked above the wood and saw
A thousand angels making festival,
Each one distinct in brightness and in function,
Which was to choreograph the universe,
Meanwhile performing it. Their work was dance.
Together, wings outstretched, they sang and played
The intellect as powerhouse of love.

John Ashbery

. . . by an Earthquake

A hears by chance a familiar name, and the name solves a
   riddle of the past.

B, in love with A, receives an unsigned letter in which the
   writer states that she is the mistress of A and begs B not
   to take him away from her.

B, compelled by circumstances to be a companion of A in an
   isolated place, alters her rosy views of love and marriage
   when she discovers, through A, the selfishness of men.

A, an intruder in a strange house, is discovered; he flees
   through the nearest door into a windowless closet and is
   trapped by a spring lock.

A is so content with what he has that any impulse toward
   enterprise is throttled.

A solves an important mystery when falling plaster reveals the
   place where some old love letters are concealed.

A-4, missing food from his larder, half believes it was taken
   by a "ghost".

A, a crook, seeks unlawful gain by selling A-8 an object, X,
   which A-8 already owns.

A sees a stranger, A-5, stealthily remove papers, X, from the
   pocket of another stranger, A-8, who is asleep. A follows
   A-5.

A sends an infernal machine, X, to his enemy, A-3, and it
   falls into the hands of A's friend, A-2.

Angela tells Philip of her husband's enlarged prostate, and
   asks for money.

Philip, ignorant of her request, has the money placed in an
   escrow account.

A discovers that his pal, W, is a girl masquerading as a boy.

A, discovering that W is a girl masquerading as a boy, keeps the knowledge to himself and does his utmost to save the masquerader from annoying experiences.

A, giving ten years of his life to a miserly uncle, U, in exchange for a college education, loses his ambition and enterprise.

A, undergoing a strange experience among a people weirdly deluded, discovers the secret of the delusion from Herschel, one of the victims who has died. By means of information obtained from the notebook, A succeeds in rescuing the other victims of the delusion.

A dies of psychic shock.

Albert has a dream, or an unusual experience, psychic or otherwise, which enables him to conquer a serious character weakness and become successful in his new narrative, "Boris Karloff."

Silver coins from the Mojave Desert turn up in the possession of a sinister jeweler.

Three musicians wager that one will win the affections of the local kapellmeister's wife; the losers must drown themselves in a nearby stream.

Ardis, caught in a trap and held powerless under a huge burning glass, is saved by an eclipse of the sun.

Kent has a dream so vivid that it seems a part of his waking experience.

A and A-2 meet with a tragic adventure, and A-2 is killed.

Elvira, seeking to unravel the mystery of a strange house in the hills, is caught in an electrical storm. During the storm the house vanishes and the site on which it stood becomes a lake.

Alphonse has a wound, a terrible psychic wound, an invisible psychic wound, which causes pain in flesh and tissue which, otherwise, are perfectly healthy and normal.

A has a dream which he conceives to be an actual experience.

Jenny, homeward bound, drives and drives, and is still driving, no nearer to her home than she was when she first started.

Petronius B. Furlong's friend, Morgan Windhover, receives a wound from which he dies.

Thirteen guests, unknown to one another, gather in a spooky house to hear Toe reading Buster's will.

Buster has left everything to Lydia, a beautiful Siamese girl poet of whom no one has heard.

Lassie and Rex tussle together politely; Lassie, wounded, is forced to limp home.

In the Mexican gold rush a city planner is found imprisoned by outlaws in a crude cage of sticks.

More people flow over the dam and more is learned about the missing electric cactus.

Too many passengers have piled onto a cable car in San Francisco; the conductor is obliged to push some of them off.

Maddalena, because of certain revelations she has received, firmly resolves that she will not carry out an enterprise that had formerly been dear to her heart.

Fog enters into the shaft of a coal mine in Wales.

A violent wind blows the fog around.

Two miners, Shawn and Hillary, are pursued by fumes.

Perhaps Emily's datebook holds the clue to the mystery of the seven swans under the upas tree.

Jarvis seeks to manage Emily's dress shop and place it on a paying basis. Jarvis's bibulous friend, Emily, influences Jarvis to take to drink, scoffing at the doctor who has forbidden Jarvis to indulge in spirituous liquors.

Jarvis, because of a disturbing experience, is compelled to turn against his friend, Emily.

A ham has his double, "Donnie," take his place in an important enterprise.

Jarvis loses his small fortune in trying to help a friend.

Lodovico's friend, Ambrosius, goes insane from eating the berries of a strange plant, and makes a murderous attack on Lodovico.

"New narrative" is judged seditious. Hogs from all over go squealing down the street.

Ambrosius, suffering misfortune, seeks happiness in the companionship of Joe, and in playing golf.

Arthur, in a city street, has a glimpse of Cathy, a strange woman who has caused him to become involved in a puzzling mystery.

Cathy, walking in the street, sees Arthur, a stranger, weeping.

Cathy abandons Arthur after he loses his money and is injured and sent to a hospital.

Arthur, married to Beatrice, is haunted by memories of a former sweetheart, Cornelia, a heartless coquette whom Alvin loves.

Sauntering in a park on a fine day in spring, Tricia and Plotinus encounter a little girl grabbing a rabbit by its ears. As they remonstrate with her, the girl is transformed into a mature woman who regrets her feverish act.

Running up to the girl, Alvin stumbles and loses his coins.

In a nearby dell, two murderers are plotting to execute a third.

Beatrice loved Alvin before he married.

B, second wife of A, discovers that B-3, A's first wife, was unfaithful.

B, wife of A, dons the mask and costume of B-3, A's paramour, and meets A as B-3; his memory returns and he forgets B-3, and goes back to B.

A discovers the "Hortensius," a lost dialogue of Cicero, and returns it to the crevice where it lay.

Ambrose marries Phyllis, a nice girl from another town.

Donnie and Charlene are among the guests invited to the window.

No one remembers old Everett, who is left to shrivel in a tower.

Pellegrino, a rough frontiersman in a rough frontier camp, undertakes to care for an orphan.

Ildebrando constructs a concealed trap, and a person near to him, Gwen, falls into the trap and cannot escape.

Three Poems by Dawn Corrigan

Letter to Lt. Demaree

You dismiss the *tiny, protesting fraction*
back home, claim you've learned a nation

and its *customs, people, mores.* Did you and your
company of fellow swaddies line up for a tour

of a Bedouin family's desert-hugging tent?
(A family randomly selected by the government,

whose women offered demonstration
of chastity to the reluctantly sober battalion.)

Your sheepish aside denies that you really know
more about the Arabs than my vision from a TV show:

Actually, we've had extremely restricted interaction.
But Cassandra's empty satisfaction,

brought on by the free-postage letter, fades
like the riyal's king, seen in faint traces.

The gossip of old mutual friends, not you, carried
news to me that last year you remarried.

The Princess

The poets have all told my story wrong
thought there was a well, and me out all alone.
The well was deep and so the rope was long.

I had a golden ball, a pretty song;
nothing's so lovely as what is one's own.
The poets have all told my story wrong.

I tossed my ball, I tossed it far and strong
with consequences that would make me moan.
The well was deep and so the rope was long.

Then, from the well, climbing rung by rung,
a toad retrieved my ball like a dog's bone.
The poets have all told my story wrong,

he said, *I am no prince. But I was wondering*:
Is the moon the great bucket, or is the sun?
The well was deep and so the rope was long.

I kissed him. Now, two toads, we hang
here on the dry land, as we call wet stone.
The poets have all told our story wrong:
our well is deep and so our rope is long.

Demaree Farm

Knoxville, Tennessee

We look for a place to pick
   our favorite apples:
no luck under *Apple, Farm* . . .

   O for *Orchard* leads only
to *Orchard Hill Miniature Horses*,
   then *Orchid Coiffeurs*.

In this strange directory
  of half-dreams at noon
just seeing the orchid man's

  listing is like walking
into his epiphytic living room,
  a room that's the same

as one where Dad makes scenes:
  perched winking owl, fox
with fat partridge in her mouth.

  That was the den
where I was finally accepted
  by one arthritic in-law

when he unwrapped
  his Elvis music box
collection for me. Amid

  crumples of tissue
we danced a little as Elvis
  on a dais spun slowly

to *Hound Dog*.

David Jauss

Lemons

Kierling Sanatorium, May 11, 1924

Each swallow scalds his throat, the lesions
on his larynx burn. There's nothing
to eat or drink but air. Skin

thin as parchment over bone,
when Max Brod visits he's revising
"A Hunger Artist." Neither mentions

that hack, Fate, his trademark
irony. What they discuss
is thirst. On a scrap of paper, the only voice

he has left, he writes, "The worst
is that I cannot drink a single glass
of lemonade. But the craving itself

gives some satisfaction." Then,
of the flowers in a vase beside his bed,
"How marvelous that lilac. Even dying

it goes on guzzling." In three weeks
he'll scrawl his last words to Dr. Klopstock—
Kill me, or you are a murderer—

but today he's cheerful: the alcohol
injected into his laryngeal nerves
makes drinking seem almost possible

and he can think of nothing but lemons.
"At work there was a woman
who ate butter sandwiches every noon.

Can you imagine? I told her lemons
were the perfect food, so much sweet fructose
they confuse the tongue into thinking

they're sour." A disciple
of Jens Peter Mueller, the Danish bodybuilder,
all that winter he ate lemons

and exercised by an open window,
boasting to his diary, *The lighter I get
the more I weigh asleep.*

Now even his stories are weightless
compared to his merest dream. He smiles,
imagining Max feeding his manuscripts

to the fire, the words rising,
smoke and ash now, lighter, almost,
than air. The only words that deserve to last

are the ones that disappear
when pen touches paper . . .
"When I was young," he writes now,

"I squeezed invisible ink from a lemon
and wrote my sister a secret message."
(How little Elli's brow wrinkled

when he asked her to read the blank paper!
And how her mouth opened, like a starving bird's,
when he held the page over the candle flame

and the words appeared . . .)
"If only I had that juice now," he adds,
"I would drink it, every drop."

Two Poems by Karen Volkman

The Case

Old wolf, I said,
leave a tatter
for my family:
a scrap, a rag,
a bone, a button—something
to bury.
        Because, I said,
I've chased
the fast fox from
the henhouse, and twisted
the livid blossoms
from failing stems,
mercy, spare a rag,
a bone, a button,
for my family.

And because, I said, I sang
the names of saints
on Sunday, and lay
with another woman's
husband Monday eve, leave
a scrap, a rag,
a bone, a button—
to bury.

And he said:
It will take
whatever it is given. It will
be still.

Chronicle

The sea's tedious soliloquies
drone and repeat
against the rinky-dink dock

where a tethered rowboat wrestles
an inexpert knot,
and wiry fish bones

stir in soggy air below
the shambled seawall not yet repaired.
Don't think *learn* or *listen* —

this speaks alone.
The jellyfish know,
splayed on waves, seeped

in seaweed, dividing,
joining. The starfish
know it, taut

in their mending dream.
Only *that one*
with its fists and its footsteps

wails regret: two legs,
one mind, and nothing
to be done.

O lost regeneration!
O saline amoeba! Elements
and gods have no words

for isolation,
though they're known to break
from the skull or thigh

a disquieting,
gray-eyed child
who bides her time.

Roderick Townley

Wave

A trick of October light
made festive the trek we
took to the empty beach,

the four of us (five
counting the box
tucked in the knapsack).

You to thank, Mother,
for my bare feet in the sand,
brother beside me, wives

to the right, the sea's
blue cylinders rolling up,
rolling slowly away.

We fought open the lid,
looked at each other,
and waded in, two brothers

for once shoulder to shoulder
in an enterprise. He
dug in first, flung fistfuls

into the wind, flecks of
crushed bone sinking at once,
finer granules riding

in little cloud puffs, as if
from a last cigarette.
Then I joined in, gripped

by a wild, grieving joy,
till the thing was done. I let
receding water run

over my numb fingers,
and stared out: blue, blue.
Lovely to turn, then,

and see the women
waiting on higher ground,
windblown and waving us home.

Three Poems by Carl Phillips

The Swain's Invitation

The barn is warm, come inside, lie down,
sleep. Here, no sheep ever fails

in jumping, tears its dug or anything
else tender on the fencing's barbed wire

and, losing all the grace that true
jumping is made of, leaves you, flushed,

to start all over again counting.
If later on in the night one sheep, over

another, appeals, stirs in you, somewhere,
something, be easy, no gate will fall

closed, forbid you trespass; what you want—
why shouldn't you, why can't you? Take it:

the easy-to-grip flank that has always
worn your mark on it; for pillow,

the woolly side, still trembling,
after; the broad tongue, meat-pink,

for washing a thing back toward clean,
that place where, at last,

there's no trouble in sleeping, or
dreaming, or in remembering, by dawn,

only how tired you were, how warm the barn.

On Morals

Naturally, the preference is for
victory, not persistence
which, like fire if not put out,
in time will burn itself out.

Mere watching is not, of course,
particularly victory, but it need not,
either, signify perversion.
One tends increasingly to think

on one's first flasher in the park,
that first uncircumsized, ungainly
cock—how, as when some trick is
near, not to watch was the impossible

thing, waiting for what the pulled
bandanna, what the dove might next
turn into—and to feel guilty, as
if Lucretius had never written of joy

attendant, too, upon the witnessing
of violence, horror, any shame
when it falls on those not ourselves.
It is part of the nature of things

that from the grafting of distance
upon failure comes a pleasure for which,
sadly, one is more and more meant
to feel compelled to seek forgiveness—

which last, if it occurs at all,
generally does so at that angle
at which the sun has never, in fact,
risen. That is, it appears to.

Youth with Satyr, Both Resting

There are certain words—*ecstasy, abandon,*
surrender—we can wait all our lives,
sometimes,

not so much to use,
as to use correctly;
then the moment at last comes,

the right scene but more impossibly
different than any we'd earlier imagined,
and we stumble, catching

instead at nouns like *desire*, that
could as easily be verbs,
unstable adjectives like *rapt* or *unseemly*.

We find that for once nothing at hand
serves quite as well as the finger doing
what it does, pointing:

at the wine whose slim remains
the two glasses—tipped slightly, given
over to the grass as to their own sweet brand

of longing—look like any moment
letting go of;
or the boy's hand, fallen in such a way as

to just miss
touching the predictably stiff phallus—no
other word here will do—of the satyr;

or at how the O of the boy's mouth,
barely open,
is the same O that the satyr's beard, abruptly

arching away from his shag-covered chest, and
on, skyward,
seems most like wanting to curl into, if only

it could . . . which in turn is
the same O repeated by those the grapes'
twisting vines—too artificially, perhaps—

string above and,
to either side of the two sleepers,
in the manner of any number of unresolvable

themes, let dangle.

Charles H. Webb

Marilyn's Machine

She bought it because her baseball player didn't want her to,
because her playwright and her President and her Attorney
General disapproved. You're a star, they said — the one
thing they agreed on. Stars don't wash their own clothes.

Too timid to defy them, she rented a little room
and left her machine there, safe in its cardboard box.
Disguised in a black wig and flowered muumuu,
she sat and stared at the machine, imagining the famous

bras, nylons and panties, tight sweaters and skirts
sighing as they rocked, settling down into the warm,
detergent bath. Sometimes she cried, thinking
of the men who dreamed about her clothes and what

went in them. How may orgasms had she inspired,
who'd never had one of her own, her breathy voice
warding off "Was it good for you?" She loved
selecting temperatures: hot/warm, warm/cold, cold/cold,

and her favorite, hot/cold. She loved the brand name
"Whirlpool Legend." She loved the cycles,
especially "Rinse" and "Spin." She whispered their names,
thinking of a man thinking of her some distant day

when she is nothing but an image made from movies,
photos, gossip, exposés — an image thinking of him
thinking of her in her black wig and flowered muumuu,
rinsing, spinning till all the dirt is washed away.

The Craft of Poetry: A Semester with Allen Ginsberg

Elissa Schappell

The news that Allen Ginsberg was going to be teaching at New York University was passed around campus like a joint, making some people giddy and euphoric, others mildly confused, and still others paranoid—teachers and students alike. The waiting list to get into the class was extraordinary not only in length, but for the sheer number of times students eagerly checked it to see if they had moved up. As a graduate student in the creative writing program I was given first dibs. I was curious to meet Ginsberg, curious to see how he would commandeer the Craft of Poetry class, which in the past had been taught by Galway Kinnell and William Matthews. The following excerpts were culled from a diary I kept during the semester.

January 25

It's hard to think of Allen Ginsberg as "Professor Ginsberg." His work, as well as his ubiquitous persona, breed a kind of familiarity, not only because you may have sat next to him as he ate pierogis at the Veselka Coffee Shop, or seen him at St. Mark's Bookshop, but because he's a pop icon and his work (and there's a lot of it) is classically American.

Ginsberg is smaller and grayer and older than I expected, much more conservative looking, nay professorial in his gray flannel jacket and dark blue knife-creased trousers. His eyeglasses are clear plastic, his salt-and-pepper beard is neatly trimmed. He is wearing what seem to be thick-soled Rockport walking shoes, sensible shoes. Although he is sixty-nine he manifests few overt signs of old age. Perhaps it is the company he keeps—young attractive men who seem to be talismans against aging. I remember someone telling me that when Ginsberg was a mere youth he slept with someone who slept with Walt Whitman, the degree of sexual separation between those two bawdy bards was that close.

The tiny classroom is cramped—full of people who have dropped in as if it were a coffee house. Those who can't find a desk sit on the floor. I haven't seen most of these students anywhere else on campus, not in Victorian Lit. or even the Derrida lectures. There are the ubiquitous poetesses in flowing gauze skirts who write in purple ink and the self-serious poets with their smudgy eyeglasses and ravel-sleeved blazers. There is also a sprinkling of pseudo-Beats in black berets and uniform goatees and kohl-eyed women in black stretch leggings, and though it's cold outside, Diane Di Prima sandals.

Professor Ginsberg sits behind his wide desk frowning up at the low ceiling as though the harsh fluorescent light were assaulting him. Without further ado he begins to take roll. Somehow I thought it would be a hey, drop-in-drop-out-whenever-the-mood-suits-you kind of arrangement. As he calls off the names, I realize that half of the people crammed into this tiny room aren't even enrolled in the class. They're just here to catch a glimpse of Ginsberg, to get some kind of Beat benediction.

Then to confuse those of us who thought this class would be beating on bongos and barking haikus into the ether, he passes out the standard old literature class standby—a syllabus.

An Allen Ginsberg self-portrait.

In fact, there were *two*, one a "Survey of Historical Poetics from Pre-Literate Oral Traditions to Multiculti Poetics," the other a "Conversational Syllabus" dated spring 1994, which surprisingly only lists the first seven weeks of classes — only half the classes scheduled. The "Conversational Syllabus" instructs the student to "Read as much as you can of book titles bibliographed above. Consult photocopied anthologies by Allen Ginsberg when you can't find or finish books. Look up your English language anthologies for authors mentioned in passing. Use your research head for others not so obvious: Kalevala, Cavafy, Sappho, Cavalcanti, Bunting, Catullus, etc. Check out whatever you can, but take it easy. You can't do everything."

After passing out the papers Ginsberg lays out the nuts and bolts of the class. We are responsible for either a term paper

("I don't want no academic jargon, just tell me what's on your mind."), plus five pages of our own poetry ("No more or I'll never get through them.") a bibliography of outside reading that relates to the class. Eyes flicker hungrily at the suggestion that Ginsberg will actually read our work.

Ginsberg announces his office hours: "My office is over in the English Department. Everyone should sign up for an interview. So, whenever you feel like it come by my office, we can talk poetry, we can rap, we can make love . . ." at this a few raised eyebrows and titters.

"So," he continues, "Gregory Corso will be teaching class on February 22. He is provocative, he might try to push your buttons." He grins. Someone jokes that Corso, one of Ginsberg's longtime chums, will try to get us to take our clothes off. Ginsberg enigmatically smiles, then says, "Bone up on Homer, and the *Iliad.*"

He continues: "Gregory Annuncia Corso . . . Annuncia or 'the announcer of the way' Corso. Poetry is the seeking of the answer. . . . Let's start with Corso's theory of oxymorons — the yoking together of opposites. Corso takes very ordinary archetypes and plays with pop-art ideas, takes a one-word title and explores all the kinds of thoughts about it. He uses stereotypes and turns them inside out. He combines disparate ideas to make a little firecracker — he is not one of those high teacup poets."

Ginsberg then reads aloud some of Corso's work from *The Happy Birthday of Death*. He tells us that the title poem was written from notes Corso took after blacking out from laughing gas. Thanks to a cousin who was a dentist, Ginsberg has also experimented with laughing gas. He then reads a poem he refers to as Corso's most famous poem, "Marriage."

"In this poem he takes a one word title and explores all the kid thoughts about it, you know — rice, lobby zombies, Niagara Falls — everybody knowing what's going to happen on the honeymoon. This is a very anthologized poem, it's an easy poem, it's *cornball*, it's like trenchmouth, one anthology passes it on to the next."

Class breaks up; half the students file out into the hall.
The other half, mostly attractive adolescent boys with wispy
suggestions of facial hair, loiter and circle his desk, some in
a rather proprietary way. Some hold out books to be signed,
others just gaze as Ginsberg politely fields their attentions.

February 15

Tonight class meets in the same squalid little room. The
ceiling is poked full of holes where kids have been whipping
sharpened pencils up into the cork panels of the ceiling. I've
brought my tape recorder; a few other students have done the
same. Tonight he's in a blue shirt, red necktie, and a dark
blue wool blazer. He looks like a very tidy union organizer,
or a podiatrist. There are fewer gawkers.

"Today we'll continue with Corso and Creeley and more
on oxymoronic poems, the notion of poetics as a poet's magical
ability to hypnotize people," he says. He interrupts himself
as a straggler tries to sneak quietly into the back row, "Are
you in the class?"

"Yes."

"Are you going to be late often?"

"Uh, no."

"If you can make it, try and be on time. Otherwise there's
this constant interruption of people drifting in late, and I
have to find them on the roster."

He looks up to spot yet another latecomer. "What is *your*
name?" he asks in irritation peering over the top of his glasses.

"Joe"

"Are you in the class?"

"No."

"*Please* try and come on time because I constantly have to
interrupt the discourse to accommodate your lateness. It's not
like we've got that much time, it's just a measly hour and a
half."

At this grouchy outburst, everyone sits staring down at their notebooks. Ginsberg sounds more like a high school gym teacher than the Dharma Lion.

He hands out a copy of "Mind Writing Slogans." The sub-head is a quote from William Blake, "First thought is best in Art, Second in other matters." Then comes a wild array of aphorisms:

I. *Ground* (Situation or Primary Perception)
"My writing is a picture of the mind moving." — Philip Whalen
"My mind is open to itself." — Gelek Rinpoche
"Catch yourself thinking." — AG

II. *Path* (Method or Recognition)
"The natural object is always the adequate symbol." — Ezra Pound
"Show not tell." — Vernacular
"Only emotion objectified endures." — Louis Zukofsky

III. *Fruition* (Result of Appreciation)
"What's the face you had before you were born?"
"The purpose of art is to stop time." — Bob Dylan
"Alone with the alone." — Plotinus

Ginsberg starts with Corso's later work, reminiscing about the notorious 1959 Columbia University poetry reading where Corso, Orlovsky and Ginsberg were put down rather conde-scendingly in a long essay by Diana Trilling in the *Partisan Review*. They were invited back sixteen years later, and Corso wrote a poem about it, called "Columbia U Poesy Reading 1975" which Ginsberg describes as "a sort of retrospective of the Beat Generation that presents its own personal and medical history."

"What a sixteen years it's been since last sat I here with the Trillings . . . sixteen years ago we were put down for being filthy beatnik sex commie dope fiends . . . Well I guess I'll

skip ahead — there is laughter — *Bill's ever Bill even though he
stopped drugging . . . Dopey-poo, it be a poet's perogative.
. . ."*

"A lot of Corso's poems are pieces of mind candy, a jaw-
breaker; you really can't figure them out any more than you
can figure out Einstein's theory of relativity — is it inside or
outside? Is the external phenomenal world inside or outside?
It's the classic proposition. It goes back thousands of years and
is a subject of Buddhist discourse."

A student pokes her hand up, then seeming to think the
gesture too formal, slowly lowers it, her ears pinkening in
embarrassment. "So, what is Corso's method? How does he
work?"

"Corso's method is to write on a typewriter with two fingers,
one phrase at a time, breath-stop in the lines, a mental or
physical breath. Spontaneous composition, little revision. It
makes incremental sense verse to verse, so there are surprises
to the reader as well as to him. You can see his mind working
line by line. Corso composes out of an idea or a conception
turned inside out."

He goes on, "He stays a lot at home, and thinks. He tends
to critique a convention and refine the idea over and over
again until he finds exactly the right formulation of it. He
had this idea that he worked with for about ten years, 'I'll
never die, because when I'm dead I won't know it. Only other
people die but I'll never die.' It's built on the paradox of
subject-object again, external or internal, phenomenal or
whatever. He then works on them, again taking classic abstrac-
tions and turning them on their heads like the thing Heraclei-
tus did — 'Everything is flowing. You can't step in the same
river twice.' Right? Corso altered it to, 'You can't step in the
same river once.'" He pauses for a moment to let this sink
in.

"What Corso tries to do is to bring abstraction down to an
idiom comprehensible to the man in the street . . . living
language rather than a literary language. Most contemporary
poetry is under the spell of the more elegant — and in some
respects inauthentic — living speech of Wallace Stevens rather

than William Carlos Williams's spoken vernacular. So in Corso there's an element of street wisdom mixed with classical references and philosophy and common sense."

The door opens and a face peers in briefly. Wrong class.

"There's an old American tradition from Thoreau saying, Most men lead lives of quiet desperation. Well there are millions of poems of quiet desperation and they are all published in *The New Yorker*." Ginsberg chuckles derisively. "So, onto Creeley."

Then out of the blue he says, "Let's take five breaths."

What's this about? Weren't we all in fact just breathing? One person is even sleeping and actually breathing rather deeply. Ginsberg closes his eyes and instructs us, "Follow your breath from the tip of your nose until it dissolves for five breaths."

The thought crosses my mind that this deep-breathing exercise is like a metaphysical sorbet, a brain palate cleanser. I shut my eyes, then open them as I hear Ginsberg draw his first deep inhalation through his nose. Most of the class have their eyes shut, the rest are, like me, furtively peeking out from under their lashes, looking away in embarrassment when our eyes meet.

Ginsberg finally breaks the uneasy silence. "Robert Creeley was born in 1926. He was a northeastern poet; his style is kind of minimal, in short verse lines, haltingly slow. He was very much influenced by Miles Davis's phrasings on the trumpet, early Davis of the forties. He's from New England so there's a kind of reticence like in Emily Dickinson, not wanting to overstate his case . . . minimalism not *my* bullshit.

"The other influence on Creeley was Thomas Campion; he was the Bob Dylan of poetry, of the Renaissance. Performing lyric poems on his tortoiseshell lyre, he created a renaissance all over Europe. Lyric poems should be performed with a musical instrument, or else they lose their muscle. They become lax without that kind of exquisite, delicate hovering accent."

Ginsberg recites some Campion from heart. "All Whitman is 'I celebrate myself, and sing myself.' It's self-empowerment.

He's not scared of his own body there in the midst of nature. Campion does the same thing.

"There's an undercurrent of abrasiveness, a kind of turn-the-apple-cart-over in Creeley's work. Generally he types the figure a phrase at a time, until the next phrase comes to him, so there's a kind of break in the line or breath stop as he calls it. Like Corso, each line he writes modifies or alters the previous line, so he doesn't know what he's going to say until he's said it. His method, like Kerouac's, is that of spontaneous composition, and relatively little rearrangement or revision."

Wrapping up class, Ginsberg reminds us that next week he is reading at the DIA Center downtown and that he's gotten free tickets for the class. He also reminds us, "If you don't have, or can't find any of the writers on the syllabus, or any of these books, let me know and I'll lend you my own books." There is a pervading sense that he is a kind of poetry pusher, the intellectual candy man.

The DIA Center Reading

Allen reads a poem that includes a line about getting out of bed after having sex with a young man who has turned his body to face the wall. There are two attractive guys sitting in front of me, neither of whom I've ever seen in class. One turns to the other: "Is that Billy he was talking about?"

"No," the guy proudly replies, "that's me."

February 23

Tonight we are liberated from our dinky classroom, upgraded to a small amphitheater in the Main Building. Once again a bunch of odd people have turned up in the class; perhaps they've heard through the groovy grapevine that Corso is at the helm tonight. Corso slouches into class with the quick anxious step of the hunted man, a man unhappy to have left his apartment. His long snaggly gray hair is pulled back in a low ponytail. He sits down, and hunching over the desk, nervously tugs and strokes his little beard. He's wearing a blue denim work shirt, khakis and a ratty black jacket. He *looks* like a Beat poet. One of the boys perpetually buzzing around Ginsberg passes around an attendance sheet.

By way of introduction Corso begins with a question, "Does anyone know where the Trojan horse is from? The Cassandra myth?"

No one says a word.

"Big big man Mr. Homer. Homer is the daddy of all mythology. You should have read Homer, there is no excuse for it, if you haven't. No excuse for not embracing Homer. If you haven't gone through Homer . . ." he throws up his hands in dismay.

"Homer wrote the *Odyssey* at the base of Mt. Olympus. He wrote the *Iliad* right on top. He wrote about the bickering of men, like the bickering of gods. Here was a man who dealt with the *gods*, who put his own voice in the mouth of gods — quite fantastic. Big big man Mr. Homer. Hindu gods don't bicker." Corso strokes his chin and fidgets in his chair. I have the feeling he isn't accustomed to lecturing. "What do you want to talk about?" he asks, nervously drumming his fingers upon the desktop.

The room is silent.

In a heartbeat he launches back in on Homer. "It is just basic knowledge for a writer; you should *all* know your Homer."

No one says a word.

"I find somebody dumb who doesn't know Homer — that's how I feel. Check him out; he brought the Greek gods on the scene, that is for sure. But then again I just happened to be reading that book that afternoon when Ginsberg called. We don't have to be stuck with the *Iliad*. There are insights in that book that are stupendous." He rocks in his chair and checks his wrist for a non-existent watch, "How long have I been here?"

"Twenty minutes."

"That's a long time man!" he sighs in exasperation, "Let's get on to something else."

There is an uneasy silence in the room. Nervous giggling.

No one knows what to do, least of all Corso. "Take a look at the Greeks and their hell," he says desperately. "Their hell was like their weather. Their weather was not too cold, not too warm, it was *moderate*. Look at the Gilgamesh hell—that was a funny hell. That hell is a desert. Different kinds of hells for different seasons."

"Where is your hell?" someone calls out from the crowd.

"Right here, believe me," he laughs uncomfortably. The class laughs along with him.

"I always figured a guy who is a philosopher would never go and tell people he was a philosopher," he says lighting on a new topic. "Others had to tell him he was a philosopher. But a poet has to tell people he's a poet. If you don't, they don't know. It's like Anne Waldman, whom I love, who made the mistake once of showing me a poem. She asked, 'Is this a poem?' And I said, 'Hell no.' She hasn't forgiven me for 10 years. I don't want her wrath on me. I never expected poets to be that sensitive," he says rolling his eyes. "I thought you could screw around with them. My god. I made it worse by trying to apologize. I tried, and oh, I was so embarrassed. I didn't mean it, really. One day she will see. That shows you how careful you have to be of what you say.

"I think as a poet you have to have certain things under your belt—the Cassandra myth, the Trojan horse. You've got to have the essentials in your head; even if they aren't essential, they're at least beautiful. I'd rather have a little bit of knowledge than a whole lot of faith. I'd rather have knowledge, an encyclopedic head. Of course to be a poet you don't have to know *nada*."

This seems to cheer the class.

"You've said poetry was a saving grace to you, how so?" a student asks.

"Because it educated me. Poetry is a study of the head. You use your head for pondering and worrying, working things out. I was alone. I didn't have some of the people others have, like parents—so I worked it out for myself. Then poetry came along."

Corso seems noticeably more at ease answering questions than lecturing.

"When did you realize you were a poet?" someone inquires.

"I realized I was a poet around fourteen, fifteen. I never got a chance to be rejected. I said I was a poet—so I was. First poem I wrote was about my mother. I used to ask people what happened to her. Sometimes they said she had died, other times they told me she was a whore, or that she just disappeared. To this day I don't know. So I took the disappearance, and figured she went back to Italy, a shepherdess in Calabria, tending sheep around the lemon trees. That was my mother. The poem was called 'Sea Chanty.' " He recites it, "*My mother hates the sea, my sea especially. I warned not to, it was all I could do . . . Upon the shore I found a strange yet beautiful food, I asked the sea if I could eat it, and the sea said I could . . .*'

"You know it would be easier to be a painter," he laments. "You have to show your ass in writing. It is embarrassing when you have to face people and read poems; they see how you look, they see you—*oh my god,*" he raises his hand to his cheek in mock horror. "Whereas a painter just puts his stuff in a gallery and walks away."

"How do you work?"

"I get a certain poem-feeling in my gut. I watched Tennessee Williams once in Greece when I was staying at his house. He'd get up every morning at seven and pull down the shades and play schmaltzy music on tapes he had from America and start typing away. The time I usually work is when people are sleeping; it is always in the middle of the night, the hour of the wolf, while the world is asleep. Not that I do it every night, but I like the dark, I don't like the bright sunlight. I'd rather be in the shade."

"How do you feel about rewriting?"

"At the time of writing I don't rewrite. First thought best thought. We were always into that. You know, first words that are down, best words that are down. The first thought is the purest thought. The purest stuff is spontaneous. But sometimes I do rewrite. Why not make it better? Why not?"

"Do you share work with other writers?"

"I've read poems on the phone to Ginsberg. He read me 'Howl.' Sharing the work is good. Why hoard your words? Poetry is *hard*," he says with a grimace.

"Do you like to read work aloud?" someone in the back calls out.

"You get more out of reading a poem than from hearing it read to you. You get more out of me in print than in a reading, yeah. Because usually I don't read the heavyweight stuff that I write. I just can't bear it. It would take too much out of me. So I read the light stuff, the funny stuff. To make them laugh. Oh boy, they love you when you make them laugh. I've got to have a couple of drinks before I do it. To face this horde, this is like death, this is the darkest nights of our souls, it is horrific, and then there is Ginsberg up there like it's a great come-on. Oh boy, he can be like a clown up there." He pauses, "It diminishes poetry, I think. It diminishes poetry by reading it and playing the clown, or entertainer. But I've done it to make money. I prefer the nice quietude of poetry. For me poetry comes from here," he points to his sternum. "If not, it doesn't mean anything—it don't mean *nada*. You can't sneak the miracle. There is no way that you're going to write a better poem just because you want to be remembered for it.

"As a kid I knew when I grew old I'd always have poetry. Old age didn't bother me because I'd always have poetry to go to—it was a standby. Whenever you have pain, or trouble, or things upsetting you, try to write poetry, it will be your greatest friend. In many ways poetry benefits you, and it could benefit others. It's a good thing. It doesn't hurt anybody en masse."

Having made this proclamation Corso rises to his feet as if to leave. A clock watcher calls out, "Uh, you've got forty-five minutes left."

Corso groans and sinks back in his seat. "I can't get out of here!"

The class cracks up. No one wants him to stop talking.

An addled-looking blond woman stands up in the back, "Do you ever have anybody else read your poetry out loud?"

"No. I never have, but I bet they have. Why, you wanna read one?"

"Yeah."

"Which one?"

"I want to do the one about the stains. The stains. I really like the thing about stains, you know that one?"

Corso knits his brow and rubs his forehead in contemplation.

"Do you know the one I'm talking about?"

Corso shrugs. "*You* don't know the poem you're talking about?" He laughs.

"I remember the *concept*," she says. "I don't remember the words. You don't remember it?"

"I don't remember my poetry that well, other than that sea chant. Who recites American poetry by memory? No one does that anymore," he says.

"Do you read criticism of your work?" a man with a shaved head asks, as the blond woman slides, as if in slow motion, back down into her chair.

"I don't see much of it. The message is either going to be heavily down, or all the way for it. They don't know how to handle it. But I have no doubts, I mean if I died now, I wouldn't feel that I wasn't accomplished.

"I could write a volume of poetry in a week—if it hit me. But I don't want to throw out poetry like that, one after another. People say, 'People are going to forget you.' I don't give a damn, I'm not a movie star. I'm a poet. Today poets have all got to be famous. It's all changed, the ball game has changed. It is only a new thing that's happened with poetry that poets are known while they are alive. Allen Ginsberg got it, nailed it so well. He knows how to handle it and put it to good use. Check it out. The man has been *beneficial* to people. If I look at history, I can't see where poets have caused any hurt en masse—I can't see where a drop of blood's been spilled, except among themselves. Verlaine with Rimbaud shooting him in the wrist, okay, Villon cutting the priest's neck because the priest wanted to seduce him, well okay— family quarrels.

"I'm facing old age," he says gently nodding his head, "I'm sixty-three. I hope poetry will stand by me. Look at Blake. Before he died, he was singing in his bed to his wife Kate, dying and just singing. The years they go like that. I saw my nine year-old kid the other day and I didn't recognize him.

"Poetry is when you are all alone in a little room and you have to write the fucker down." He pauses for emphasis. "It's all there. Remember, it's a game being a writer; you are taking a gamble there. I really admire people who do it, even hack writers, I admire them, because they can create attitudes, time spans." He nods. Then, rising to his feet for the last time, he signs off, "I hope I gave you something."

Corso left the class twenty minutes early. Nobody seemed to notice.

March 1

Tonight's class is greatly diminished. The regular core plus one or two stalkers. Ginsberg unloads a pile of books from a tote bag. He seems anxious to hear about last week's class. "Anybody take any notes?" he asks, rubbing his hands together gleefully. "I'd be curious to see what happened. What did he have to say?"

"He spoke about growing old and the Trojan horse," a student in her seventies says.

"We talked about his *craft*," murmurs a kohl-eyed woman in long dangly earrings.

"It was *great!*" says an eager note-taker in the front row. Ginsberg nods in satisfaction.

"Today I want to talk about Creeley, his growing older, middle-aged poems, and his realization of aging. So, we'll begin with "Self-Portrait," his realizations about himself:

He wants to be
a brutal old man,
an aggressive old man,
as dull, as brutal
as the emptiness around him.

He doesn't want compromise
nor to be ever nice
to anyone. Just mean,
and final in his brutal,
his total, rejection of it all.

It's a rare and brutal self-portrait, and it is very much him. It reflects his recollections of his earlier life, when he did drink quite a bit, and was quite mean to people when he got drunk. Some drunken people are very sweet, some are dopey, some are maudlin — some get really really mean. Fortunately, he never turned it on me, but I've seen him in that situation. He is actually alcohol-free now, I think."

"Incrementally, almost monosyllabically, the meaning of a Creeley poem accumulates, changing everything that goes before it. His method of writing is to put paper in the typewriter and begin with whatever phrase or insight he started with, a retroactive small instance of feeling, and then accumulate detail and reach for common ground."

Ginsberg reads aloud Creeley's poem "Memories":

Hello, duck
in yellow

Cloth stuffed from
inside out,

Little
pillow

"That's all there is," he laughs, then reads it aloud again. "It's very *intimate* poetry. Some people say its incomprehensible, but I don't think so. If you look long enough it will make sense. The work couldn't be more real or concrete. Like the duck—it's a real baby cloth duck. It is a play of pure language, but there is always some substantive matter there."

"What do you think when people call him abstract?" someone asks.

"Well, it *is* abstract. I wouldn't want to write that way myself, so abstractly, except I really dig it when I read it. I'm almost crying it is so cool.

" '*Go*' is another minimal one," Ginsberg says, then reads aloud:

Push that little
thing up and the
other right down.
It'll work.

"It sounds like instructions for a baby toy, doesn't it? It is also slightly erotic; it might read as some suggestion about the whole process of creation, Push that little thing up." He laughs uproariously. "It's so beautiful! It is actually the memory of a child's toy but it is also parallel to God, or a divine messenger telling man, *Push that little thing up, it will work.* He trembles with laughter. "It is your generic instructions for existence, or am I reading too much into it? It *is* there," he insists. "If anybody here doesn't get it, it's all right. It took me forever to get them myself."

Next we read "Age," which is from Creeley's collection *Windows*. It's the most explicit poem we've read. Ginsberg begins to crack up over the line, "probe into your anus." He has to stop at "roto-rooter-like device" to catch his breath, and by the time he reaches "like a worn out inner tube" his voice is a high-pitched squeak, and he's laughing hysterically at the line "to snore not unattractively." After he wipes the tears from his cheeks he continues, "I guess what I like about his poems is that they are a trip. It's really the mind laid bare. He may do some tinkering, but I think his method is if it doesn't work, it doesn't work and he throws it away. This poem is like a mind trap in a way. Creeley's poems are like jokes that crack themselves."

After he has composed himself Ginsberg adds, "Creeley takes from Campion the rhythmical subtlety, the musicality characteristic of English song and lyric poetry. The delicate cadence in Creeley comes from Campion. His care for the syllable is like the poets of the Black Mountain School, who composed their work conscious of every syllable and how it fits into the cadence."

The subject of cadence and rhythm leads us to Sappho, whom Ginsberg refers to as "the first Rimbaud." We listen to him read some of Sappho's most famous poems like "Invocation to Aphrodite" and some other fragments.

"Sappho invented a number of stanza forms, like the sapphic stanza," he says, then begins to chant, "Trochee trochee dactyl trochee trochee." He waits for a second as if expecting us to jump in, but the class is speechless. The woman next to me whispers, "Is he having some kind of flashback?"

"Okay," he says in his best patient Cub Scout leader voice, "Let's do it together!" and leads the whole class in a chorus of sapphic stanza form. At first we are timorous and shy, then after a few rounds our voices become loud, even celebratory. This singing makes class seem more like day camp than a literature class.

"These are dance steps," Ginsberg tells us. "Ed Sanders and The Fugs use these. These have a cadence so powerful and inevitable that they outlasted Troy — the monuments of marble, brass and iron and the Parthenon — and they're good for love poetry — good for poems of *yearning*. They're not far from the blues in terms of structure. Actually, they're very similar to twelve-bar blues.

"For next week," he calls out as everyone gathers up their books, "I want you to write a sapphic poem!" As we file out of class I can hear people humming trochee trochee dactyl trochee trochee . . .

March 8

I'm early for class. Ginsberg hasn't arrived yet. The woman next to me is visibly peeved. She's riffling through some papers,

and sighing in exasperation. I can see that they're sheaves of
poetry which have been corrected in cramped handwriting—
I think it's Ginsberg's hand. She looks over at me and rolls
her eyes.

"Have you had your meeting with him yet?" I ask.

"Oh, *yeah* . . ." she says, sucking in her breath and raising
her eyebrows. "I got completely clobbered. He hated it. He
was *so* critical—I don't think he likes women. At least he sure
doesn't like my work, it's too *girly* for him."

I confess to her that I'm nervous about my meeting. She
smirks, "You should be. I couldn't wait to get out of there.
I know these are good, I've workshopped one of them even,"
she says, sliding the poems out of my sight and into a purple
folder.

One on One with Ginsberg

I sit in the hall outside of Ginsberg's office, along with
several other students. A platinum-haired boy with a black
goatee scribbles in his journal. A woman with long black Me-
dusa locks twirls a snake of dark hair around her finger, looking
pained as she reads a slender volume of Sappho. I can see,
through the crack in the door, a boisterous fellow in cowboy
boots sitting in the chair alongside Ginsberg's desk. He is
leaning across the desk jabbing his finger into what I suspect
is his poem. In his lap is a large pile of papers, more poems
I assume. I can't hear the conversation, but as I watch I can
see the man slowly deflating, his gestures becoming larger as
he struggles to explain the intention behind his art. I feel
sick. I read over my own poems, stumbling over obvious meta-
phors and silly turns of phrase. I want to flee. I can hear
Ginsberg's voice, "okay," he says in a wrapping-it-up voice,
"there are other people waiting." My heart is pounding. The
man bounds out of the office.

Ginsberg looks down at his sign-up sheet. "Schappell?" he

asks, peering over the rims of his clear plastic glasses. I nod and shut the door tightly behind me, I don't want anyone to witness my artistic evisceration. He waves me into the chair next to his desk. My heart is pounding as I hand over my work.

He reads silently, tipping back in his chair. Then he leans forward across the desk and smiles. To my surprise he is incredibly generous and complimentary. Perhaps my contemporaries have just worn him down so his critical faculties are muted. Perhaps he's just in a good mood. He makes insightful comments, and does a quick edit that vastly improves my poem. He suggests a few writers for me to read and asks me questions about my poem, which is about my experiences with olfactory hallucinations. He's curious about them and nods as I tell him about the strange and unsettling phenomena of smelling smoked meat and alcohol when none are in evidence. He writes down the name of a neurologist who might be interested in my case and suggests I stop by again. I leave his office feeling greatly relieved, and a bit elated.

March 29

When I show up for class, the amphitheater is full of strange faces. Another class has hijacked our room. Ginsberg looks annoyed. Tonight he's wearing a hand-knitted dark blue, white and red cardigan with chunky hand-wrought silver buttons. It looks like a Tibetan Perry Como sweater.

"Just sit down and let's get going," he says in irritation, and gestures at the floor for us to sit down. "We have a lot to do." At his bidding people sit cross-legged on the floor just outside the open door of the ampitheater as though in peaceful protest. The other class peers out the door at us. Just as Ginsberg starts to take roll, a uniformed security guard appears and sternly informs us that there are too many of us to sit in the hall. *We're a fire hazard*. Ginsberg insists he has the paperwork needed for the room, and pats his pockets as though he carries the documents with him. The guard disappears, then reappears a few minutes later saying he has found another room for us. We move en masse to an auditorium on another floor. The new room is a lecture hall for the sciences, its main source of decoration being an enormous periodic table of elements.

Without waiting for the stragglers to find seats, Ginsberg plants himself on the edge of the stage and starts in on John Wieners. "Wieners is the great gay poet of America. He's in hardly any anthologies, but he's so emotional and truthful." Ginsberg reads us "A Poem For Trapped Things" in a voice that is full of intense appreciation.

"Wieners is like Cavafy, a Greek modern poet of the twentieth century who died in the twenties or thirties. His work gives us glimpses into his love life, his homosexual bent . . . it's a similar aesthetic to Whitman's poetry."

He quotes from Wieners's tragic American poem "The Acts of Youth": "*I have always seen my life as drama, patterned after those who met with disaster or doom,*" then reads the poem in its entirety. Ginsberg compares Wieners with Hart Crane, who he describes as "a doomed powerful poet whose low self-esteem led him to commit suicide."

Ginsberg reads more Wieners, interjecting comments on his sexual infatuation with Robert Creeley and how this pissed off Creeley's wife. He tells us of Wieners's time spent in and out of various asylums, his shock treatments and awful nightmares, and how he experimented with peyote and "loco weed," which makes you lose your memory and then your mind. "He had been over the abyss before," Ginsberg says and pauses. "There's a thread of Marlene Dietrich glamor in Wieners's poetry."

He describes Wieners's trips to New York to do poetry readings. "Sometimes he would just read one," Ginsberg recalls. "He'd read one, sit down and wait until they applauded and he was called back onto the stage. Then he'd get up and read another, then go sit back down. Sometimes he would read the gossip columns as poetry. He wrote some of his poetry under the nom de plume Jackie O."

© Allen Ginsberg

Allen Ginsberg, John Wieners and Gregory Corso in 1986.

Class ends too soon. "For next week think about Kerouac and vowel delicacy, meditation and poetics," he cries out.

April 5

Tonight we're in yet another classroom — a cramped but bright little space with many more chairs than students, so people are fanned out all over the room, mostly lingering in the back. This seems to annoy Ginsberg, who insists, "Come closer, come closer, I don't want to yell." We pull our chairs up in a circle and surround him like disciples.

"What was the face you had before you were born?" Ginsberg asks. "That question, the theme of a Zen poem, is the heart of Beat poetry. It could be called the 'golden ash' school, as Kerouac said, 'A dream already ended, the golden ash of dream.'"

"Has anyone ever heard of the Paramita Sutra?" he asks. Everyone shakes their head no.

Someone jokes, "Isn't that like the Kama Sutra?" The class giggles.

"This is the basis of much Eastern thought, particularly in the Buddhist world through Indo-China, Burma, Ceylon, Tibet and China itself. This is a translation by Shunryu Suzuki Roshi, a Zen master from San Francisco who was a big deal in the fifties and sixties. It was tinkered with by myself and a Tibetan lama to make it maybe a little clearer. Generally it's chanted in a monotone, so I'll chant it."

Ginsberg chants the Paramita Sutra in a strangely pretty monotone.

"First time I ever heard anything about Buddhism was Kerouac crooning the Buddha refuge vows; he was singing these, crooning them like Frank Sinatra." Ginsberg, with his eyes downcast sings the refuge vows, repeating them three times.

He describes the four vows of the bodhisattva then chants them for us. This is all to prepare us for Kerouac. Of the books *On The Road*, *Visions of Cody* and *Dr. Sax*, all published in a three-year period, Ginsberg believes that *Visions Of Cody* contains some of his best writing. "By then he had discovered his method of spontaneous writing. He'd written the huge novel *On The Road* and had rethought it. He decided he would do it even better and bigger, by going back over the same characters, same plot, not making it a chronological narrative, but according to epiphanous moments. He'd write a series of discrete epiphanous moments, then string them together. Different experiences and moments popping up in whatever order would be the structure of the book. It wouldn't have the linear quality of a regular novel, with a beginning, middle, end. It would be as the mind sees a cubist painting. Cody Pomeray is Dean Moriarty is Neal Cassady, all based on a real person, all real happenings but fictionalized.

"His next book, *Dr. Sax*, was written on marijuana, so it has an elaborate marijuana openness. Dr. Sax was the Shadow, a bogeyman, the shrouded stranger, the figure you see through your window at night who follows you down the street and makes you want to run home fast after it gets dark. He even made a drawing of him, a comic strip. Like science fiction, he emerges out of the dots of the Brooklyn waterfront; he comes up out of the water with his hair long and glistening in a shroudy cape, and goes to the Pyramid club and dances on the bar. So here's the situation, little Jacky Kerouacky from Lowell, Mass. at the age of twelve or thirteen is befriended by Dr. Sax, the bogeyman. In the daytime he's a football coach, but at night he puts on his shrouded cape and goes around the city performing miracles, and the big plot of this is that the millennium is approaching, the apocalypse, or Armageddon, and at Snake Hill in Lowell, Mass. the great snake of the world is going to emerge and devour the planet. This is a recording of Jack reading *Dr. Sax* made in 1961 on an old tape recorder at his house."

Ginsberg pushes down the play button and Kerouac's voice booms out of the battered tape recorder as if possessed. Despite the scratchy static his voice is clear and mesmerizing, his nasal New England accent rattling the room, his cackle electric. The whole class is rapt. Ginsberg's face softens and gets a little dreamy-looking.

"That's beautiful isn't it?" He repeats and savors Kerouac's sentences, biting the consonants and mouthing the vowels, emphasizing the oral qualities and rhythms. "It has a subtlety of both language and ear that comes from a virginal, or rather somewhat youthful marijuana fantasy.

"The writing of *Visions of Cody* was influenced by Thomas Wolfe, Thomas Mann, Proust's madeleine and tea, and Joyce's *Finnegans Wake*. It has the extended sentences, panoramic awareness and interesting narrative like *On the Road*." Ginsberg then reads us bits of *Visions of Cody*. He thankfully doesn't try to sound like Kerouac, or read like him.

"These are sort of Whitmanic descriptions aren't they?" he points out. "This is an experimental, exuberant book. It's broken down into sections like jazz sessions. It might mean one sentence, or it might mean pages. Each section is written in a session of writing like a jazz musician. It's like blowing until the energy is gone. Gertrude Stein also did this. She'd write it all out in a focus of attention. Kerouac didn't always write it all down. It was mostly babbling in bars or under the Brooklyn Bridge. We used to walk under the Brooklyn Bridge and improvise a lot, trading lines, riffing poetry. There are a

couple specimens between me and Kerouac and Peter Orlovsky. They're not all that interesting," Ginsberg confesses, but
he shares them anyway. "'*Oh my baby tip my cup all my
thoughts are open, no? all my doors are open.*' Burroughs and
Kerouac did a collaborative novel back in the forties, set in
the St. Louis zoo. It was called *And the Hippos Were Boiled
in Their Tanks.*"

This recollection gets Ginsberg on to the subject of Burroughs. "Burroughs thinks in pictures—he spends long sessions just sitting at the typewriter, seeing images moving
against the dark. He sits with his hands hovering over the
typewriter thinking about *hands pulling in nets in the dark*
like in Interzone. He does cut-ups and revises a lot. He follows
his dreams, follows them visually like a movie camera and
writes the images down. His material often comes from dreams
or visual daydreams, and are filed according to subject matter
in manila folders. All writing is spontaneous, you don't know
what the next word is going to be until you write it, unless
you're like the Russians who work it all out in their heads."

Ginsberg ends class by reading Kerouac's mea culpa in *Visions of Cody*. In the middle of it he nearly begins to weep,
"I never thought it would be published."

April 12

Ginsberg is eager to start class today. "We'll begin with a
recording of blues and haiku done by Kerouac in 1959 with
Al Cohn and Zoot Sims, two vanguard hard bop white saxo-
phonists. Kerouac would pronounce the haiku and they would
make up a little saxophone haiku. With the push of a button
Kerouac is alive reciting haikus accompanied by slithery sax
music that compliments the verse:

In my medicine cabinet the winter fly has died of old age.

"Nice huh?" Ginsberg nods appreciatively. "Did you notice
his enunciation? It's like real mature mouthing. I mentioned

last week that the master of intonation and enunciation, Frank Sinatra, was actually an influence on Kerouac. Sinatra, I think, learned his technique from Billie Holiday. So the lineage is Billie Holiday through Sinatra to Kerouac."

Drunk as a hoot owl writing letters by thunderstorm.

"I've a series of poems of my own, which instead of calling haiku I've called 'American sentences.'" The trouble with most of the traditional haiku is the way they're synthesized into English; they're not a complete sentence. They sort of hang in the air. The advantage of 'In my medicine cabinet the winter fly has died of old age' is it's a straightforward active sentence with a subject, verb and object. It just goes right into your head without that *arty* sound of *translationese.*

"The next recording is 1959, a time when Steve Allen, then a popular television personality, *somewhat* literate, really dug Kerouac and understood that he was a little better than the beatnik image given in the press. He actually made friends with him. He asked him to come into the recording studio. It was lucky that Steve Allen had that intuition because there are not so many recordings of Kerouac. He made some on his own home machine like the *Dr. Sax* that I played you last week, but that's quite rare and not issued. There's another I have of him reading *Mexico City Blues*, but he's really *completely* drunk and the timing is not good, though it's still him.

"At the time of *Mexico City Blues* Jack was reading a book called the *Buddhist Bible*. Did we ever do sitting practice and meditation here?" he suddenly ask us.

"That might be interesting to do that. So you know what Kerouac's talking about when he talks about Buddhism and meditation and all that crap. So if you will sit forward in your seats with your hands on your knees, *sit up straight*. The reason I say sit *forward* is to keep your spine straight so that you're not slumping over, you're *erect*. Okay, top of the head supporting heaven (so to speak), so it's not quite marine military; the

chin is down, somewhat more relaxed, eyeballs relaxed, so
you're not staring at any specific point, but letting the optical
field hang outside of your skull, looking through your skull
at the outside. We are led to believe a lie when we see with
not through the eye, says William Blake, so you're looking
through the eye, with *perhaps* awareness of the periphery of
the optical field.

"We're *not* leaving the world, we're *here*; we're just resting
within the phenomenal world and appreciating it. Shoulders
relaxed, nose in line with belly button, ears in line with your
shoulder blades. Sitting forward actually on the edge of the
chair is best, balanced on your feet, hands resting on thighs.
Mouth closed, putting the tongue toward the teeth and roof
of your mouth, *eliminating the air pocket* so you won't be
disturbed by an accumulation of saliva forcing you to swallow.
Gaze tending toward the horizon, resting in space, or, if it's
too bright, at a forty-five degree angle down in front of you
toward the floor. So the basic classical practice is paying attention to the breath leaving the nostril and following the breath
until it dissolves, not *controlling* the breath, just any regular
old natural breath that comes along will do. What you are
adding is your *awareness* of the breath rather than any control.
On the *in* breath you can let go of your observation, maybe
check your posture, if you're slumped you will tend to be
daydreaming, if you are upright you will tend to be alert. So,
let's try that. Ignore other parts of the mind. When you notice
you are thinking, label it thinking and take a friendly attitude
toward your thoughts. That is the nature of the mind to think
thoughts, but when you become aware of it observe it, acknowledge it, notice it, then return your attention back to
the breath, and it will restore your focus."

We sit on the edge of our seats, hands on our knees. If
someone were to peek through the window in the door, they
would see what I am sure looks like an army of zombies
awaiting instructions. The room hums with silence. A smoker
begins to hack, everyone else sits still, drawing deep breaths.

"Okay" Ginsberg says, disturbing our pleasant revery. "*Mexico City Blues*. In Chorus 63 Kerouac's commenting on his own

poetics, 'Rather gemmy, Said the King of Literature Sitting on a davenport at afternoon butler's tea.' " Ginsberg guffaws, the class laughs too. Ginsberg's reading it in a very funny high-tone sniffy British voice. " 'Rather gemmy *hmmm* . . . always thought these sonnets of mine were rather gemmy as you say, true perfect gems of lucid poetry, poetry being what it is today, rather gemmy . . .'

"It's sort of like a midtown intellectual ninny or somebody reading *The New Yorker*," he says. "Kerouac was really a master of camp. Very few people realize that a lot of Kerouac is campy voices, or getting into other people's heads, very common archetypal people like a *New Yorker* reader, or Burroughs, or W. C. Fields, very often he goes into W. C. Fields mode.

"Kerouac is often accused of being naive macho but this is very sophisticated camp he's laying down." Ginsberg then reads Chorus 74, which he recites in a lockjawed English accent he confesses is Gore Vidal's.

"I think Jack had slept with Gore Vidal by this time, or so Gore Vidal said. Why, I don't know. Kerouac wasn't really gay, but on the other hand I think he dug Vidal as a sort of ultra-sophisticated person and wanted some of it to rub off, or maybe it was just drunken lust, but I think it was more a sort of envious inquisitiveness and curiosity and amusement."

Ginsberg starts the 64th Chorus, " 'I'd rather die than be famous,' " he reads, then mutters, under his breath, "fat chance."

He moves on to another point about *Visions of Cody*. "The first forty-two pages are a series of little sketches. A friend, Ed White, who studied architecture at Columbia when Kerouac was hanging around there in 1948–1949, told him what he ought to do is go out with a pencil, a sketch pad and make verbal sketches just like painters make sketches, little quick sketches, little salient lines, to capture the motif or subject, to capture the ephemera of the moment . . . sketch. It's actually quite a good exercise. Sit in front of a window and sketch what you see within the frame of the window. It ain't so easy, but it ain't so hard either. So that's your homework. Jack died,

© Allen Ginsberg

William Burroughs and Jack Kerouac, 1953.

I believe, sitting in a chair verbally sketching the action on a
TV quiz program. Making a little prose poem sketch of what
was going on."

April 19

Despite the overcast gray sky it feels like spring. The consen-
sus is to have class out of doors. This evening there's a journalist
from *The New Yorker* in our class. She's doing a piece for
their upcoming fiction issue. Like some ragtag tribe following
a prophet, we are led outside to the Leonard Stern business
building. Ginsberg sits down in the lotus position on the
walkway beneath an overhang and takes off his shoes. His
socks are dark blue with no holes in the toes or heels. We sit
around him on the pavement and grass. A few students try to
imitate his pretzel-pose. He is the only one who looks remotely
comfortable, especially when it begins to drizzle, forcing us
all to huddle under the cement lip of the building where
there's a decidedly dank odor of urine and wet dog.

"This week or next I'd like to lay down the materials for
Kerouac's rules for writing—because that is essential to the

writing aspect of the Beat Generation. It is also essential to understand in relation to earlier work like Gertrude Stein's and see how it reflects back into Shakespeare."

Ginsberg reads a few of Kerouac's verses from *Mexico City Blues*, 104, "I'd rather be thin than famous," and 110 and 111, which deal with Buddhism. "Is this making sense at all? Or is it gobbledygook? Is there anyone who feels this is totally unclear? I confess I don't always know what the hell Kerouac is talking about in his poetry."

"It seems like a totally different attitude than *On the Road*," comments a guy in a baseball cap.

"Well this *is* five years later. In *On the Road* you'll also find moments of perception of the whole phenomenal world as delusion also. In *On the Road* there's one point where he's coming out of Mexico or into Texas and he sees an old lonely shrouded stranger walking the road looking like death or God or a prophet and his prophetic word is, *Wow*. I am so glad we're having this class out of the building so I have this vast space to point to—endless space, going beyond the sky, beyond what we can see, beyond the clouds, galaxies. . . . Everybody has already accomplished their existing in vastness, or some form of eternity whether they know it or not; everybody is already a Buddha in infinity, already placed in the infinite, so it's a question of whether they know they're in the infinite, or they're just stuck with their nose in a bank book, or somebody's cunt or whatever. . . . There's no attainment because there's no non-attainment. It's already happened, it's already *here*. The ordinary mind in the place of transcendental mind if you catch on, which is the purpose of sitting and the practice of meditation, to catch on to that. To catch on to the vastness of your own mind, to see that inside space is the same as outside space, so therefore everything is ignorant of it's emptiness."

As it continues to rain, Ginsberg discusses meditation at some length. Most of us are a bit befuddled.

"So when you meditate you're trying *not* to think?" someone asks shyly.

"No. You're observing the thought, you observe the breath. Let's do that for just a moment now. I was going to do it inside, but now that we've got the open space. . . . I don't know how comfortable you can get. It doesn't require a straight back. Just relax your mind, and maybe focus attention on the out breath, out through the nose if you can, unless you've got problems . . . Follow your breath if you can, then as you find yourself thinking, or conceptualizing, notice it, touch on it, like anger when you notice it; it dissolves, then you're back here in the space where you are, and then latch onto your out breath again, which should keep your mind here in this space until it drifts again. So it's a question of observing your thought, rather than stopping it. Trying to stop your thought is only another thought. You can go into an infinite regress of thought. The only way is to actually switch your attention to the breath, become conscious of breath and soon your mind is out there in space. The formula is mixing breath with space, mixing mind with breath, mixing mind with space. Let's go for four minutes."

We sit up straight. I remember to think of balancing heaven on the top of my head. We close our eyes, and breathe deeply through our noses, trying to filter out the yipping dogs and the chatter of sorority girls.

We sit and meditate, some of us more deeply than others. The journalist from *The New Yorker* falls deeply asleep, her mouth hanging gently agape. She doesn't rouse herself until a good fifteen minutes have passed. Ginsberg looks amused and a little annoyed.

To wrap up Kerouac we look at a handout, composed by Kerouac in his own unique shorthand, perhaps intended as a letter.

Belief & Technique For Modern Prose a List of Essentials

1. Scribbled secret notebooks, and wild typewritten pages, for yr own joy
2. Submissive to everything, open, listening
3. Try never get drunk outside yr own house

4. Be in love with yr life
5. Something that you feel will find its own form
6. Be crazy dumbsaint of the mind
7. Blow as deep as you want to blow
8. Write what you want bottomless from bottom of the mind
9. The unspeakable visions of the individual
10. No time for poetry but exactly what is
11. Visionary tics shivering in the chest
12. In tranced fixation dreaming upon object before you
13. Remove literary, grammatical and syntactical inhibition
14. Like Proust be an old teahead of time
15. Telling the true story of the world in interior monolog
16. The jewel center of interest is the eye within the eye
17. Write in recollection and amazement for yourself
18. Work from pithy middle eye out, swimming in language sea
19. Accept loss forever
20. Believe in the holy contour of life
21. Struggle to sketch the flow that already exists intact in mind
22. Dont think of words when you stop but to see picture better
23. Keep track of every day the date emblazoned in yr morning
24. No fear or shame in the dignity of yr experience, language & knowledge
25. Write for the world to read and see yr exact pictures of it
26. Bookmovie is the movie in words, the visual American form
27. In Praise of Character in the Bleak inhuman Loneliness
28. Composing wild, undisciplined, pure, coming in from under, crazier the better
29. You're a Genius all the time
30. Writer-Director of Earthly movies Sponsored & Angeled in Heaven

As ever,
Jack

April 26

"How many of you write some form of open verse? Most of you. Well, for you kids who want to write it there are some rules and regulations. Now, Robert Frost, he made one notorious comment that writing free verse was like playing tennis without a net. And I think T. S. Eliot was quoted as saying no verse is really free. Ezra Pound has endless suggestions for experimenting with verse forms. William Carlos Williams's effort was to find an 'American measure' as he called it, or a variable measure. Nobody seems to know what that is. So at one point or another I began toting up all the different considerations that might be weighed in the balance in laying out your verse lines on the page, and I'd like to go through some of them. Does anybody know Marianne Moore's method of composition of the stanza? Well, you know her stanzas are kind of cute, like butterfly wings, or very irregular, but they all have some kind of shape when you look at them, like the famous poem 'Poetry' which begins, 'I, too, dislike it. . . .' Let's look at that poem."

It becomes apparent no one in class has a Marianne Moore book with them. A few people are lugging their Norton anthologies of modern poetry, but most of the class is either empty-handed or have brought their Kerouac books. According to our "Survey of Historical Poetics" we are to be looking at *Post-literate Oral Tradition: Preacher, Spirituals, Hymns, Blues, Calypso, improvisation; Signifying Monkey, Rap, African-American and Caribbean poetics, Bop.* What book should one presume to bring to class for "Signifying Monkey?" The class has been proceeding organically, for want of a better word, growing and evolving along the ecstatic tributaries of Ginsberg's passions and obsessions. There is no schedule. From week to week we have no idea what he is going to do, this free-associative format can be confusing, but it's also exciting.

Ginsberg sighs in exasperation, "Oh man, how can I teach if you're all spaced out."

"You said this week we were doing Kerouac," someone offers in our defense.

"We're not doing Kerouac."

"We just never know," says a nervous-looking poet who gnaws his pencils.

"Okay . . . I just wish you would always bring your fucking books," he says ruefully, "because I'm trying to improvise to *some* extent and have it *real* rather than just a rote thing."

Ginsberg begins to discuss the ways Marianne Moore constructed her verse and laid it out on the page. "The basic principle is that each verse, stanza to stanza, maintains the same number of syllables, or can be divided arbitrarily into syllables with no particular significance to the count of the syllables line by line except to make an interesting look, like a butterfly's wing on the page; or there may be some counter rhythm the way the line runs."

Ginsberg then gives a long explanation of how various poets lay their work out on the page according to syllables, accents, breath stop, units of mouth phrasing and division of mental ideas. In a burst of inspiration Ginsberg springs to his feet and goes to the blackboard.

"You might begin a poem on, uh, hair. Let's do that. Let's write a poem on . . . bald heads." He turns to the board and begins to compose on the board, improvising aloud. He first writes "Bald Heads."

My own with a fringe of gray
Corso's mop salt and pepper
Eisenhower's dome

"Now something just occurred to me relating to Eisenhower, so I'll put it over here on the board. That will lead on to other skulls,

Alas poor Yorick
Nixon's skull-to-be

"Do I want Yorick or first thought, best thought, or should I say alas poor Lincoln, or alas poor who? . . . Alas, poor

Warren Harding!" He laughs as he scribbles it on the board.
"And his girlfriend's skull, or mistress. Harding was famous
for having a mistress wasn't he? Remember that? What was
her name? I knew it once.

and his Lilly's skull
Again my own

"You see, one thought comes from another thought, so
that this opens up like a telescope along the line. What is the
next thought I have? It is that movie star, Johnny Depp, has
long hair, so I go back to the margin: *Johnny Depp has long
hair*. You just diagram your thought out. So this is division
of mental ideas.

"No." He scowls and erases the line about Johnny Depp,
"That doesn't work. Anyway these were the ideas that came
to me while I was standing here at the blackboard. So I was
laying them out, with a space in between each idea as it arose,
maybe making a line. But if I had two thoughts coming together fast like Corso's mop salt and pepper, I left them on
one line. It is like diagramming your mind. But you have to
focus your mind on the subject, exhausting all the variations
that arise in your mind." He turns to the board and reads his
poem. "Not bad," he shrugs. "So you can divide the lines the
way they are spoken or the way you think them up. Sometimes
it's simultaneous and identical, sometimes it might not be."

"When you changed Yorick to Warren Harding, do you
think that you lost any of the sort of electricity of your natural
thought process?" someone asks.

"Maybe, but I think it was an even trade. Yorick, it's too
formulaic . . . I was on Eisenhower: Nixon and Warren Harding
made it more common, universalized it in a way, unexpected.
You were fresh from the drama of Eisenhower, Nixon, and
Warren Harding is not very dramatic at all; he's very ordinary,
but it brings it back to the ordinary skull; so does his Lilly's
skull, his girlfriend's skull . . . it means it's *everybody's* skull
and that leads again to my own."

"So is it a combination of a natural thought process and control?" the student asks.

"Well, it's a natural thought process and then something quick, shrewd, swift." Ginsberg laughs. "Spontaneity. I mean how did I get to Warren Harding? *He rose up.* So it's sort of a nimble skill during the time of composition in making substitutions and hopping it up a little bit."

"Is this how it really happens with you?" someone else asks incredulously.

"Yeah. I wouldn't mind copying that down and having a little poem out of it. Some little magazine asks me for a poem, I could send them that 'Bald Heads'." Everyone laughs. "A little meditation on bald heads," he shrugs and grins. We believe him.

Towards the end of class—after we have discussed the aesthetics of laying work out according to typographical topography, original notation, and pure chance—someone asks about Ginsberg's punctuation.

"There are some dashes here and there. The first person to get rid of punctuation, the first modern poet was Apollinaire, who went over the proofs of his book which included the poem 'Zone' and eliminated all the punctuation to get it a little closer to his stream of thought. I tend not to punctuate too much. One thing I really avoid for some reason or another is being too finicky. I rarely use a semicolon in a poem, sometimes a colon, but a semicolon? I don't get it. It just sounds like a lot of extra spaghetti. I don't know exactly what spoken idiom or cadence would require a semicolon in actual speech. That's my own prejudice. George Bush doesn't like broccoli, and I don't like semicolons. Maybe semicolons are good for you. Maybe semicolons help you avoid radiation sickness.

"Another matter we should look into is how to revise poems written in the principle of absolutely spontaneous verse. How do you revise poems? A total contradiction in terms." Ginsberg chuckles gleefully. He takes out the handout we received the first day. Things are actually coming full circle.

Fourteen Steps for Revising Poetry

1. Conception
2. Composition
3. Review it through several people's eyes
4. Review it with eye to idiomatic speech
5. Review it with eye to the condensation of syntax (blue pencil and transpose)
6. Check out all articles and prepositions: are they necessary and functional?
7. Review it for abstraction and substitute particular facts for reference (for example: "walking down the avenue" to "walking down 2nd Avenue")
8. Date the composition
9. Take a phrase from it and make up a title that's unique or curious or interesting sounding but realistic
10. Put quotations around speeches or referential slang "so to speak" phrases.
11. Review it for weak spots you really don't like, but just left there for inertial reasons.
12. Check for active versus inactive verbs (for example: "after the subway ride" instead of "after we rode the subway")
13. Chop it up in lines according to the breath phrasing/ ideas or units of thought within one breath, if any
14. Retype

Ginsberg explains, "Well, you have the conception of the poem, then the composition of the poem, which we just had. Then the next thing I generally do is read it through a lot of different people's eyes. I have a new book out. I spent several times reading it once with Burroughs's eyes, once with Bob Dylan's eyes, once through my stepmother's eyes, various people's. I see what will hook them into the poems and see what flaws the poems have according to people's intelligence I am familiar with and which have been imprinted on me. For instance, reading my own poetry through Burroughs's eyes I get much more cynical and much less tolerant of sentimentality. Reading it through Dylan's eyes I'm wondering if it's surprising enough, or if it's pedestrian. Looking through Corso's eyes I wonder if it's condensed enough and tailored interestingly so that I'm not prosaic. Reading it through the eyes of the editorialist at *The New York Times*, I wonder does it make some political sense. . . . Intuitively I end up reading my work through several hundred people's skulls. It's a way of accumulating a lot more intelligence than your own, because what you are doing, to the extent that you are sensitive to other people's swiftness, and intelligence and sensitivity, is empathizing with them as you're reading your own poems to improve them and figure out where your poems are weak. Take the highest intelligences you know, the people you most admire and read it through their eyes. The people you really *dig,* the people you really want to please or communicate to, and then go through it with an eye to *could you say this out loud to your mother or your friend without sounding poetic, or arch, or literary or artificial?* and without sounding like you are copping a poetic attitude of some sort. Review the whole thing through idiomatic speech. Can you say it without embarrassment either to an audience, or your best friend or to your mommy? Intense emotionally charged fragments of idiomatic speech people won't question, but emotionally charged moments that sound highfalutin or literary or hand-me-down literary, people will suspect the genuineness and sincerity of it. So review it with an eye to idiomatic speech and that will correct the whole attitude of the poem. Then the next is condensation of syntax. Let's look at my poem," he says hopping up and going back to the blackboard, this time with an eraser. He snuffs out the words "with a" from the first line.

"'*My own gray fringed*' . . . that's better. I don't need all those syllables.

"'*Corso's mop salt and pepper*' that's impeccable, '*Eisenhower's dome,*' '*Nixon's skull to be*' that's all right, '*Alas, Poor Warren Harding*' do I need *and* there? Nah—comma *his Lilly's skull* I don't know that I need *again?* Maybe dash *my own.* So I would review it. Do I need all the articles, the conjunctions, connectives, *the*'s, *them*'s, *of*'s. . . . *Of* particularly, you can often get rid of the *of* which is more French. You examine every single syllable, especially the small ones, the monosyllables that have no substantive information, and see if you can transpose and reconnect things a little more solidly without the extra articles and particles. Don't reduce it to Chinese laundry talk where you eliminate all the articles, you don't want to do that. . . .

"Next, I generally review for abstraction. Nailing the thing down, grounding the generalizations. Very often generalizations are like a blank in a form that you can fill in."

"Okay, next week is our last class, we'll do the other steps. And be prepared to do Shelley's 'Ode to the West Wind!' "

May 3

I wondered if class might start off with some acknowledgment that this is our final class, or perhaps some hash brownies and jug wine. Instead class begins in a pedestrian way with Ginsberg passing out copies of open form poems. He takes roll, of course, then launches into the texts.

A guy walks in late. Ginsberg in typical fashion asks the latecomer, "What's your name? Are you in the class?" The guy has been in the class since the first day.

Ginsberg takes us through the process of how poets such as Philip Whalen, Gary Snyder, Lawrence Ferlinghetti, and William Carlos Williams lay their poems on the page. He then eagerly passes out copies of Shelley's "Ode to the West Wind."

"There was one other thing that I wanted to do that we hadn't done, which was to do a choral recitation of this poem. My suggestion is that we read it together. Pay attention to the punctuation, so that where you have a comma, a colon, a parenthesis, an exclamation point, a period that indicates a pause, you take a pause and breathe so that we will all be doing it at the same time. We'll do *everything* at the same time or it will be chaos . . . with some people stopping and some people going on. The run-on lines, where there's no punctuation, read as run-on lines. But where there's punctuation, please observe it as a sign of breath. This poem is about the subject of breath, or wind. He's asking the west winds to enter him and let the spirit of the west wind be his spirit, meaning the breath of the west wind be his own breath, and that using the breath of that wind and his own breath make the poem immortal, so that other people after he's dead can chant the same poem using the same periods of breath that he employs in the poem itself. The subject is spirit or breath, (spirit means breathing in Latin), his observation is of his breath, the means of vocalization is breath, and if you do that you can get high, you can get a little buzz out of this poem, quite literally if you follow his breaths. It's like taking a pill . . . where you internalize the actual breathing that Shelley has set out for you. All you have to do is follow his notational instructions and you'll get a hyperventilated buzz." Ginsberg laughs. "So we'll just do it all together. One two three . . . '*O wild West Wind, thou breath of Autumn's being* . . .'"

We start off in sync and go in and out of it as the poem progresses. I feel decidedly lightheaded, and a little giddy. It's not exactly a party trick, but it is a pleasant experience. As soon as we finish people begin clapping.

"Well, I got a buzz!" He laughs. "It's really a terrific piece. To get to, '*Drive my dead thoughts over the universe/Like withered leaves to quicken a new birth!*' you have to do some abdominal breathing to get that whole line through, because that's a long, long breath. How many have read Shelley?" A couple of students grudgingly raise their hands. "Well, how was it?" he asks the way one might ask a first time drug-user how the trip was. Judging by the laughter and murmurs the experiment was a success.

"Better late than never, I guess," he sighs, "Shelley is supposed to be the acme of romantic expostulation in poetry."

Seeing how turned on everybody is by the reading he launches in on Hart Crane's *The Bridge*, focusing particularly on the "Atlantis" section, which he describes as "one of the great rhapsodies in the English language." He reads it aloud with gusto. After he finishes, his face is flushed, his eyes gleaming.

"It tends to rise then come to a plateau, then drop a bit in tone, then rise again, then drop a bit in tone, then rise all the way up to a sort of prayer in ecstasy and then kind of *come* in an orgasmic series of breaths, then a coda, or postcoitus treatise, the end. Basically an iambic pentameter eight verse stanza."

The class sits in amused shock. Did he say *"come?"* Perhaps we appear unconvinced or maybe Ginsberg is just enjoying himself, but he rereads what I imagine to be the "come" part with great drama—"white seizures!" he cries out, then says professorially, "So you get some kind of power breath there, like in the 'Ode to the West Wind.' It's one of the best pieces of music of this century, I think, in terms of a machine that begins to levitate and finally take off. I think probably to some extent *The Bridge* is almost a substitute for Eros in a way. . . . Ultimately, I think, this mouthing is a variety of cocksucking. It's the same emotional devotional adorational impulse displaced into musical language. Crane was gay and also into sailors (like Genet, sort of), but this is almost the acme of sublimated eros into poetry. When this was published, his good friends, Yvor Winters and Allen Tate, both academic poets, objected that there was no object that could contain his emotions, that it was an idealism that had no location . . . so much adoration, so much emotion, so much buildup, so much orgasmic mouthing—so to speak—that they denounced the poem as a great failure. It kind of broke Crane's heart. He found himself not only a pariah, but as a gay in a time when to be gay was to be somewhat of a pariah in those circles of academic poets who were all tending toward Eliotic conservatism and undemonstrative cool poetry. That general rejection of his feelings was one of the elements that I think led him to jump off the rear of an ocean liner and drown himself two years later. I also think the constriction of the form didn't allow him full play of all of the emotions that he kept in a kind of emotional and mental prison. I think he would have survived better if he had opened up the form and taken in more detail like William Carlos Williams. He certainly was a great ear, a great poet, and I think that *The Bridge* is one of the great long poems of the century, certainly a big influence on my own work and Kerouac and other writers. One of the most exciting pieces of music in the last fifty to sixty years. Pound's "Uzura" has some of that excitement, and so do the *Cantos*, and Dylan Thomas's "Fern Hill." You have to go back to when T. S. Eliot is kidding with '*OOO, that Shakespeherian Rag — /It's so elegant/So intelligent*' . . . that has a little bit of the rhythmical excitement in it. You get it in other languages, you might get it in some blues, you might get it in Ma Rainey in that long extended spiritual breath, but it's rare, and that is what Shelley is noted for particularly. You get it in Kerouac certainly, and I try to imitate it in the "Moloch" section of *Howl*.

"It is an aspect of poetry that really people don't pay too much attention to. Of course the sound poets do. You'll find it in Dada poetry and in Bob Dylan. Actually "A Hard Rain's Gonna Fall" has a buildup like that." Ginsberg recites the song from memory.

"So this is, you know, our last meeting — I had started last time on the fourteen steps for revising and left midway at number seven, and so I'll just say a few more things about that then leave some time open for conversation.

"Wherever you find yourself generalizing or in abstraction, you can examine it for generalization. If you can tell the difference between particularity and generalization, if you can tell the difference between minute particulars and vague reference, it might do to check for elements that have no special pictorial value or special sound value, just general moo, moo, moo. Of some suggestion of smell, like Resnikoff's '*a pot of fish hissed and bubbled on the stove the smell of the fish filled the basement*' or some sort of tactile, sight, smell, sound, taste, touch anything palpable. You can find a lot of Latinate words that have no sensory suggestion. They're like blanks in a bureaucratic form to be filled in with particulars. What were you really referring to when you spoke of being lonesome in the city? What city? On the roof? Where in your bedroom? Can you particularize a little?

"I myself date compositions so that I know where the origin was, when I first thought something up; if I work on it a long time, I'll put a date showing the finish. If it's your ambition to be a great poet, you'll want to help your scholars and professors a hundred years from now. They're all lazy. If you date it yourself, they won't have to shuffle through all your papers. Dating your work means there'll be a greater accumulation of term papers on your work, masters theses, graduate theses, which means that you'll get more attention in the future. So, if you want to be immortal, date your mortality."

The class laughs, not sure if he really means what he is saying.

"The question of getting a title. Usually I go through a poem and I find two interesting words that combined together might give the gist of the poem. The title actually begins to magnetize or get people into your poem.

"Then one interesting thing, I found really useful is that in reading my work aloud I'll tend to hasten through parts that are not quite so interesting till I get to the meat of the poem, to the parts I *really* like. If you can detect that difference, you might examine the weaker parts and perhaps eliminate them altogether. If they bore you, they might bore other people too. It might be a little phrase, a whole sentence, or even a section of the poem that isn't as good . . . so why not just eliminate that and get to the point fast? Williams's phrase for that was 'one active phrase is more valuable than pages of inert writing.' Reading aloud is a good bullshit detector. I read poetry aloud a lot. I may read a poem a hundred times before it's published in a book, and I found after many years that was a really good way of editing. So get rid of the cool parts and leave yourself a hot fragment, like in Sappho. Readers might never get to your great fragment because they got stuck with the first ten lines.

"So now the floor is open—does anybody have anything they want to talk about, as we are in our last breaths here?"

"Why would you want to be immortal?" asks one of the boys who periodically shows up in class.

"Remember that line from Zukofsky," Ginsberg replies. "'Nothing is better for being eternal nor so white as white that dies in the day.' Well, if the purpose of your poetry is to assuage your suffering or relieve the sufferings of others, then you want to build a machine which will operate after your death. In a way you could say that Poe did that by liberating consciousness once and for all to experience its own paranoia and feedback, and to experience guilt and conscience, to articulate it so clearly that everybody thereafter would have their minds opened up. What is the purpose of Christ laying down the Golden Rule, or the Sermon on the Mount, or Buddha or Allah? Their function is not so much that they are immortal but that their spirit, their gentility, generosity, openness can be more widespread. Poetry is not an ego trip that preserves your ego in the amber of the poem, but rather that you've made your own ego transparent, conquered it. Your battle against selfishness begins with yourself, to enlighten others to the techniques of liberating yourself from your ego.

"In Yeats's books it is really interesting to see the progression of his mind from beginning to end, and how he ends up with Crazy Jane and very spare things. His last poem actually turns out to be, 'How can I . . . My attention Fix . . . on Russian or on Spanish politics? . . . But Oh that I were young again And held her in my arms.' the final thought that he wanted to leave behind. It's interesting to know that's where he concluded and to see how he got there. It's interesting to know in what part of Keats's life, what sequence those poems came on, how he developed and at what point he got to that last little poem "This Living Hand." Do you know that? It's to Fanny Brawne, his girlfriend, and he knew he was dying. It's really kind of uncanny. It's one of Gregory Corso's favorite poems. Well, when you know it's the last poem it adds a dramatic flair, as well as a kind of ghoulish presence."

Someone calls out, "How do you reconcile your mind-writing slogan—first thought best thought—with rewriting?"

"I don't know. As I get older, I get more schizophrenic about it," Ginsberg confesses, then quotes Whitman, *Do I contradict myself? Very well then I contradict myself, I am large, I contain multitudes.'* The answer is embedded in what I said before about dating. If the poem, the original skeleton of the poem, retains it's integrity, that's it.

"Kerouac allows for revision, for certain afterthoughts or mistakes. I don't feel as sure of myself as Kerouac, and maybe his assurance came from his vow not to return to the poem. So that it pushed him to the limit during the time of writing, but I don't feel the same absoluteness, or courage, and yet I like it in him. And what *is* the first thought? The first thought isn't necessarily the first thought you notice, it's the first thought you sub-notice. People edit their awareness of what is underneath their minds.

"I remember when I was a boy in grammar school my brother and I had a chemistry set. One of the mysterious miracles of grammar school chemistry was sodium. If it's pure, a little fragment of sodium in water fizzes, burns, gives off hydrogen which will pop, or explode if you put a match next to it. We had a whole pound of sodium which we kept in a bucket of kerosene. While cleaning the chemistry set, I got some water in the kerosene. My father had to carry the whole thing steaming and bubbling out of the house just before it exploded. Why that arose in my mind right now, I don't know. I was looking for a first thought . . . an early significant thing that I remember at least once a month, maybe three times a month, because it was a moment that I got away with something. I was lucky. I could have blown the house apart.

"If I wanted to write it as a poem I might want to recall how the water got into the bucket. I think it was some stupid attempt to clean up the whole pantry shelf where we kept all our chemicals. It would pertain to the first thought. Second thought would be, Young kids do foolish things around the house. Third or fourth would be the generalization: Parents are always there to rescue their kids who do foolish things around the house. Or something wittier like, Wise father puts out the son's fire. First thought does not necessarily mean don't correct at all, it just means that your model should be the interior form that you glimpse, rather than the superficial level of mind. If the mind is shapely the art will be shapely."

With that final pronouncement the semester formally ends. There's an awkwardness. No one knows what to do — everyone seems to be waiting for something else to happen. Finally someone calls out, "What about our paper, our poetry?"

"Oh yeah, yes," Ginsberg answers loudly as though he had almost forgotten to collect them. "I'll take them all now if you have them," he says clearing a space on the edge of the cluttered desk for the proliferation of colored folders and slim sheaves of cream-colored paper. Students linger around the desk, hands extending books to be signed, notebooks to be autographed.

"Your name again?" Ginsberg asks with a hint of embarrassment, as he signs his name, then doodles inside the flyleaf, a sun and a crying hot dog. A few students dawdle, backs pressed up against the wall like they're waiting to be asked to dance. Slowly the class filters out, and Ginsberg bundles up his books and papers. As he starts to shuffle out of class, one last student reaches out to touch his elbow.

Experience

Rick DeMarinis

"Consider, if you will, the ancient Egyptians," Stan Duval said, just as we were sitting down to dinner. "They had the correct attitude, in my humble estimation."

I usually acted as though I hadn't heard him. He made me nervous; I couldn't get used to him being around. My mother had married him in Yuma, Arizona, a year ago. I couldn't figure out why. He was twenty years older than she was and he always wore his green pin-striped suit at the dinner table even if he'd been walking around the house in stained underwear a half hour earlier.

Stan always characterized his estimations and assessments as humble. "In my humble way, I believe I am one of the most valued employees at Ryan." He'd said this more than once, as if he suspected we had our doubts. He was in charge of an equipment shed at Ryan Aircraft. His job was to check out machine tools, and then check them back in again. Inventory Control Engineer. That's what he called himself.

Mom had fixed fried chicken, lima beans, and scalloped potatoes, Stan's favorite meal. He made a point of bringing up obscure subjects at the dinner table in order to educate us. Mom had quit school after the eighth grade, and I was going to be a freshman at Lowmont High School, a school Stan had no respect for.

"What do you mean, dear?" Mom said. She didn't care about Egypt, but she knew Stan liked to be drawn out after he'd made a thought-provoking statement. It was a routine of theirs.

Mom's eyes were glazed. She was still young-looking and almost pretty, even though she'd gotten thick around the hips and had developed a sizable double chin.

Stan leveled his fork at her. "Firstly, their social organization—*sine dubio*," he said. "Secondly, their thoroughly worked out religious bureaucracy. Thirdly, their corps of civil engineering professionals, *par excellence*. Those chaps knew who they were and had no doubt about their self-worth."

He forked some potatoes into his mouth and chewed them thoughtfully, jaws rotating side to side, camel-style, his heavy-lidded, Levantine eyes studying the ceiling. His phony British accent got on my nerves. Stan grew up in Boise, Idaho and had lived in California most of his life. He'd never been to England, or anywhere else, as far as I knew.

"They had slaves," I said.

"Ah, slaves," he said. The word seemed to stir up favorable memories for him. The long syllable slid down his tongue like gravy. "As an institution, slavery was not the social horror the present day liberal thinker makes it out to be," he said, smiling abruptly.

The accent was bad enough, but it was this smile that unnerved me most about him. Out of that gray, half-collapsed face came a sudden specter of long, black-edged teeth that animated his entire being with a parody of life-loving vigor. It was a smile meant to charm and convince. But it was as if a corpse in its coffin had leered flirtatiously at the passing line of mourners.

"Take some more chicken, Tony," Mom said to me. "There's more than enough for your lunch tomorrow."

"I'm not hungry," I said. In fact, my stomach was jumpy. Dillard Burdett was coming over in a few minutes. We were

going to have Cokes in my basement room. My stomach was
jumpy because Dillard's sixteen-year old cousin, Wanda
Schnell, from Escondido, was coming with him. Dillard had
told me incredible stories about Wanda. Once, when he was
visiting his aunt and uncle in Escondido, he and Wanda went
out into a grove of avocado trees where she took off her under-
pants for him.

"I — saw — it — *all*," Dillard had said. He spoke gravely, with
arresting eloquence. "I — shit — you — not — Tone," he said.

"Did you show her yours?" I had asked. This question was
out of line, but my curiosity got the better of me. Dillard,
like me and most of our friends, preferred the mutual pre-
sumption of experience. Innocence and fear, our true condition, could not be admitted. This was the unstated given
that made our friendship possible. We never challenged each
other's boasts in the area of sexual experience, though we
understood that none of us had any. Of course the boasts
had to be reasonable — flights of fantasy were shouted down
instantly.

"What do *you* think, turd?" he'd said, annoyed with me.
We dropped the subject, lit cigarettes.

"The slaves of Egypt were well taken care of," Stan continued. Stan was a speedy eater. He took large bites and worked
his sideways-grinding jaws fast. He usually finished minutes
ahead of me, and I was often reprimanded for inhaling my
food and bolting from the table. But I couldn't finish tonight.
I was too jumpy.

Stan lit a Chesterfield and blew a cloud of smoke into the
hanging lamp above the table. "Slaves were highly prized
possessions. And most certainly they were not excessively
abused. You do not abuse your valuable possessions. It would
make no sense to do so," he said. "Are there any vestiges of
doubt in your mind, Antonio?"

I hated my name. The way Stan dragged it out made me
hate it more. He gave it the correct foreign pronunciation.
It made me feel like an immigrant. My real father *was* an
immigrant, a barber from Palermo who now cut the hair of
movie stars in Beverly Hills. "Georgio Castellani — Modern

Hair Styling." He wore his hair long, like the TV wrestler, Baron Leone. When I visited him, which was three or four times a year, he would give me a haircut that made me feel like a scented and oiled Sicilian hit man. I'd seen him just a week ago, and my hair was still squared-off and crisp. I could still smell pine trees and lemons.

"I guess not," I said, wanting to leave the table. I didn't like to argue with Stan. He was an educated man, having graduated from Cal Poly at San Luis Obispo. He spouted Latin at us as if it were our second language.

"*Quae nocent docent*," he said. "'That which hurts, teaches.' You need to be a realist in this turbulent world of ours. Slavery was cradle-to-grave welfare, all needs and wants attended to." He flashed his dark smile engagingly. "Now, Antonio, I've often mentioned how adamantly I am against the socialistic welfare system inspired by our late president, Franklin Delano Roosevelt. However, in ancient Egypt the social structure required a ready-and-willing force of considerable proportions. And remember, the Egyptians did not have the gasoline-powered machinery to do their work for them such as is available to the so-called modern world." He leaned back in his chair and puffed his cigarette. He held it in the European style—cradled between thumb and forefinger, palm up. He blew a cloud of smoke toward the ceiling and squinted into it as if he could see pyramids and Pharaohs assembling in the haze.

I saw Egypt in my mind, 3000 years ago. I saw myself as Mark Twain's Connecticut Yankee making modern devices for the astonished Pharaoh, such as the two-way radio, television, the internal combustion engine, and the airplane. Diesel powered vehicles trucked stones the size of bungalows through the desert as the astonished Pharaoh applauded. Pharaoh's daughter thought I was some kind of god. She came to me bearing gifts. "I'm not a god, Laura," I told her. "I'm just a guy with some American know-how."

I liked the name Laura.

My rumbling stomach interrupted my daydream. I needed to get ready for Wanda Schnell. I couldn't believe Dillard was

bringing her over. I'd seen a snapshot of Wanda wearing a
bathing suit. Though she was only fourteen years old in the
photo, she already had the full breasts and flared hips of a
grown woman. Her face was blurry, but she seemed to be
smirking at the photographer, her slitted eyes dark with knowledge. She was now sixteen, two years older than me.

"What about freedom?" I said.

"Freedom?" Stan passed his hand over the table, like a
magician casting or removing a spell. "Bloody hocus-pocus,
Antonio. Freedom is an earned condition of the mind. It has
nothing to do with the ideals and schemes of a society. Socrates
in his cell, staring at his cup of hemlock, was freer than you
or I shall ever be. Freedom, Antonio, cannot be conferred
upon the *profanum vulgus* — that is to say, the common riff-
raff — by fiat alone."

Mom snatched up her wine glass and drank it down in
audible gulps. "What about their creepy ole zombies?" she
asked, laughing with a kind of merry desperation. Stan was
her fourth, and worst — I thought — husband.

He flinched as if someone had flicked ice water in his face.
Blatant ignorance always took him by surprise. He regarded
her with his big, moon-yellow eyes. "I believe you mean *mum-
mies*, dear. The so-called *zombie* is a vulgar Hollywood exploi-
tation of a West Indies folk myth."

I pushed away from the table. "Well, I've got to cut out,"
I said. "Dillard's coming by."

"Clean your plate first, Antonio," Stan said. "Food such as
this is the exception, not the rule. In Ethiopia or Zanzibar,
the peasants are often forced to eat insects for want of grain
and meat."

"Did you really like it, Stanley?" Mom said. She looked
hopeful, and a little nervous all of a sudden.

Stan looked confused. "The chicken? Of course I liked it,
dear," he said. "You *know* it's my favorite meal. Why do you
ask?"

"Because, well, it's not really chicken."

Stan looked at his plate, frowned, then looked at Mom.
"I'm afraid I don't . . ."

"It's bunny rabbit, honey, not chicken. Safeway had a wonderful sale, and . . ."

Stan jumped up from the table, his face turning a lighter shade of gray. He brought his napkin to his mouth and made a dash for the bathroom. He didn't have time to close the door. We heard him vomit.

"Guess he doesn't like rabbit," I said.

"He had three helpings," Mom said. "Of course he liked it."

Stan moaned horribly between upchucks.

"*Lepus cuniculus*," I said. "A burrowing rodent. He liked it as long as it was chicken. When it was *lepus cuniculus* he hated it. He's vomiting an *idea*."

Mom tapped a cigarette out of a pack of Lucky's and lit up. "I suppose you think that makes sense, smarty pants," she said.

I heard Dillard's shrill whistling out in the street. Then he yelled my name in big baritone shouts. His voice had changed in the last year. He sounded like a fully grown-up man, and he vocalized the change whenever the opportunity presented itself.

"See you later, Mom," I said.

"Does he have to bellow like that?" Mom said.

"He's showing off," I said.

I gave her a kiss and then smelled the booze. Even under the rabbit, potatoes, lima beans, and cigarette it was strong. Vat 69. She'd been drinking it most of the afternoon. When you considered who she'd married, it was easy to figure out why. What did she ever see in him? I felt sorry for her, wished she could have the man of her dreams, whoever that might be. I pictured someone like Gary Cooper, a tall, quiet man of unshakable integrity who never in a million years would lecture us about the ancient Egyptians or socialistic welfare. Gary Cooper, the brave yet modest man of *High Noon*, who didn't like to fight but could if forced to. Not a man full of fancy ideas, but a man who was silently wise. A man who ate slowly and chewed his food with good square jaws that went up and down, and who did not puke at the thought of eating rabbit.

I flooded and combed my hair at the kitchen sink, then went out to meet Dillard. His cousin, Wanda, lagged a few yards behind him. She seemed to be examining the neighborhood—the houses, the shrubs, the cars parked in the street. "Hey, neato," she said. "Whose Stude?" She didn't direct her question to either me or Dillard, content that someone would feel obliged to answer her.

"My stepdad's," I said.

"Neat car," she said, still not addressing anyone in particular. She touched the long sleek fender, then began to stroke it.

It *was* a neat car, a brand-new 1948 Studebaker Champion, pearl gray and fast-looking. I oftened wondered how Stan had managed to pay for it since he was always complaining about how much it cost to support even a small family like ours.

"You wanna see his stuff?" Dillard said. He meant my radio gear, which was down in the daylight basement where I had my room.

Wanda shrugged indifferently and sauntered toward us. I got my first clear look at her as she moved into the glow of our porch light. She was wearing flip-flop clogs and a loose-fitting cotton dress. Her face was round and puffy, and she had short fleshy arms that she kept folded against her breasts. Her eyes were small and deep-set. I couldn't see them even when she faced me. She looked like a mature woman who'd already had her quota of disappointments.

I led the way down the driveway to the basement. The house was built on a slope, and my room, along with the garage, was under the daylight end. I switched on the lights.

"What's all this *junk*?" Wanda said.

"That's his radio stuff," Dillard said. "Tone's a ham, a radio head. He got his license last year. Hey, isn't that right, Tone?"

"Right," I said. It always embarrassed me a little when strangers came into this room. My radio gear was a very personal thing. When strangers looked at it I felt naked.

The gear did look like junk, to the untrained eye. My homemade worktable was crowded with steel chassis studded with vacuum tubes, power transformers and coils. Tangles of green, red, and yellow wires were strung between them. Large-faced ammeters and voltmeters gleamed from hammered aluminum panels. A wall was covered with QSL cards from other hams around the world.

"Show her how it works, Tone," Dillard said.

Dillard and Wanda sat on my bed, a war surplus cot covered with surplus wool blankets. I kept a big Westclox alarm clock under it. When I wanted to raise stations in New Zealand or Australia, I'd set the clock for three or four in the morning, the hours when darkness covered most of the Pacific Ocean. That was the best time for long-distance communication.

I switched on my receiver, a Hallicrafter S-40A, and tuned it to one of the busy ham bands. A garble of voices mixed with Morse code whined from the speaker.

"*Yuck!*" Wanda said.

I turned down the volume and spun the dial to one of the commercial shortwave bands. A suave British voice was giving news items in brief sentences, pausing after each one to let the foreign listeners catch up. "Cairo's response to the Crown was ambiguous at best," the suave voice said.

"Pretty cool, huh?" Dillard said.

"Parliament will take up the question of policy concerning future relations with our former protectorate," the slow-speaking Englishman said.

Wanda was looking around the room. It wasn't much of a room — the walls were concrete blocks, except for the far back one which was just dirt. I'd been digging in that dirt to increase the size of the basement — Stan wanted more storage room — but I hadn't made much progress. Stan paid me fifteen cents for every wheelbarrow of dirt I hauled out.

My worktable was against a wall. High up on that wall was a short window at ground level. Antenna wires passed through this window and into the backyard. I'd nailed some two-by-fours together, braced them with one-by-four splints, set them in three-foot deep holes sixty-four feet apart, and cemented them in. A folded dipole antenna hung between these masts, suspended on pulleys. Guy wires anchored to wood stakes webbed the backyard, which made careless strolling hazardous. Neither Mom nor Stan spent much time outside, so it didn't matter.

"What's all this stuff for?" Wanda said. She'd shoved Dillard off the cot so she could have it for herself, and was now lying on her side, her head propped on her hand. Her puffy face and stringy hair made her seem exotic. The great arc of her hip rose and fell slightly as she dangled her foot over the side of the cot and kicked rhythmically. Her flip-flop hung precariously from her toe.

Dillard sat on the concrete floor, spinning a king-size marble he'd found. His legs had outgrown his torso. They took up most of the space between the cot and my worktable. His size twelve shoes scuffed against my chair. He was only about five-feet seven, but he had the legs and feet of a six-footer. "Hey, talk to somebody, Tone," he said. "Show her how you do that."

I put on my earphones and turned on my homemade transmitter. When the tubes got hot, I tuned it. The electrical smell of hot insulation filled the room. It was a smell I liked. I liked the smell of hot solder, too. I glanced quickly at Wanda to see if she had noticed the change. Her nose crinkled a bit, so I guessed she had.

I tapped out a series of CQs with my telegraph key. I got an answer right away. I pulled the earphone jack out of the S-40A so that the code would come over the loudspeaker. It was a strong station in Bakersfield, someone I'd contacted before. I didn't like this guy because he used a Vibroplex semi-automatic speed key and sent his messages too fast. He had a lousy "fist." His dashes were too short — you could easily take them for dots — and his spacing between word groups was erratic. He also bragged too much about his rig. A thousand watts generated by a pair of big Eimac tetrodes in the final amplifier. Anybody could do that if they had the money.

"There it is," I said, as code thumped through the basement. "Bakersfield, California. Over two hundred miles north." I was a little vain about my ability to send and receive Morse code over long distances.

"Bakersfield, huh?" Wanda said. "You actually *want* to talk to somebody you don't even know in Bakersfield?"

I tapped out the usual greeting with my old-fashioned brass key, a relic of the 1920s spark-gap days, a present from my Uncle Lamar. Then I turned to Wanda. Her small dark eyes seemed Oriental to me. Her flip-flop had dropped off and her little painted toes splayed and unsplayed in time to some rhythm she was hearing in her head. "I've raised stations in Japan," I said, trying to recover lost ground.

This seemed to interest her. "How can you do *that*?" she said. "You don't even speak Japanese."

"It's just the same as Bakersfield," I said. "It's just farther away. You have to wait until the atmospheric conditions are right. Radio waves bounce off the ionosphere, hundreds of miles up. It's like banking a pool ball. And language is no problem. We just use international Q signals."

"Oh, I'm sure," she said, rolling her eyes.

"Tone's a whiz, no lie," Dillard said. "He can tell you how the stuff works, can't you Tone?" He flipped the marble all the way into the dirt hole at the back of the basement. He went to look for it. "Tell her how it works!" he yelled from the dark excavation.

"It's actually pretty simple," I said. I signed off with Mister Vibroplex from Bakersfield and unplugged the crystal from my transmitter. "This is a quartz crystal. It vibrates at about seven million times per second once you excite it with a small amount of electricity. Then this seven megacycle oscillation is amplified by this Pierce oscillator—" I tapped on a glowing vacuum tube. "And the signal is fed into a final amplifier—" I tapped on the bigger of the two tubes in my transmitter. "This boosts the power of that seven megacycle oscillation to about twenty-five watts. Next, I tune the final amp with this knob here, which is connected to a variable capacitor under the chassis. This plug-in coil is designed to match the crystal's frequency—" I tapped on the forty-meter coil at the back of the chassis. "And then the tuned signal goes into the half-wave

folded dipole antenna out in the backyard where it is radiated
into space. You understand any of this, Wanda?"

She was lying on her back now, hands behind her head and
chewing gum methodically. "Any of what?" she said. She
stared into the joists of the kitchen floor, which was directly
above us. It was an indolent, small-eyed gaze.

"How I can talk to Japan," I said.

"How do you know if it's really Japan?" she said. She blew
a bubble, popped it. "How do you know if it's even coming
from Bakersfield? Maybe it's just some joker down the street
yanking your chain." She raised up a little and looked at me.
"Hey, Tony. Does that radio of yours play music?"

The sound of my name coming from her lips made me feel
strange. My stomach lurched. I switched the Hallicrafter to
the broadcast band and tuned in a local station. Dick Haymes
was singing "Together."

"That's more like it," she said. She flopped her arms out
to her sides and her bare legs dangled off the cot. She swung
her feet lazily to the music. The thin cotton material of her
dress gathered in the valley between her round thighs. The
contours of her lower body were amazingly visible. Dillard
crawled up to me on his hands and knees, pushing the big
marble ahead of him. He tugged my arm hard. I bent down
so that he could whisper in my ear. "I think she wants to show
it to you, Tone," he said.

"You said we were going to get Cokes, Dill," Wanda said.

Dillard's words made my mouth go dry as paper. "I'll get
them," I whispered.

When I came back down, Wanda was sitting in my chair,
fooling with the dials of the S-40A. She had my earphones
on. I looked at Dillard. He was sitting on my cot. He shrugged,
then winked. I passed out the Cokes. Wanda pulled the earphones off and got up. "All I can hear is noise," she said.

We sat there, sipping our Cokes. Dillard burped every few
seconds. He was swallowing air to do it. Wanda didn't seem
to mind.

Dillard punched my arm. "*Ask* her, numb nuts," he said.
My face got instantly hot.

"Ask me what?" Wanda said.

"*You* ask," I said, shoving Dillard away.

The chair she was sitting on swiveled and she began to push herself in slow circles. "I'm dizzy," she said, letting her head loll about helplessly, as if her neck had been snapped.

"Tone here wants to see it, Wanda," Dillard said.

I could have killed Dillard on the spot. I couldn't swallow my last mouthful of Coke. It backed up into my nose.

Wanda got up and stretched, her woman's breasts rising inside the cotton dress. The she turned her back on us and strolled to the dark end of the basement where I'd been excavating. Dillard and I sat on the cot.

"Go on," he said.

"*You* go on," I said.

"I've already seen it," he said.

"Sure, two years ago."

"It was last year, chicken." He made a clucking chicken noise.

My heart was beating fast and a burp was trapped halfway between my stomach and throat.

"We'll stroll the lane . . . *together*," Wanda sang, at the dark end of the basement. Her voice contradicted her mature body. It was small and high, the voice of a little girl.

Dillard set his Coke down and pulled me off the couch. He gave me a hard shove toward Wanda, which gave me the momentum I needed, physical and mental.

"Sing love's refrain . . . *together*," she sang.

Then I was standing next to her on the dark dirt floor, our shadows looming large and formless against the unevenly excavated area.

"What do you want, Tony?" she asked.

"You know," I mumbled. "What Dillard said."

"What did he say? I forget."

My pickax was stuck in the wall of compacted dirt. I grabbed it and took a few energetic swings. I hadn't worked down here in a week. I'd run into some rocks and the going was slow. Fifteen cents a load wasn't half enough. For all his money, Stan was a cheapskate.

I hit a rock and big red sparks flew down toward our feet. I put the pick down. "He said that you were going to show it to us," I blurted out.

"Dillard's a geek," she said. She folded her arms against her breasts. She bent and unbent a knee impatiently. "In fact, both of you are geeks. I bet you two are the geekiest freshmen at Lowmont." The knee rocked faster and faster, building up speed.

I started to leave but she grabbed my arm and spun me toward her. She kissed me. Her hard lips were cold from the Coke and tasted of Double Bubble. She pushed me away but held me in place with her eyes. Even wide open they were small. But I couldn't turn away from them.

She drew up her skirt as if squaring a tablecloth. I saw it all—the trembling pink thighs, the anonymous dark where they met.

The skirt dropped. "You've got a real neat haircut, Tony," she said. "Does your old man let you drive the Stude yet?"

"No, I won't be sixteen for almost two years."

"Gee, *that's* hard to believe," she said.

This made me feel good for a few seconds. Then not so good.

I went back to the cot. Dillard had an idiot grin spread across his face. "Shut up," I said.

He grabbed me and wrestled me down to the floor. We rolled around, each trying to get an advantage. I could usually best him at wrestling, but now that his legs were long and his feet were size twelves, it was hard to handle him. We held each other in stalemated headlocks, unable to move.

Wanda put her bare foot on my shoulder and rocked our knotted, headlocked bodies back and forth. "Hey, geek," she said. "Time out. You got a toilet around here someplace?"

"Upstairs," I said. "Let go, Dillard."

He didn't. I got his arm behind his back and pulled his hand up to the nape of his neck. He made a squawking noise. Then let go.

I led the way out of the basement. The path to the front of the house was steep and unlit. Wanda grabbed my hand.

It was surprisingly small in mine. It was also damp. She held on tight, as if she needed my guiding strength. I was embarrassed, but also flattered.

Mom and Stan were watching television and didn't pay any attention to us. We had an Admiral with a three-and-a-half inch screen, and they were sitting up close to it, trying to watch "The Toast of the Town." I stood behind them while Wanda went to the bathroom. Mom was sipping her Scotch and Stan had a glass of Bromo Seltzer. Every so often he let loose a complaining belch.

Wanda finished peeing. We went back outside. Dillard was sitting on the curb, throwing pebbles into a storm drain. "You're a nice guy, Tony," Wanda said. "There's not many nice guys left."

She had a bruised look in the pale streetlight. She was only sixteen, but she seemed to know what was in store for her. There wouldn't be very many nice guys in her life.

"Stay fine, Tony," she said.

I cleared my throat once, then twice, but couldn't think of anything to say. My jaws felt wired shut.

There was something just out of reach in this stopped moment between us. She knew what it was but could not articulate it. And if she could have, I could not have grasped it. It was this: She knew her fate. I did not know mine.

Lucie Brock-Broido

How Can It Be I Am No Longer I

Winter was the ravaging in the scarified
Ghost garden, a freak of letters crossing down a rare

Path bleak with poplars. The yew were a crewel
Of kith at the fieldstone wall, annulled

As a dulcimer cinched in a green velvet sack.
To be damaged is to endanger—taut as the stark

Throats of castrati in their choir, lymphless & fawning
& pale. The miraculous conjoining

Where the even air harms our self & lung,
Our three-chambered heart & sternum,

Where two made a monstrous
Braid of other, ravishing.

To damage is an animal hunch
& urge, thou fallen—the marvelous much

Is the piece of Pleiades the underworld calls
The nightsky from their mud & rime. Perennials

Ghost the ground & underground the coffled
Veins, an aneurysm of the ice & spectacle.

I would not speak again. How flinching
The world will seem—in the lynch

Of light as I sail home in a winter steeled
For the deaths of the few loved left living I will

Always love. I was a flint
To bliss & barbarous, a bristling

Of tracks like a starfish carved on his inner arm,
A tindering of tissue, a reliquary, twinned.

A singe of salt-hay shrouds the orchard-skin,
That I would be—lukewarm, mammalian, even then,

In winter when moss sheathes every thing alive
& everything not or once alive.

That I would be—dryadic, gothic, fanatic against
The vanishing; I will not speak to you again.

Two Poems by Tom Disch

The Fireworks

One moment the sky is its usual dark,
Dimensionless self, and the next, with a double burst—
Two spreading spheres of radiance, phosphor
Chrysanthemums—it is shown to be as large
In every direction as any mathematician
Might wish, an infinite emptiness
In which all trajectories are possible.

We groundlings gasp in sympathy
With each new illumination, becoming,
Momentarily, a mob of Archimedes
And Pythagorases, to whom the heavens
Have opened to reveal axiom after axiom
Of higher geometry.
                              In the chord
Of that communal Eureka a deeper secret
Trembles to be released, a sphere
That is only hinted at by the explosions
We are sharing: the sphere of our selves,
Gathered here beside the lake, unknown
To each other in the darkness, united
Not by any common task but by the great Ah!
Of this awareness of something so large,
So high, so lucid, and—this must enter
Into it—so potentially lethal, too.

For this might be Sarajevo,
And not the Fourth of July, and we might be
Receiving these messages instead of sending them.
Our dark streets might be filled with anatomy
Lessons like Dr. Tulp's, our separate

Intelligences sliced open like white gourds,
Our dazzling blood sprayed across the movie screen
Of eternity, each mayfly life allotted
Only this single expression of glory,
Before the night sky resumes its usual
Everlastingly cool demeanor,
All instruction spent.

                         Ah, but the god
Of holidays has been kind. He has unveiled
Only as much of his terror as will strike us
As seeming lovely in a largely abstract way,
Celestial bouquets with no stench of decay—
Though as the display continues
And the smoke accumulates above, to mirror,
In its tangled wreathes, each new flare,
We do become aware of a gunpowdery smell,
And we know there's a cost for this pleasure.
We gather up the cans and blankets,
While we still can breathe, and go home
To our TVs and the comfort of a shared delusion.

The Moon on the Crest of the New-Fallen Snow

These are those same trees you saw six months ago.
I've drawn them in a way that will explain
Not only their nature, but the nature of snow,
And my own—removed, yet not unaware. Pain

Has its place—and pity, too—but it is not here.
Here all is calm and cold and luminous.
The snow has smoothed over the tracks of the deer.
The moon—I am the moon—would rather be oblivious

Of what lives, since the moon itself is not alive.
It enjoys superior—some might say supernal—
Pleasures. It is confident it can survive
The loss of leaves, of love, of life. Eternal

As the miracle it mirrors, the moon
Transcends, and maps, all circumstances.
It is at midnight as it is at noon.
It sits alone and smiles, as the snow dances.

John Hollander

Variations on a Table-Top

for Saul Steinberg

(Whose carved and painted
Balsa table-tops
Were sculpted drawings
Of the table-tops
They were drawn upon.)

I

The varnished, waxed, mahogany veneer of the table-top
Where he sat, unable to write truthfully of what truth was,
Shone back at him, uninvitingly showing only his own
Reflectiveness, standing for all its wide mirroring of mind.
The plain deal table in the kitchen, where the vegetables get
Chopped, stood for nothing but what was rightfully done on
    it, and
Thereby—how splendidly exemplary this was!—for itself.

Locke's *tabula rasa* was blank only if you couldn't see
The intricate structures of possibility—a landscape
Of openness, (imprisoned in contingency nonetheless,
Locked in the very jail of what it could ever be open to)?
A still life of quick motionlessness? a *tableau vivant* of
The heretical panel of *The Creation of the World*?

On the Multiplication Table, X and Y were going
Away at it, following the biblical injunction. But
Was it truly fruitful? alas we ask, (and more and more we
Have to ask). But here is another question, set for us by
That great examiner, Late Morning: Consider that

The discussion of the nasty matter was tabled in Great
Britain, and thereupon the back benchers started to shout,
   some
At once and others in quick succession, very nasty things.
But on this side of the Atlantic the very same motion
Was tabled and everyone there heaved a great sigh of relief:

What did the respective tables look like? Was the British one
All of metal, or perhaps even tiled, so that whatever
Blood was involved could easily be cleaned up? Was the one
   in
Washington placed high up on a dusty balcony where few
People ever went, save for the night watchman, on his sad
   rounds?
(Be specific. Do not write on more than two sides of the page.)

He lay there at the end of things; what was it he still could
   see:
A table of green fields, laid out in squares with hedgerows
   and small
Brooks? Or was it the squares on the quilt he could make out
   beneath
His nose (sharp as a pin? as a pen?) stretching out sadly toward
The distant and inaccessible hills of his covered feet?

II

But Babel crashed in a thunder of wreckage and the mortared
Syntax which held words fast to harder (but no less durable)
Things crumbled into bricky chunks: the world fell into its
   own
Grand aphasia and we had to make allowances for
Almost everything; still, in the twilight of meaning one could
Glimpse momentary sparks of sense, like the cold and lovely
   blue-
Green of fireflies benignly but significantly flashing,
So that there was at least something to go on. For example

Untwisting the mystery of the Bower of Tabel, the
Lost place of light, highest garden of eloquence — with
The consequence that words like table lost some of their grip
   on
Things, and neighboring words moved in for the referential
   kill:

"See here, now! I'm going to lay my cards on the sable!" But
Did he mean the last remaining pelt, let-out, but not needed
For Mrs. Blasenkopf's coat? we knew that whatever he thought,
   it
Was all shifting sand; meanwhile the less substantial Knights
   of the
Round Fable were spoken of, told of, as if they had been
   there;
(Or, if you prefer *arrosto d'Ariosto*, Fancy munched
On the fast food of the open-all-night *favola calda*.)
It was said of the late wise Professor that, young and foolish,
He had a local whore in the Society of Fellows'
Rooms, upon a celebrated and highly-polished Mabel
(As in *"Get off the Mabel, the two bucks is the waiter's tip"*);
Something untoward about the green baize of the billiard
   gable
Caused all the balls to hasten to the side cushions as if they
Were caught in one of two adjacent gravitational fields;
And when the enraged curmudgeon pounded the unyielding
   oaken
Stable (but not the sort that had ever even heard of the
Horse), his hand hurt, but we all acknowledged his authority:
The sturdy, old, ugly "golden" oak that had come to him from
Some turn-of-the-century schoolroom quite legibly proclaimed
The contents of his character as he pounded once again
On the label around which sat his intimidated peers.

On the walls above, gazing out over the tedium of
This scene was a faded sepia print that might have been one
Of J.H. Tischmann's *Moses Bearing the Cables of the Law*;

—And so forth. But were these all examples of the very same
Phenomenon? Were they, too, variations on some theme,
   some
Enigma at the center? (I imagine it lying there
Like some crazy lazy Susan, pre-Copernican, who knew
Just that the table of the world whirled about her fixity.)

III

How to turn the tables on these turns of designation, though?
Playing on the name and with the palpable surface itself
Is to play variations "on" it as on a piano
And as on a theme, the motif of itself in its great, flat
Capacity for taking on the work of our minds, our hands
Our eyes; and taking pen in hand—unmindful that, were it
   not
For the flat opacity of yielding paper which prevents
Any mirroring of that writing from the tabletop, all
Might be lost in the distractions of self-regard—is at last
To climb to the table land and see, not a fancy prospect
As from a mountaintop, or across a bay at sunset, but
Again the broad true plain, ungirded by any lofty hills.

Three Poems by William Logan

Mother on the St. Johns

The palms looked wary even in broad afternoon,
thin women in fancy ribbed hats.
Beyond them the hooded sweep of the St. Johns

gathered home the overweight mariners,
yachting caps askew as the afternoon broke up
and boats shuddered to the bank.

Indoors, beside your chaise longue, the cigarettes
were burning mad, their heads alight.
You lit them one after another,

as if you could torture them all.
The condo's wide-screen TV blocked your view.
All life was now a miniseries,

overlong and full of minor actors,
and the Florida sky, that great brocaded curtain,
was about to be drawn over the closing night,

the children unnamed lakes of pain,
and the widow a thorny, ungrateful gator
wallowing on a shared ledge of bank,

home, or willing to call it home,
the incoherent kingdom. And then a heron took off,
beating its wings like a broken angel,

its neck crooked backward in a childlike Z.
Its arc hesitated above the palms.
Darker, but not so injured now.

Insects

Those heavy, drowned-washrag, still moonless nights
our hands would test the blindness of our faces,
tourists scratching their names on marble columns
valued for the old Ionic pallor.
Ah travelers, your unmarked passports held
down for the inky stamp and the waved hand.
Where had we been, what hopes had we abandoned?
That was the summer when we couldn't sleep,
naked each night—your breasts aglow at dawn,
your clammy skin a glistening repeat.
The neighbors' mournful country-western songs
echoed across the lawn at three A.M.
to anything awake to mate, to breed,
to summer's insects with a geisha's feet.

The Fates

Deep in the house your Singer sang its dirge,
one more thread clipped stealthily from conscience.
Who sewed the gowns and blouses of the Fates?
We read ourselves in history, out-of-date
as spiders chasing sunlight on the chrome.
Where were its lessons, its eerie rapt temptations,
for mouths so thin-lipped, corrupt, and curious?
Pages turned down at sleep, where men had wept
or armies met their slaughter in the night,
the nervous ticking before the blood surrenders.
Despair, at times, is history's only exercise—
vain, self-approving, the mirror in easy reach.
Like the snails drawing across a rain-slick window,
tired of making enemies, we were enemies.

Grace Schulman

American Solitude

Hopper never painted this, but here
on a snaky path his vision lingers:

Three white tombs, robots with glassed-in faces
and meters for eyes, grim mouths, flat noses,

lean forward on a platform like strangers
with identical frowns scanning a blur,

far off, that might be their train.
Gas tanks broken for decades face Parson's

smithy, planked shut now. Both relics must stay.
The pumps have roots in gas pools, and the smithy

stores memories of hammers forging scythes
to cut spartina grass for dry salt-hay.

The tanks have the remove of local clammers
who sink buckets and stand, never in pairs,

but one and one and one, blank-eyed, alone,
more serene than lonely. Today a woman

rakes in the shallows, then bends to receive
last rays in shimmering water, her long shadow

knifing the bay. She slides into her truck
to watch the sky flame over sand flats, a hawk's

wind arabesque, an island risen brown
Atlantis, at low tide; she probes the shoreline

and beyond grassy dunes for where the land
might slope off into night. Hers is no common

emptiness, but a vaster silence filled
with terns' cries, an abundant solitude.

Nearby, the three dry gas pumps, worn
survivors of clam-digging generations,

are luminous, and have an exile's grandeur
that says: in perfect solitude, there's fire.

One day I approached the vessels
and wanted to drive on, the road ablaze

with dogwood in full bloom, but the contraptions
outdazzled the road's white, even outshone

a bleached shirt flapping alone
on a laundry line, arms pointed down.

High noon. Three urns, ironic in their outcast
dignity—as though, like some pine chests,

they might be prized in disuse—cast rays,
spun leaf-covered numbers, clanked, then wheezed

and stopped again. Shadows cut the road
before I drove off into the dark woods.

Four Poems by Susan Wheeler

Landscaping for Privacy

I wanted the gigando set in this corner here,
the 36 incher under the row of cornapples
hung just as the greasy greasy grannies done.
I like to collect copper, and here it's found
beside blue hyacinth forcers, in clumps of pans.
Something's always on the stove when a visitor comes.

The kilim fans make fine lampshades for those days
when birds swarm the greening shingles lined
with that vermiculite dusting we did last week.
Repeat: your burdock dishrags will last you a life
if you sun them slowly in a makeshift pan.
The visitor should always be encouraged to eat.

Those small doilies woven from maidenhair ferns?
Just the ticket on a happ'nin' day when the crow-
house takes you hours just to rake the dung,
or thickets of linens haul slow in the wringer,
or terns pinned on the landing grouse, unsung.
Visitors are allowed to eat with their fingers.

I've filed a grievance of the nuisance brand
on the new neighbor who provided a violate view:
what once dressed eaves in honeysuckle decor
now, a dish, satellite, with camouflage crochet.
The pressings book per gingerbread's good for more.
Decorate the bluefish and the visitors they stay.

Run on a Warehouse

What he had said came back to him.
Sectioned seat, sectioned seat.
The lift caught wind and swayed him in.
Big armoire, big armoire.

For some time he had felt it stir.
Sideboard door, sideboard door.
He sashayed through the conifers.
Dad's chair, dad's chair.

He had not known how far he'd come.
The blanket chest, the blanket chest.
A sourceless light suffused the run.
Love seat, love seat.

He had not come for his own sake.
All fixtures new, fixtures new.
Before the end he'd need to break.
Wall to wall, wall to wall.

So buckily he bore his load.
Filigreed frame, filigreed frame.
He could not see the lodge for snow.
Canopied bed, canopied bed.

He'll not forget the moment soon.
Cuckoo clock, cuckoo clock.
Now over snow a glimpse of moon.
Savvy desk, savvy desk.

There were but two things he required.
Glass breakfront, glass breakfront.
The slope was steep and he was tired.
Just a hutch, just a hutch.

Knit in Your Will

It was dumb luck the airline went bust
and he had to change his flight. It was
fortuitous that they were passing by
the dumpster in the dark. *It was a real break*
that the agent's steak had to cook some more.
Had you not come, I wouldn't have gone
to the acres beyond Fuller Peak.

Gentlest hull of bond, tendons that bear
to work a gait, sentiment that brought you here:
at the window in the dark, speaking tongues
that I can't hear. A bayou slush and slop
against the shore, the stiffened call of a
callou bird, the wading in a break might bear:
storm, I see the order there.

Tenderly, repeated Flo, as though she knew
the words. The gate's unstuck, and now the flock
wheels out overhead.

Alphabet's End

So I'll speak ill of the dead. A was crooked,
planting the small left finger of the raccoon in the upholstery
before he sold the car. B made certain to point out Celia's
bewildered look before her pink slip came in the flimsy institu-
    tion.
In the videos of C, a jejune overwhelmed the cast.

D built dollhouses. Even Lonnie down at Shell
found him less a man for it, the night they went off to see
    the stock
cars break. I wanted E's hair, but by the end it was no more. F
refused alms, pulling the man up by his shirt in the street,
    and
G sought rewards. Marybeth said H fondled her for sport.

Now you, I, Smokey, hell
bent on a village version of Club 21, embarrassed by our
    attentions.
Mistrust it was. Dig me a chamber of preparedness.

Two Poems by Richard Lyons

Symmetry

I remember erecting a screened-in porch
for a house I lived in, the staple gun
all afternoon like a giant mosquito

whirring above a sleeper's ear.
One month later, to the day, I found a hummingbird, dead,
and I thought *be careful*

as I turned it over with a long yellow pencil.

It was terrifyingly symmetrical, each wing an inch,
its torso, even its needle nose compass an inch.

Its neck an iridescent emerald.
Its underside a burnt sandalwood ash

coming off a bit with the pencil.

The Corpse Washing

What is this shame we feel for her, being dead,

as she lies there, her flesh cooling, on a table,
what blush easing the furniture of her body
toward the invisibility in a mirror

where no shadow is turning, nothing, not even a wasp
burrowing an exact inkspot in the curve of a pear?
This is the way Augustine says that it is

with God, when the breath stops—no red poppies
bobbing senselessly through their shadows
like mutineers. In one impossibility

my mother & I are sitting on cool blue shale above the Pacific,
watching a few men kiss basketballs off a backboard.

Flushed with sun & adrenaline, their damp bodies dry in the
   wind.
They drive, pull up & shoot. We hoot & clap,
the smack of shale on shale all the way down into the sea.

Sketches of Paris

Edmund White

I

One of our neighbors is the famous couturier Azzedine Alaïa, the minuscule "architect of the body," as he's often called because he creates his garments directly on his models, whereas someone like Christian LaCroix dashes off a sketch which he tosses at a trained team of seamstresses who interpret and realize even his most far-fetched inspirations. Alaïa works sometimes late into the night, his mouth full of pins, as he drapes and pulls and turns and twists and dances around the dais like Pygmalion dressing an already transformed and fully alive Galatea.

I remember one night when the Galatea was a ravishing, pouting, smiling teenager, Naomi Campbell, who would later become the world's most famous model but who then was just a sumptuously beautiful, shy English adolescent. She kept turning and turning as Azzedine ordered her to do, though

when he stuck a pin in her she shouted lustily and tapped
the tiny maestro on the head.

That night the chubby, charming American painter Julian
Schnabel was also in attendance, he who'd made his mark
by gluing broken crockery to his imposing canvases. He and
Azzedine are best friends, although curiously neither can
speak the other's language. Julian, who's very rich, invited us
all to dinner—and with Azzedine "all" includes his entourage
of at least four or five models, his aristocratic German business
manager and two or three gofers. Over dinner I asked them
how they'd met and Julian and Azzedine gave me conflicting
versions, each happily insulated in his own language. Julian
said, "I dropped in on Azzedine's shop with my then wife
Jacqueline and asked to see Mr. Alaïa. When he came downstairs I introduced myself and offered to exchange one of my
paintings for a fur coat. He was overwhelmed, since obviously
one of my paintings is worth twenty fur coats, but he gratefully
accepted."

Azzedine's almost simultaneous version: "This man came
to my shop and I'm so embarrassed to say it but I'd never
heard of him and when he offered me one of his paintings I
just shrugged, but Jacqueline was so beautiful I thought I'd
love to have her wearing my coat in New York so I agreed."

Each man finished his answer with a big smile, sure he'd
just confirmed what the other had said.

Azzedine, who's from Tunisia, hates it if you say he's a
typical Arab businessman who lives over the shop, but in fact
he bought an immense, 4,000-square-meter workshop and
warehouse that was built in the nineteenth century and he
converted it into a boutique, an enormous showroom with a
runway for his style shows, a dormitory for the models, work-
shops for fabricating clothes—and he lives above it, ready to
come swooping down at a moment's notice.

Just as dancers like to smoke, models like to eat and nothing
is more delightful than watching Azzedine's cook prepare a
succulent leg of lamb covered in mint leaves and coated in
honey or some other North African delicacy for these skinny,
ravenous beauties.

Over dinner Azzedine loves to speak of the great women he's known or adored from afar. His first idol was the Egyptian singer Oom Kalsoum, whose concerts would be broadcast in the evening once a month throughout the Arab world during the 1950s. The most celebrated and respected Arab performer of this century, she was as worshipped as Maria Callas and as powerful as Margaret Thatcher at the time of the Falklands' invasion. On the morning of her monthly recital the little Azzedine would be sent to the local café, which possessed the only radio in town, to reserve a chair as near the radio as possible for his grandfather. There his grandfather would install himself with a jasmine flower behind his ear and sigh and weep as Oom Kalsoum improvised verse after verse, hour after hour, of her lovesick ballads. On that day, once a month, no business was conducted throughout the Arab world, all misdeeds were overlooked and no war could have been fought. Oom Kalsoum taught Alaïa his first lesson about the power and mystery of female artistry.

When he arrived in Paris in the 1960s he became a private dressmaker to Louise de Vilmorin, a well-known poet and

hostess and Malraux's mistress. Vilmorin had lived for a while in America and her daughter had married and settled down there. One day Vilmorin's nine-year-old grandson, whom she'd never seen, was expected and Vilmorin, ever the seductress, was obsessed about what she should be wearing when the child arrived, where she should be standing and which profile she should present him with. Azzedine had to advise the coquettish grandmother on every detail. As her confidant, he also got to hear all the gossip about fashionable Paris during the preceding half century.

His favorite private client was Greta Garbo. Just at the beginning of the 1970s he was making clothes for Cécile Rothschild, who was living in Coco Chanel's old townhouse on the rue Faubourg St-Honoré. One day Cécile said to him, "I have a special customer for you, but if you make a big fuss over her or are indiscreet I'll be very disappointed." Curiously enough, Azzedine had been watching *Queen Christina* on television only the night before and when he entered Madame Rothschild's salon, there was the same immortal face greeting him.

"At the time," Azzedine recalled, "around 1970, human taste was at a historic low and since I was part of my era I, too, liked orange and black and horrible fabrics and cuts. Miss Garbo, however, was outside or above history. She wanted me to make her a military greatcoat. She described what she wanted in detail and even gave me the fabric, which was very heavy. At the time I was living in a little room but I made my German business manager walk back and forth in Garbo's coat as we worked through the night, night after night, trying to imagine how the coat would move and drape and how she could bear the weight. But after many fittings and hundreds of suggestions from Miss Garbo, at last the design worked like a charm—and I felt Garbo had *purified* my taste of all the follies of that terrible period."

One of Azzedine's idols was the actress Arletty, star of all those black-and-white pre-war films with Michel Simon. She was the quintessential *Parisienne*, with her plucked eyebrows, racy laugh and penetrating, nasal voice always ready to deliver a wisecrack. Jean-Pierre Grédy, the playwright, recently told me that whereas Arletty had the body of a goddess painted by the School of Fontainebleau, her voice was that of a gutter rat. Gerard Depardieu, he pointed out, has exactly the opposite combination of characteristics: his body is that of a peasant, whereas his voice is almost feminine.

By the time Alaïa knew Arletty she was already old and blind, but he revered her. And he'd been directly inspired by the dress she wears in *Hôtel du Nord*, which unzips from top to bottom on the diagonal.

Alaïa has a masterful eye when he turns it on old clothes. In New York once he was led through the clothing archives of the Fashion Institute of Technology and was unimpressed by everything until he suddenly chanced upon beautifully elegant clothes from the 1930s and 1940s. He exclaimed, "But these clothes must have been designed by a European!" The curator told him that in fact they had been designed by Charles James, the great eccentric and, indeed, America's most revered dress designer.

Alaïa was called in by the fashion museum at the Louvre when it wanted to dress some display dummies in dresses from the 1930s made by Madame Vionnet. The curator didn't know what to make of all these odd bits of white fabric, but Azzedine, who'd studied old fashion photos and who admires Vionnet more than any other couturier of the past, was able to drape them and tuck them and fold them expertly and to create the most striking display in the whole museum.

His favorite fashion icon, however, he's never met: the Queen Mother. He's awestruck by her fashion sense, especially her penchant for Nile green.

Once Julian Barnes and his wife Pat Kavanagh came to visit me in Paris. When I suggested we all go to an Alaïa fashion show, Julian snorted, "Edmund, you've been in Paris too long. Fashion show indeed!" But Pat and I persuaded him and he was not only enthralled by the long-legged beauties on the runway but delighted when I introduced him to Alaïa-faithful Tina Turner. She exclaimed, "I haven't yet read *Flaubert's Parrot* but I have it on my bedside table, Mr. Barnes."

II

In the rue des Lombards just below the windows of my study, seven or eight very old, matronly prostitutes work in shifts. According to our concierge, Madame Denise, they don't live here but have rented an . . . *atelier*, strictly for work purposes, between the Japanese and Chinese restaurants and across from the sex shop. Between customers they often amble into the local bar, downstairs, Les Piétons, where Madame Denise likes to drink her glass of white wine of an afternoon.

Two of the prostitutes wear mink coats and sweep their white hair up into chignons off the neck. In Paris, it's true, the only women who wear minks are Italian tourists and local prostitutes, but the Italians usually carry a cordless telephone as well, so there's generally no confusion (*Ciao, Mamma, siamo a Parigi!*) Another local prostitute, also in her sixties, wears a shiny rubber dress and matching cape, as well as scary, lickable boots. Since God made lots of male masochists and very few female sadists, a prostitute who's willing to be a *dominatrice* can continue her career well into her golden years. No sex could be safer than making Monsieur Micheton dress up in frilly lace panties and dust the *atelier* while treated to a shower of insults and a taste of the whip. As Madame Denise confides in a whisper, "She can even sit down in an armchair and relax, poor thing."

One of the snowy-haired matrons, still according to Madame Denise, lives in a distant neighborhood with her grown son, a proud and respectable *garçon de café*. For years she has told her son she works at the Les Halles branch of the giant book store, the FNAC, and he has never doubted her story.

One of the prostitutes is slightly younger, wears a gray floor-length coat over-printed with the Hapsburgs' double eagle, and has a yappy dog named Mickey. Ceaseless dog-walking is a good reason to live in the streets and two of the other women have dogs too—always tiny, beribboned puppies, I've remarked, as though an obese aging dog would invite unwelcome comparisons.

During the day three or four of the women stand in their doorway and gossip with each other and scold their puppies. They seldom seem to be troubled by clients as they clobber stiffly down the stretch of cobbled street in their stiletto heels. It crosses my mind that prostitution is just an innocent excuse for hanging out and chewing the fat with the girls. At night, however, young men in search of maternal love do stand in the street, even under the rain, looking longingly up to the *atelier*.

One afternoon I saw a respectable young mother in a pleated navy-blue skirt hurry past with her daughter. She was aghast when the whores started waving in their grandmotherly way to the little girl and the child went running toward Mickey and all that shiny rubber, so much prettier than a twin set and pearls.

III

One August evening I was having dinner at our place with Peter Kurth, the American biographer. We were comparing notes about all the difficulties in researching the biography of someone like Jean Genet or Peter's current subject, Isadora

Duncan, people who turned their own lives into myths and had a creative approach to the truth.

Peter was on his way back from Russia, where he'd been investigating Isadora's relationship to Esenin, the flamboyant bisexual poet. The next day he'd be heading home to the States. He was discouraged by the sinking level of culture throughout the world. "No one even knows who Isadora was any more," he said gloomily.

"Oh, surely," I said, "they've all heard about the American modern dancer who danced barefoot and nude for the Bolsheviks or who was kept by Singer of the sewing machine or who strangled herself when her scarf was caught in the wire wheels of a roadster."

"Not really," he said. He looked belligerently at Fred, who was sleeping on his back with all four paws in the air though folded back gracefully. "God, is that dog fat!" he said.

"He is not. The winner of the Westminster Dog Show this year was a basset and he was much more jowly."

But Peter was determined to lash out at a being so infernally relaxed as Fred, even inert, free of all a biographer's worries. "And how banal to name him Fred the Basset."

"We didn't even know about that comic-strip character," I protested. "We named him after a French psychiatrist friend, Frédéric."

Fred's right front paw twitched insouciantly with a ghostly Pavlovian response to the mention of his name.

Just then a young woman's voice, penetrating and perfectly pitched, free of all accompaniment, rang out in the old streets below. We went to the open window and watched her barefoot, shiny hair streaming down her back, as she belted out one show tune after another in English. Her voice was strong and clear and not to be confused with anyone else's. The diners sitting under the awning on the curb didn't appear to appreciate her, perhaps because they'd just been dazzled by three tap dancers dressed up as ducks, a tough act to follow.

Peter and I, however, adored her voice and called out to her to wait for us as we came down to the street. She nodded, looking somewhat confused.

When we joined her with Fred, we invited her to the Café Beaubourg. She told us her whole story—how she'd come from Australia and was now studying song and dance. "I'm determined," she said, "to become the new Isadora!"

NOTES ON CONTRIBUTORS

FICTION

Rick DeMarinis teaches creative writing at the University of Texas at El Paso. His last novel, *The Mortician's Apprentice*, was published in 1994 by Norton.

C.M. Mayo lives in Mexico City. She received the Flannery O'Connor Prize for her collection of stories, *Sky Over El Nido*, which will appear this fall from the University of Georgia Press.

Francine Prose's new novel, *Hunters and Gatherers*, will be published by Farrar, Straus and Giroux this summer.

POETRY

John Ashbery's new collection of poetry, *Can You Hear, Bird*, will be published this fall by Farrar, Straus and Giroux.

Lucie Brock-Broido's second book of poetry, *The Master Letters*, will be published this fall. She teaches in the School of Arts at Columbia University.

Katharine Coles's second book of poems, *The Walk-Through Heart*, will be published this fall. She lives in Salt Lake City, where she teaches English at Westminster College.

Dawn Corrigan's work has appeared on the buses in Salt Lake City, where she lives.

Tom Disch has published seven books of poetry. A book of essays on poetry, *The Castle of Indolence* is forthcoming.

Stephen Dobyns teaches creative writing at Syracuse University. Viking will publish his ninth book of poetry, *Common Carnage*, in 1996.

Thom Gunn is the subject of an interview in this issue.

John Harvey's poetry is forthcoming in *Grand Street* and *The Gettysburg Review*.

John Hollander's latest volume of poetry, *Tesserae*, was published in 1993. Next year a volume of critical writing, *The Gazer's Spirit*, will be published. He teaches in the English department at Yale.

David Jauss's first collection of poems, *Improvising Rivers*, will be published this fall.

Cynthia Kraman is the author of three volumes of poetry, including *The Mexican Murals*.

Gwyneth Lewis writes in both Welsh and English. The poem in this issue is from her first collection of English poems, *Parables and Faxes*.

William Logan has a collection of poems, *Vain Empires*, and a collection of essays and reviews, *Reputations of the Tongue*, forthcoming.

Richard Lyons received the Devins Award in 1988 for his book of poems, *These Modern Nights*. He teaches at Mississippi State University.

James McManus's first collection of poems, *Great America*, was published in 1993. He is currently a Guggenheim fellow in poetry.

Sandra McPherson will have two collections of poetry, *The Spaces between Birds* and *Edge Effect*, published next year.

Christopher Middleton's books include *The Balcony Tree* and *Andalusian Poems*, the latter a collection of translations.

Carl Phillips teaches literature and creative writing at Washington University in St. Louis. He is the author of *In the Blood* and *Cortège*.

Dan Quick is a student at the University of Denver.

Adrienne Rich has received the Harriet Monroe Prize and a MacArthur Fellowship. Her new collection of poems, *Dark Fields of the Republic*, will be published this fall.

Daniel Rifenburgh's poems have appeared in *The New Republic* and *Western Humanities Review*. He served in the Army from 1972–1975.

Peter Sacks is the author of *The English Elegy* and two volumes of poetry. His new book, *Woody Gwyn: an Approach to the Landscape*, will be published this year.

Grace Schulman is Poetry Editor of *The Nation*. Her books of poetry include *For That Day Only*, *Burn Down the Icons* and *Hemispheres*.

Maureen Seaton's two poetry collections are *The Sea Among Cupboards* and *Fear of Subways*. She received an NEA fellowship in 1994.

Cathy Stern teaches at the University of Houston. Her work has appeared in *The New Republic* and *Shenandoah*.

Roderick Townley's publications include a novel, *Minor Gods*, and two collections of poetry, *Three Musicians* and *Final Approach*. He lives in Kansas.

Charles H. Webb is the editor of *Stand Up Poetry: the anthology*. He lives in Los Angeles.

Susan Wheeler's first collection of poetry, *Bag 'o' Diamonds*, appeared in 1994. She is Director of Public Affairs for Arts and Sciences at New York University.

Charles Wright's two latest books are *Chickamauga*, a volume of poetry, and *Quarter Notes*, a collection of improvisations and interviews.

Karen Volkman's collection of poetry, *Crash's Law*, was a National Poetry Series selection for 1995.

INTERVIEWS

Stephen Becker (Patrick O'Brian interview) is a novelist and translator.

Shusha Guppy (P.D. James interview) is the London editor of *The Paris Review*.

Clive Wilmer (Thom Gunn interview) is writing a critical study of Thom Gunn's poetry. His *Selected Poems* will be published this year by Carcanet Press.

FEATURES

Bernard Cooper is the author of *Maps to Anywhere* and *A Year of Rhymes*. His collection of memoirs, *Truth Serum* is forthcoming from Viking.

Elissa Schappell is senior editor at *The Paris Review*. Robert Creeley's poems from *Memory Gardens*, copyright © 1986 by Robert Creeley, are reprinted by permission of New Directions Publishing Corp.

Matt Steinglass (Daniil Kharms) writes for television and studies multimedia at NYU's Interactive Telecommunications Program.

Edmund White is the author of ten books, including, most recently, the story collection *Skinned Alive*, as well as a biography of Jean Genet. The pieces in this issue will appear in White's forthcoming book, *Our Paris: Sketches from Memory*. **Hubert Sorin**, an architect and illustrator, died in March 1994.

ART

Graham Gilmore was born in Vancouver, British Columbia and lives in New York. He has exhibited in New York, Canada, Germany and England.

Judy Glantzman has exhibited her work throughout the United States and internationally. Her drawings appear courtesy of BlumHelman Gallery in New York.

Raffaele lives and works in Fiesole, Italy. His work is represented by Paolo Baldacci Gallery, New York.

The Paris Review
Booksellers Advisory Board

THE PARIS REVIEW BOOKSELLERS ADVISORY
BOARD is a group of owners and managers of
independent bookstores from around the
world who have agreed to share with us their
knowledge and expertise.